The Indian Rebellion of 1857

Compiled by
Kiera Mccune

Scribbles

Year of Publication 2018

ISBN : 9789352979202

Book Published by

Scribbles

(An Imprint of Alpha Editions)

email - alphaedis@gmail.com

Produced by: PediaPress GmbH
Limburg an der Lahn
Germany
http://pediapress.com/

Contents

Indian Rebellion of 1857

Indian Rebellion of 1857	
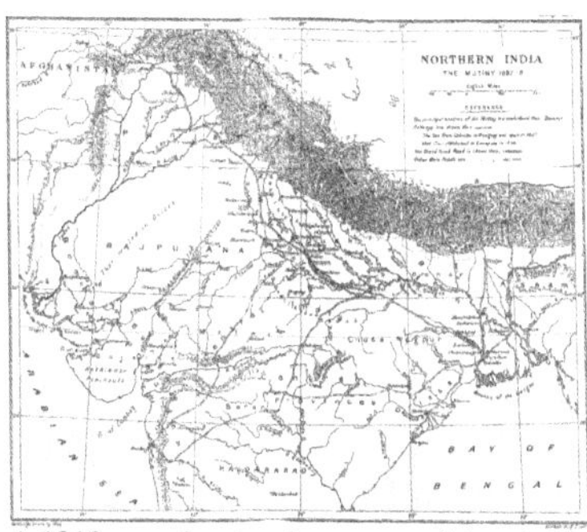 A 1912 map showing the centres of the rebellion	
Date	10 May 1857 – 1 November 1858 (1 year and 6 months)
Location	India
Result	British victory • Suppression of revolt • Formal end of the Mughal empire • End of Company rule in India • Transfer of rule to the British Crown
Territorial changes	British Indian Empire created out of former East India Company territory (some land returned to native rulers, other land confiscated by the British crown)

Belligerents	
• Sepoy Mutineers • Gwalior Factions • Forces of Rani Laxmi bai, the deposed ruler of Jhansi • Forces of Nana Sahib Peshwa • Followers of Birjis Qadra • Oudh • Followers of Babu Kunwar Singh • Followers of Drig Narayan Singh • Forces of Ballabgarh king Nahar Singh • Followers of Rewari Chief Rao Tularam • Forces of Shahmal Tomar	• British Empire • Kingdom of Nepal • TibetWikipedia:Citation needed • East India Company • 21 Princely States:

	• Ajaigarh • Alwar • Bharathpur • Bhopal • Bijawar • Bikaner • Bundi • Hyderabad • Jaipur • Jaora • Jodhpur • Kapurthala • Jammu and Kashmir • Kendujhar • Nabha • Patiala • Rampur • Rewa • Sirmur • Sirohi • Udaipur • Mysore • Travancore
Commanders and leaders	
• Bakht Khan † • Bahadur Shah II • Mirza Mughal ☠ • Nana Sahib • Tatya Tope ☠ • Rani Lakshmibai † • Begum Hazrat Mahal • Birjis Qadr • Babu Kunwar Singh (d. April 1858)	• Lord Canning • George Anson (d. May 1857) • Patrick Grant • Colin Campbell (From August 1857) • John Nicholson † • Jung Bahadur Rana[1]
Casualties and losses	
at least 100,000[2]Wikipedia:Verifiability-nearly 806,000 and possibly more, both in the rebellion and in famines and epidemics of disease in its wake, by comparison of sketchy pre-existing population estimates with Indian Census of 1871.[3]	

Part of **a series** on the

History of India

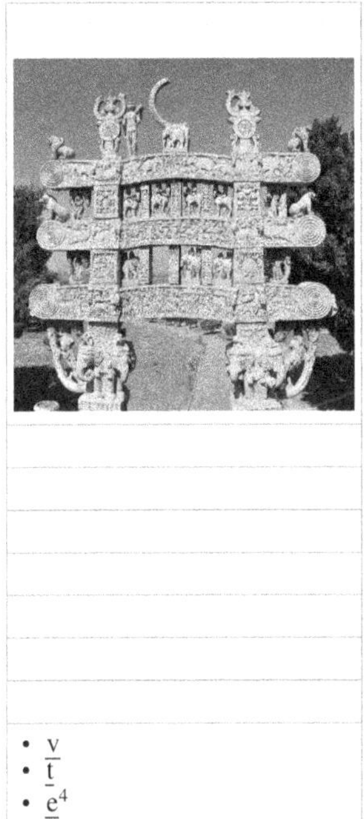

- v
- t
- e[4]

The **Indian Rebellion of 1857** was a major uprising in India between 1857–58 against the rule of the British East India Company, which functioned as a sovereign power on behalf of the British Crown. The event is known by many names, including the Sepoy Mutiny, the Indian Mutiny, the Great Rebellion, the Revolt of 1857, the Indian Insurrection, and India's First War of Independence.[5]

The rebellion began on 10 May 1857 in the form of a mutiny of sepoys of the Company's army in the garrison town of Meerut, 40 miles northeast of Delhi (now Old Delhi). It then erupted into other mutinies and civilian rebellions chiefly in the upper Gangetic plain and central India,[6,7] though incidents of revolt also occurred farther north and east.[8] The rebellion posed a considerable threat to British power in that region,[9] and was contained only with the rebels' defeat in Gwalior on 20 June 1858.[10] On 1 November 1858, the British granted amnesty to all rebels not involved in murder, though they did not declare the hostilities formally to have ended until 8 July 1859.

The Indian rebellion was fed by resentment that had emerged from British rule, including invasive British-style social reforms, harsh land taxes, summary treatment of some rich landowners and princes,[11,12] and broader scepticism about the improvements brought about by British rule.[13] Many Indians did rise against the British, but many others fought *for* the British, and the majority remained seemingly compliant to British rule.[14,15] Violence, which sometimes betrayed exceptional cruelty, was inflicted on both sides; on British officers and civilians (including women and children) by the rebels, and on the rebels and their supporters (sometimes including entire villages) by British reprisals. The cities of Delhi and Lucknow were laid waste in the fighting and during the British retaliation.[16]

After the outbreak of the mutiny in Meerut, the rebels very quickly reached Delhi, whose 81-year-old Mughal ruler, Bahadur Shah Zafar, was declared by the rebels as the Emperor of Hindustan. Soon, the rebels also captured large tracts of the North-Western Provinces and Awadh (Oudh). The East India Company's response came rapidly as well. With help from reinforcements, Kanpur was retaken by mid-July 1857 and Delhi by the end of September. Even so, it then took the remainder of 1857 and the better part of 1858 for the rebellion to be suppressed in Jhansi, Lucknow, and especially the Awadh countryside. Other regions of Company controlled India—the Bengal Presidency, the Bombay Presidency and the Madras Presidency—remained largely calm.[17] In the Punjab, the Sikhs crucially helped the British by providing both soldiers and support.[18] The large princely states, Hyderabad, Mysore, Travancore, and Kashmir, as well as the smaller ones of Rajputana, did not join the rebellion, serving the British, in the Governor-General Lord Canning's words, as "breakwaters in a storm."

In some regions, most notably in Awadh, the rebellion took on the attributes of a patriotic revolt against European presence and power. However, the rebel leaders proclaimed no articles of faith that presaged a new political system.[19] Even so, the rebellion proved to be an important watershed in Indian and British Empire history.[20] It led to the dissolution of the East India Company, and forced the British to reorganize the army, the financial system, and the administration in India, through the passage of the Government of India Act 1858. India was thereafter administered directly by the British government in the new British Raj. On 1 November 1858, Queen Victoria issued a proclamation to Indians, which while lacking the authority of a constitutional provision,[21] promised rights similar to those of other British subjects.[22,23] In the following decades, when admission to these rights was not always forthcoming, Indians were to pointedly refer to the Queen's proclamation in growing avowals of a new nationalism.[24,25]

East India Company's expansion in India

Although the British East India Company had established a presence in India as far back as 1612, and earlier administered the factory areas established for

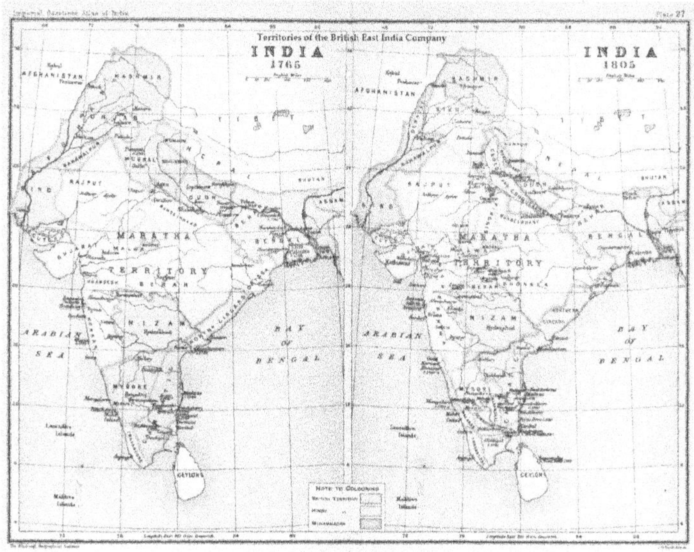

Figure 1: *India in 1765 and 1805, showing East India Company-governed territories in pink*

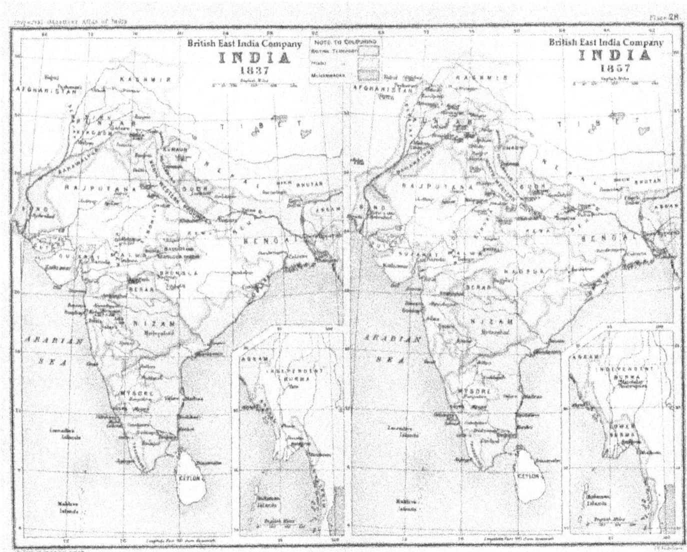

Figure 2: *India in 1837 and 1857, showing East India Company-governed territories in pink*

trading purposes, its victory in the Battle of Plassey in 1757 marked the beginning of its firm foothold in eastern India. The victory was consolidated in 1764 at the Battle of Buxar, when the East India Company army defeated Mughal Emperor Shah Alam II. After his defeat, the emperor granted the Company the right to the "collection of Revenue" in the provinces of Bengal (modern day Bengal, Bihar, and Odisha), known as "Diwani" to the Company. The Company soon expanded its territories around its bases in Bombay and Madras; later, the Anglo-Mysore Wars (1766–1799) and the Anglo-Maratha Wars (1772–1818) led to control of even more of India.

In 1806, the Vellore Mutiny was sparked by new uniform regulations that created resentment amongst both Hindu and Muslim sepoys.

After the turn of the 19th century, Governor-General Wellesley began what became two decades of accelerated expansion of Company territories. This was achieved either by subsidiary alliances between the Company and local rulers or by direct military annexation. The subsidiary alliances created the princely states of the Hindu maharajas and the Muslim nawabs. Punjab, North-West Frontier Province, and Kashmir were annexed after the Second Anglo-Sikh War in 1849; however, Kashmir was immediately sold under the 1846 Treaty of Amritsar to the Dogra Dynasty of Jammu and thereby became a princely state. The border dispute between Nepal and British India, which sharpened after 1801, had caused the Anglo-Nepalese War of 1814–16 and brought the defeated Gurkhas under British influence. In 1854, Berar was annexed, and the state of Oudh was added two years later. For practical purposes, the Company was the government of much of India.

Causes of the rebellion

The Indian Rebellion of 1857 occurred as the result of an accumulation of factors over time, rather than any single event.

The *sepoys* were Indian soldiers who were recruited into the Company's army. Just before the rebellion, there were over 300,000 sepoys in the army, compared to about 50,000 British. The forces were divided into three presidency armies: Bombay, Madras, and Bengal. The Bengal Army recruited higher castes, such as Rajputs and Bhumihar, mostly from the Awadh and Bihar regions, and even restricted the enlistment of lower castes in 1855. In contrast, the Madras Army and Bombay Army were "more localized, caste-neutral armies" that "did not prefer high-caste men."[26] The domination of higher castes in the Bengal Army has been blamed in part for initial mutinies that led to the rebellion.

In 1772, when Warren Hastings was appointed India's first Governor-General, one of his first undertakings was the rapid expansion of the Company's army.

Figure 3: *Two sepoy officers; a private sepoy, 1820s*

Since the sepoys from Bengal – many of whom had fought against the Company in the Battles of Plassey and Buxar – were now suspect in British eyes, Hastings recruited farther west from the high-caste rural Rajputs and Bhumihar of Awadh and Bihar, a practice that continued for the next 75 years. However, in order to forestall any social friction, the Company also took action to adapt its military practices to the requirements of their religious rituals. Consequently, these soldiers dined in separate facilities; in addition, overseas service, considered polluting to their caste, was not required of them, and the army soon came officially to recognise Hindu festivals. "This encouragement of high caste ritual status, however, left the government vulnerable to protest, even mutiny, whenever the sepoys detected infringement of their prerogatives." Stokes argues that "The British scrupulously avoided interference with the social structure of the village community which remained largely intact."

After the annexation of Oudh (Awadh) by the East India Company in 1856, many sepoys were disquieted both from losing their perquisites, as landed gentry, in the Oudh courts, and from the anticipation of any increased land-revenue payments that the annexation might bring about. Other historians have stressed that by 1857, some Indian soldiers, interpreting the presence of missionaries as a sign of official intent, were convinced that the Company was masterminding mass conversions of Hindus and Muslims to Christianity. Although earlier in the 1830s, evangelicals such as William Carey and William

Wilberforce had successfully clamoured for the passage of social reform, such as the abolition of *sati* and allowing the remarriage of Hindu widows, there is little evidence that the sepoys' allegiance was affected by this.

However, changes in the terms of their professional service may have created resentment. As the extent of the East India Company's jurisdiction expanded with victories in wars or annexation, the soldiers were now expected not only to serve in less familiar regions, such as in Burma, but also to make do without the "foreign service" remuneration that had previously been their due.

A major cause of resentment that arose ten months prior to the outbreak of the rebellion was the General Service Enlistment Act of 25 July 1856. As noted above, men of the Bengal Army had been exempted from overseas service. Specifically, they were enlisted only for service in territories to which they could march. Governor-General Lord Dalhousie saw this as an anomaly, since all sepoys of the Madras and Bombay Armies and the six "General Service" battalions of the Bengal Army had accepted an obligation to serve overseas if required. As a result, the burden of providing contingents for active service in Burma, readily accessible only by sea, and China had fallen disproportionately on the two smaller Presidency Armies. As signed into effect by Lord Canning, Dalhousie's successor as Governor-General, the act required only new recruits to the Bengal Army to accept a commitment for general service. However, serving high-caste sepoys were fearful that it would be eventually extended to them, as well as preventing sons following fathers into an army with a strong tradition of family service.[27]

There were also grievances over the issue of promotions, based on seniority. This, as well as the increasing number of European officers in the battalions,[28] made promotion slow, and many Indian officers did not reach commissioned rank until they were too old to be effective.[29]

The Enfield Rifle

The final spark was provided by the ammunition for the new Enfield P-53 rifle. These rifles, which fired Minié balls, had a tighter fit than the earlier muskets, and used paper cartridges that came pre-greased. To load the rifle, sepoys had to bite the cartridge open to release the powder.[30] The grease used on these cartridges was rumoured to include tallow derived from beef, which would be offensive to Hindus,[31] and pork, which would be offensive to Muslims. At least one Company official pointed out the difficulties this may cause:

> *unless it be proven that the grease employed in these cartridges is not of a nature to offend or interfere with the prejudices of caste, it will be expedient not to issue them for test to Native corps.*[32]

However, in August 1856, greased cartridge production was initiated at Fort William, Calcutta, following a British design. The grease used included tallow supplied by the Indian firm of Gangadarh Banerji & Co. By January, rumours were abroad that the Enfield cartridges were greased with animal fat.

Company officers became aware of the rumours through reports of an altercation between a high-caste sepoy and a low-caste labourer at Dum Dum. The labourer had taunted the sepoy that by biting the cartridge, he had himself lost caste, although at this time such cartridges had been issued only at Meerut and not at Dum Dum. There had been rumours that the British sought to destroy the religions of the Indian people, and forcing the native soldiers to break their sacred code would have certainly added to this rumour, as it apparently did. The Company was quick to reverse the effects of this policy in hopes that the unrest would be quelled.[33]

On 27 January, Colonel Richard Birch, the Military Secretary, ordered that all cartridges issued from depots were to be free from grease, and that sepoys could grease them themselves using whatever mixture "they may prefer". A modification was also made to the drill for loading so that the cartridge was torn with the hands and not bitten. This however, merely caused many sepoys to be convinced that the rumours were true and that their fears were justified. Additional rumours started that the paper in the new cartridges, which was glazed and stiffer than the previously used paper, was impregnated with grease. In February, a court of inquiry was held at Barrackpore to get to the bottom of these rumours. Native soldiers called as witnesses complained of the paper "being stiff and like cloth in the mode of tearing", said that when the paper was burned it smelled of grease, and announced that the suspicion that the paper itself contained grease could not be removed from their minds.[34]

Civilian disquiet

The civilian rebellion was more multifarious. The rebels consisted of three groups: the feudal nobility, rural landlords called *taluqdars*, and the peasants. The nobility, many of whom had lost titles and domains under the Doctrine of Lapse, which refused to recognise the adopted children of princes as legal heirs, felt that the Company had interfered with a traditional system of inheritance. Rebel leaders such as Nana Sahib and the Rani of Jhansi belonged to this group; the latter, for example, was prepared to accept East India Company supremacy if her adopted son was recognised as her late husband's heir.[35] In other areas of central India, such as Indore and Saugar, where such loss of privilege had not occurred, the princes remained loyal to the Company, even in areas where the sepoys had rebelled. The second group, the *taluqdars*, had lost half their landed estates to peasant farmers as a result of the land reforms that came in the wake of annexation of Oudh. As the rebellion gained ground, the *taluqdars* quickly reoccupied the lands they had lost, and paradoxically, in part because of ties of kinship and feudal loyalty, did not experience significant opposition from the peasant farmers, many of whom joined the rebellion, to the great dismay of the British. It has also been suggested that heavy land-revenue assessment in some areas by the British resulted in many landowning families either losing their land or going into great debt to money lenders, and providing ultimately a reason to rebel; money lenders, in addition to the Company, were particular objects of the rebels' animosity.[36] The civilian rebellion was also highly uneven in its geographic distribution, even in areas of north-central India that were no longer under British control. For example, the relatively prosperous Muzaffarnagar district, a beneficiary of a Company irrigation scheme, and next door to Meerut, where the upheaval began, stayed relatively calm throughout.

Figure 4: *Charles Canning, the Governor-General of India during the rebellion.*

Figure 5: *Lord Dalhousie, the Governor-General of India from 1848 to 1856, who devised the Doctrine of Lapse.*

Figure 6: *Lakshmibai, the Rani of Maratha-ruled Jhansi, one of the principal leaders of the rebellion who earlier had lost her kingdom as a result of the Doctrine of Lapse.*

Figure 7: *Bahadur Shah Zafar the last Mughal Emperor, crowned Emperor of India, by the Indian troops, he was deposed by the British, and died in exile in Burma*

"Utilitarian and evangelical-inspired social reform",[37] including the abolition of sati and the legalisation of widow remarriage were considered by many—especially the British themselves—to have caused suspicion that Indian religious traditions were being "interfered with", with the ultimate aim of conversion. Recent historians, including Chris Bayly, have preferred to frame this as a "clash of knowledges", with proclamations from religious authorities before the revolt and testimony after it including on such issues as the "insults to women", the rise of "low persons under British tutelage", the "pollution" caused by Western medicine and the persecuting and ignoring of traditional astrological authorities. European-run schools were also a problem: according to recorded testimonies, anger had spread because of stories that mathematics was replacing religious instruction, stories were chosen that would "bring contempt" upon Indian religions, and because girl children were exposed to "moral danger" by education.

The justice system was considered to be inherently unfair to the Indians. The official Blue Books, *East India (Torture) 1855–1857*, laid before the House of Commons during the sessions of 1856 and 1857, revealed that Company officers were allowed an extended series of appeals if convicted or accused of brutality or crimes against Indians.

The economic policies of the East India Company were also resented by many Indians.[38]

The Bengal Army

Each of the three "Presidencies" into which the East India Company divided India for administrative purposes maintained their own armies. Of these, the Army of the Bengal Presidency was the largest. Unlike the other two, it recruited heavily from among high-caste Hindus and comparatively wealthy Muslims. The Muslims formed a larger percentage of the 18 irregular cavalry units within the Bengal army, whilst Hindus were mainly to be found in the 84 regular infantry and cavalry regiments. The sepoys were therefore affected to a large degree by the concerns of the landholding and traditional members of Indian society. In the early years of Company rule, it tolerated and even encouraged the caste privileges and customs within the Bengal Army, which recruited its regular soldiers almost exclusively amongst the landowning Brahmins and Rajputs of the Bihar and Awadh regions. These soldiers were known as Purbiyas. By the time these customs and privileges came to be threatened by modernising regimes in Calcutta from the 1840s onwards, the sepoys had become accustomed to very high ritual status and were extremely sensitive to suggestions that their caste might be polluted.[39]

The sepoys also gradually became dissatisfied with various other aspects of army life. Their pay was relatively low and after Awadh and the Punjab were annexed, the soldiers no longer received extra pay (*batta* or *bhatta*) for service there, because they were no longer considered "foreign missions". The junior European officers became increasingly estranged from their soldiers, in many cases treating them as their racial inferiors. In 1856, a new Enlistment Act was introduced by the Company, which in theory made every unit in the Bengal Army liable to service overseas. Although it was intended to apply only to new recruits, the serving sepoys feared that the Act might be applied retroactively to them as well. A high-caste Hindu who travelled in the cramped conditions of a wooden troop ship could not cook his own food on his own fire, and accordingly risked losing caste through ritual pollution.

Onset of the Rebellion

Several months of increasing tensions coupled with various incidents preceded the actual rebellion. On 26 February 1857 the 19th Bengal Native Infantry (BNI) regiment became concerned that new cartridges they had been issued were wrapped in paper greased with cow and pig fat, which had to be opened by mouth thus affecting their religious sensibilities. Their Colonel confronted them supported by artillery and cavalry on the parade ground, but after some negotiation withdrew the artillery, and cancelled the next morning's parade.[40]

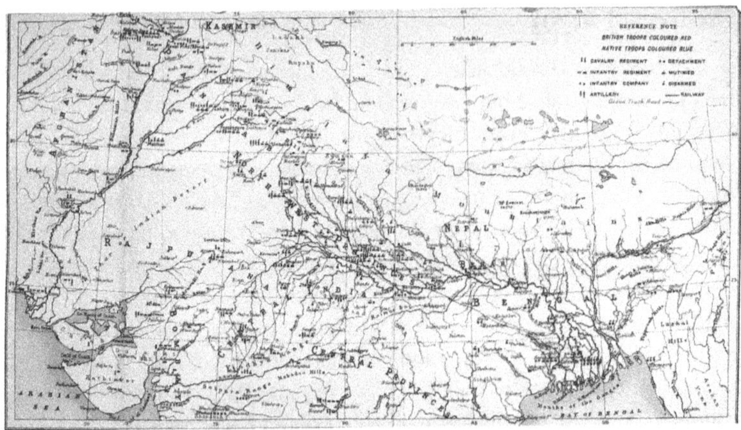

Figure 8: *Indian mutiny map showing position of troops on 1 May 1857*

Mangal Pandey

On 29 March 1857 at the Barrackpore parade ground, near Calcutta, 29-year-old Mangal Pandey of the 34th BNI, angered by the recent actions of the East India Company, declared that he would rebel against his commanders. Informed about Pandey's behaviour Sergeant-Major James Hewson went to investigate, only to have Pandey shoot at him. Hewson raised the alarm. When his adjutant Lt. Henry Baugh came out to investigate the unrest, Pandey opened fire but hit Baugh's horse instead.[41]

General John Hearsey came out to the parade ground to investigate, and claimed later that Mangal Pandey was in some kind of "religious frenzy". He ordered the Indian commander of the quarter guard Jemadar Ishwari Prasad to arrest Mangal Pandey, but the Jemadar refused. The quarter guard and other sepoys present, with the single exception of a soldier called Shaikh Paltu, drew back from restraining or arresting Mangal Pandey. Shaikh Paltu restrained Pandey from continuing his attack.[42]

After failing to incite his comrades into an open and active rebellion, Mangal Pandey tried to take his own life, by placing his musket to his chest and pulling the trigger with his toe. He managed only to wound himself. Court-martialled on 6 April, he was hanged two days later.

The Jemadar Ishwari Prasad was sentenced to death and hanged on 22 April. The regiment was disbanded and stripped of its uniforms because it was felt that it harboured ill-feelings towards its superiors, particularly after this incident. Shaikh Paltu was promoted to the rank of havildar in the Bengal Army, but was murdered shortly before the 34th BNI dispersed.

Sepoys in other regiments thought these punishments were harsh. The demonstration of disgrace during the formal disbanding helped foment the rebellion in view of some historians. Disgruntled ex-sepoys returned home to Awadh with a desire for revenge.

Unrest during April 1857

During April, there was unrest and fires at Agra, Allahabad and Ambala. At Ambala in particular, which was a large military cantonment where several units had been collected for their annual musketry practice, it was clear to General Anson, Commander-in-Chief of the Bengal Army, that some sort of rebellion over the cartridges was imminent. Despite the objections of the civilian Governor-General's staff, he agreed to postpone the musketry practice and allow a new drill by which the soldiers tore the cartridges with their fingers rather than their teeth. However, he issued no general orders making this standard practice throughout the Bengal Army and, rather than remain at Ambala to defuse or overawe potential trouble, he then proceeded to Simla, the cool "hill station" where many high officials spent the summer.

Although there was no open revolt at Ambala, there was widespread arson during late April. Barrack buildings (especially those belonging to soldiers who had used the Enfield cartridges) and European officers' bungalows were set on fire.

Meerut

At Meerut, a large military cantonment, 2,357 Indian sepoys and 2,038 British soldiers were stationed along with 12 British-manned guns. The station held one of the largest concentrations of British troops in India and this was later to be cited as evidence that the original rising was a spontaneous outbreak rather than a pre-planned plot.

Although the state of unrest within the Bengal Army was well known, on 24 April Lieutenant Colonel George Carmichael-Smyth, the unsympathetic commanding officer of the 3rd Bengal Light Cavalry, ordered 90 of his men to parade and perform firing drills. All except five of the men on parade refused to accept their cartridges. On 9 May, the remaining 85 men were court martialled, and most were sentenced to 10 years' imprisonment with hard labour. Eleven comparatively young soldiers were given five years' imprisonment. The entire garrison was paraded and watched as the condemned men were stripped of their uniforms and placed in shackles. As they were marched off to jail, the condemned soldiers berated their comrades for failing to support them.

The next day was Sunday. Some Indian soldiers warned off-duty junior European officers that plans were afoot to release the imprisoned soldiers by force,

Figure 9: *'The Sepoy revolt at Meerut," from the Illustrated London News, 1857*

Figure 10: *An 1858 photograph by Felice Beato of a mosque in Meerut where some of the rebel soldiers may have prayed*

but the senior officers to whom this was reported took no action. There was also unrest in the city of Meerut itself, with angry protests in the bazaar and some buildings being set on fire. In the evening, most European officers were preparing to attend church, while many of the European soldiers were off duty and had gone into canteens or into the bazaar in Meerut. The Indian troops, led by the 3rd Cavalry, broke into revolt. European junior officers who attempted to quell the first outbreaks were killed by the rebels. European officers' and civilians' quarters were attacked, and four civilian men, eight women and eight children were killed. Crowds in the bazaar attacked off-duty soldiers there. About 50 Indian civilians, some of them officers' servants who tried to defend or conceal their employers, were killed by the sepoys. While the action of the sepoys in freeing their 85 imprisoned comrades appears to have been spontaneous, some civilian rioting in the city was reportedly encouraged by kotwal (local police commander) Dhan Singh Gurjar

Some sepoys (especially from the 11th Bengal Native Infantry) escorted trusted British officers and women and children to safety before joining the revolt.[43] Some officers and their families escaped to Rampur, where they found refuge with the Nawab.

The British historian Philip Mason notes that it was inevitable that most of the sepoys and sowars from Meerut should have made for Delhi on the night of 10 May. It was a strong walled city located only forty miles away, it was the ancient capital and present seat of the nominal Mughal Emperor and finally there were no British troops in garrison there in contrast to Meerut. No effort was made to pursue them.

Delhi

Early on 11 May, the first parties of the 3rd Cavalry reached Delhi. From beneath the windows of the King's apartments in the palace, they called on him to acknowledge and lead them. Bahadur Shah did nothing at this point, apparently treating the sepoys as ordinary petitioners, but others in the palace were quick to join the revolt. During the day, the revolt spread. European officials and dependents, Indian Christians and shop keepers within the city were killed, some by sepoys and others by crowds of rioters.[44]

There were three battalion-sized regiments of Bengal Native Infantry stationed in or near the city. Some detachments quickly joined the rebellion, while others held back but also refused to obey orders to take action against the rebels. In the afternoon, a violent explosion in the city was heard for several miles. Fearing that the arsenal, which contained large stocks of arms and ammunition, would fall intact into rebel hands, the nine British Ordnance officers there had opened fire on the sepoys, including the men of their own guard. When resistance

Figure 11: *Massacre of officers by insurgent cavalry at Delhi*

Figure 12: *The Flagstaff Tower, Delhi, where the European survivors of the rebellion gathered on 11 May 1857; photographed by Felice Beato*

appeared hopeless, they blew up the arsenal. Six of the nine officers survived, but the blast killed many in the streets and nearby houses and other buildings. The news of these events finally tipped the sepoys stationed around Delhi into open rebellion. The sepoys were later able to salvage at least some arms from the arsenal, and a magazine two miles (3 km) outside Delhi, containing up to 3,000 barrels of gunpowder, was captured without resistance.

Many fugitive European officers and civilians had congregated at the Flagstaff Tower on the ridge north of Delhi, where telegraph operators were sending news of the events to other British stations. When it became clear that the help expected from Meerut was not coming, they made their way in carriages to Karnal. Those who became separated from the main body or who could not reach the Flagstaff Tower also set out for Karnal on foot. Some were helped by villagers on the way; others were killed.

The next day, Bahadur Shah held his first formal court for many years. It was attended by many excited sepoys. The King was alarmed by the turn events had taken, but eventually accepted the sepoys' allegiance and agreed to give his countenance to the rebellion. On 16 May, up to 50 Europeans who had been held prisoner in the palace or had been discovered hiding in the city were killed by some of the King's servants under a peepul tree in a courtyard outside the palace.[45]

Supporters and opposition

The news of the events at Delhi spread rapidly, provoking uprisings among sepoys and disturbances in many districts. In many cases, it was the behaviour of British military and civilian authorities themselves which precipitated disorder. Learning of the fall of Delhi by telegraph, many Company administrators hastened to remove themselves, their families and servants to places of safety. At Agra, 160 miles (260 km) from Delhi, no less than 6,000 assorted non-combatants converged on the Fort.

The military authorities also reacted in disjointed manner. Some officers trusted their sepoys, but others tried to disarm them to forestall potential uprisings. At Benares and Allahabad, the disarmings were bungled, also leading to local revolts.[46]

Most Muslims did not share the rebels' dislike of the British administration and their ulema could not agree on whether to declare a jihad. There were Islamic scholars such as Maulana Muhammad Qasim Nanautavi and Maulana Rashid Ahmad Gangohi who took up arms against the colonial rule. But a large number of Muslims, among them ulema from both the Sunni and Shia sects, sided with the British. Various Ahl-i-Hadith scholars and colleagues of

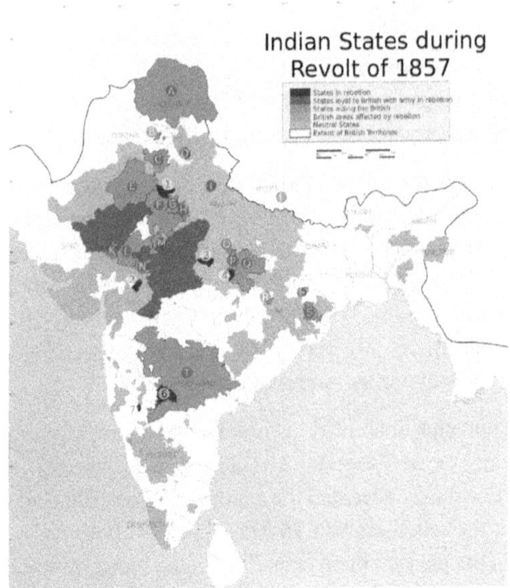

Figure 13: *States during the rebellion*

Figure 14: *Troops of the Native Allies by George Francklin Atkinson, 1859.*

Figure 15: *Sikh Troops Dividing the Spoil Taken from Mutineers, circa 1860*

Nanautavi rejected the jihad. The most influential member of Ahl-i-Hadith ulema in Delhi, Maulana Sayyid Nazir Husain Dehlvi, resisted pressure from the mutineers to call for a jihad and instead declared in favour of British rule, viewing the Muslim-British relationship as a legal contract which could not be broken unless their religious rights were breached.

Although most of the mutinous sepoys in Delhi were Hindus, a significant proportion of the insurgents were Muslims. The proportion of *ghazis* grew to be about a quarter of the local fighting force by the end of the siege and included a regiment of suicide *ghazis* from Gwalior who had vowed never to eat again and to fight until they met certain death at the hands of British troops.

The Sikhs and Pathans of the Punjab and North-West Frontier Province supported the British and helped in the recapture of Delhi.[47] Historian John Harris has asserted that the Sikhs wanted to avenge the annexation of the Sikh Empire eight years earlier by the Company with the help of *Purbiyas* ('Easterners'), Biharis and those from the United Provinces of Agra and Oudh who had formed part of the East India Company's armies in the First and Second Anglo-Sikh Wars. He has also suggested that Sikhs felt insulted by the attitude of sepoys who, in their view, had beaten the Khalsa only with British help; they resented and despised them far more than they did the British.

The Sikhs feared reinstatement of Mughal rule in northern India because they had been persecuted heavily in the past by the Mughal dynasty.

Sikh support for the British resulted from grievances surrounding sepoys' perceived conduct during and after the Anglo-Sikh Wars. Firstly, many Sikhs resented that Hindustanis/Purbiyas in service of the Sikh state had been foremost in urging the wars, which lost them their independence. Sikh soldiers also recalled that the bloodiest battles of the war, Chillianwala and Ferozeshah, were won by British troops, and they believed that the Hindustani sepoys had refused to meet them in battle. These feelings were compounded when Hindustani sepoys were assigned a very visible role as garrison troops in Punjab and awarded profit-making civil posts in Punjab.

In 1857, the Bengal Army had 86,000 men, of which 12,000 were European, 16,000 Sikh and 1,500 Gurkha. There were 311,000 native soldiers in India altogether, 40,160 European soldiers and 5,362 officers. Fifty-four of the Bengal Army's 74 regular Native Infantry Regiments mutinied, but some were immediately destroyed or broke up, with their sepoys drifting away to their homes. A number of the remaining 20 regiments were disarmed or disbanded to prevent or forestall mutiny. In total, only twelve of the original Bengal Native Infantry regiments survived to pass into the new Indian Army.[48] All ten of the Bengal Light Cavalry regiments mutinied.

The Bengal Army also contained 29 irregular cavalry and 42 irregular infantry regiments. Of these, a substantial contingent from the recently annexed state of Awadh mutinied *en masse*. Another large contingent from Gwalior also mutinied, even though that state's ruler supported the British. The remainder of the irregular units were raised from a wide variety of sources and were less affected by the concerns of mainstream Indian society. Some irregular units actively supported the Company: three Gurkha and five of six Sikh infantry units, and the six infantry and six cavalry units of the recently raised Punjab Irregular Force.[49]

On 1 April 1858, the number of Indian soldiers in the Bengal army loyal to the Company was 80,053.[50,51] However large numbers were hastily raised in the Punjab and North-West Frontier after the outbreak of the Rebellion. The Bombay army had three mutinies in its 29 regiments, whilst the Madras army had none at all, although elements of one of its 52 regiments refused to volunteer for service in Bengal. Nonetheless, most of southern India remained passive, with only intermittent outbreaks of violence. Many parts of the region were ruled by the Nizams or the Mysore royalty, and were thus not directly under British rule.

Figure 16: *Fugitive British officers and their families attacked by mutineers.*

The Revolt

Initial stages

Bahadur Shah Zafar was proclaimed the Emperor of the whole of India. Most contemporary and modern accounts suggest that he was coerced by the sepoys and his courtiers to sign the proclamation against his will.[52] In spite of the significant loss of power that the Mughal dynasty had suffered in the preceding centuries, their name still carried great prestige across northern India. Civilians, nobility and other dignitaries took an oath of allegiance. The emperor issued coins in his name, one of the oldest ways of asserting imperial status. The adhesion of the Mughal emperor, however, turned the Sikhs of the Punjab away from the rebellion, as they did not want to return to Islamic rule, having fought many wars against the Mughal rulers. The province of Bengal was largely quiet throughout the entire period. The British, who had long ceased to take the authority of the Mughal Emperor seriously, were astonished at how the ordinary people responded to Zafar's call for war.

Initially, the Indian rebels were able to push back Company forces, and captured several important towns in Haryana, Bihar, the Central Provinces and the United Provinces. When European troops were reinforced and began to counterattack, the mutineers were especially handicapped by their lack of centralized command and control. Although the rebels produced some natural leaders

AUGUST 15, 1857.] THE ILLUSTRATED LONDON NEWS 157

NYNEE TAL.

IN this hill station in the Himalaya, we learn from the recent news from India, most of the officers and English families who escaped from the insurrections at Delhi and Meerut are stated to have taken refuge.

Nynee Tal is situated in the British district of Kumaon—a town on the route from Rampoor to Almora, twenty-two miles S.W. by S. of the latter. It lies around a lake which is 6409 feet above the level of the sea. At 2323 feet above the lake is Cheenur, the highest mountain. This new settlement has been known to the English only about fourteen years. It is extensively resorted to as a sanitarium, and a market has thus been opened for the productions of the neighbouring country, which, it is represented, is of considerable advantage to its cultivators. A church dedicated to St John in the Wilderness was erected here by public subscription in 1847.

The jungle at the foot of the hill abounds with tigers, leopards, bears, &c.; and it was on a shooting excursion that a party of officers discovered the lake. The bazaar is well situated, and contains a market and several shops. The lake is well stocked with fish. The rains are heavy, but the climate is almost the finest in the world.

THE LAKE AND BAZAAR OF NYNEE TAL, HIMALAYA, THE REFUGE OF ENGLISH FAMILIES WHO HAVE ESCAPED FROM THE INSURRECTIONS IN DELHI, MEERUT, ETC.

Figure 17: *An etching of Nynee Tal (today Nainital) and accompanying story in the Illustrated London News, August 15, 1857, describing how the resort town in the Himalayas served as a refuge for British families escaping from the rebellion of 1857 in Delhi and Meerut.*

such as Bakht Khan, whom the Emperor later nominated as commander-in-chief after his son Mirza Mughal proved ineffectual, for the most part they were forced to look for leadership to rajahs and princes. Some of these were to prove dedicated leaders, but others were self-interested or inept.

In the countryside around Meerut, a general Gurjar uprising posed the largest threat to the British. In Parikshitgarh near Meerut, Gurjars declared Choudhari Kadam Singh (Kuddum Singh) their leader, and expelled Company police. Kadam Singh Gurjar led a large force, estimates varying from 2,000 to 10,000. Bulandshahr and Bijnor also came under the control of Gurjars under Walidad Khan and Maho Singh respectively. Contemporary sources report that nearly all the Gurjar villages between Meerut and Delhi participated in the revolt, in some cases with support from Jullundur, and it was not until late July that, with the help of local Jats, the British managed to regain control of the area.

The Imperial Gazetteer of India states that throughout the Indian Rebellion of 1857, Gurjars and Ranghars (Muslim rajpoots) proved the "most irreconcilable enemies" of the British in the Bulandshahr area.

Figure 18: *Attack of the mutineers on the Redan Battery at Lucknow, 30 July 1857*

Mufti Nizamuddin, a renowned scholar of Lahore, issued a Fatwa against the British forces and called upon the local population to support the forces of Rao Tula Ram. Casualties were high at the subsequent engagement at Narnaul (Nasibpur). After the defeat of Rao Tula Ram on 16 November 1857, Mufti Nizamuddin was arrested, and his brother Mufti Yaqinuddin and brother-in-law Abdur Rahman (alias Nabi Baksh) were arrested in Tijara. They were taken to Delhi and hanged. Having lost the fight at Nasibpur, Rao Tula Ram and Pran Sukh Yadav requested arms from Russia, which had just been engaged against Britain in the Crimean War.

Delhi

The British were slow to strike back at first. It took time for troops stationed in Britain to make their way to India by sea, although some regiments moved overland through Persia from the Crimean War, and some regiments already *en route* for China were diverted to India.

It took time to organise the European troops already in India into field forces, but eventually two columns left Meerut and Simla. They proceeded slowly towards Delhi and fought, killed, and hanged numerous Indians along the way. Two months after the first outbreak of rebellion at Meerut, the two forces met near Karnal. The combined force including two Gurkha units serving in the Bengal Army under contract from the Kingdom of Nepal, fought the main army of the rebels at Badli-ke-Serai and drove them back to Delhi.

Figure 19: *Assault of Delhi and capture of the Cashmere Gate, 14 September 1857*

The Company established a base on the Delhi ridge to the north of the city and the Siege of Delhi began. The siege lasted roughly from 1 July to 21 September. However, the encirclement was hardly complete, and for much of the siege the Company forces were outnumbered and it often seemed that it was the Company forces and not Delhi that were under siege, as the rebels could easily receive resources and reinforcements. For several weeks, it seemed likely that disease, exhaustion and continuous sorties by rebels from Delhi would force the Company forces to withdraw, but the outbreaks of rebellion in the Punjab were forestalled or suppressed, allowing the Punjab Movable Column of British, Sikh and Pakhtun soldiers under John Nicholson to reinforce the besiegers on the Ridge on 14 August.[53,54] On 30 August the rebels offered terms, which were refused.[55]

Figure 20: *The Jantar Mantar observatory in Delhi in 1858, damaged in the fighting*

Figure 21: *Mortar damage to Kashmiri Gate, Delhi, 1858*

Figure 22: *Hindu Rao's house in Delhi, now a hospital, was extensively damaged in the fighting*

Figure 23: *Bank of Delhi was attacked by mortar and gunfire*

Figure 24: *Capture of Bahadur Shah Zafar and his sons by William Hodson at Humayun's tomb on 20 September 1857*

An eagerly awaited heavy siege train joined the besieging force, and from 7 September, the siege guns battered breaches in the walls and silenced the rebels' artillery.:478 An attempt to storm the city through the breaches and the Kashmiri Gate was launched on 14 September.:480 The attackers gained a foothold within the city but suffered heavy casualties, including John Nicholson. The British commander wished to withdraw, but was persuaded to hold on by his junior officers. After a week of street fighting, the British reached the Red Fort. Bahadur Shah Zafar had already fled to Humayun's tomb. The British had retaken the city.

The troops of the besieging force proceeded to loot and pillage the city. A large number of the citizens were killed in retaliation for the Europeans and Indian civilians that had been slaughtered by the rebels. During the street fighting, artillery was set up city's main mosque, neighbourhoods within range were bombarded; the homes of the Muslim nobility that contained innumerable cultural, artistic, literary and monetary riches destroyed.

The British soon arrested Bahadur Shah, and the next day the British agent William Hodson had his sons Mirza Mughal, Mirza Khazir Sultan, and grandson Mirza Abu Bakr shot under his own authority at the Khooni Darwaza (the bloody gate) near Delhi Gate. On hearing the news Zafar reacted with shocked silence while his wife Zinat Mahal was content as she believed her son was now Zafar's heir. Shortly after the fall of Delhi, the victorious attackers organised

Figure 25: *Tatya Tope's Soldiery*

a column that relieved another besieged Company force in Agra, and then pressed on to Cawnpore, which had also recently been retaken. This gave the Company forces a continuous, although still tenuous, line of communication from the east to west of India.

Cawnpore (Kanpur)

In June, sepoys under General Wheeler in Cawnpore (now Kanpur) rebelled and besieged the European entrenchment. Wheeler was not only a veteran and respected soldier but also married to a high-caste Indian lady. He had relied on his own prestige, and his cordial relations with the Nana Sahib to thwart rebellion, and took comparatively few measures to prepare fortifications and lay in supplies and ammunition.

The besieged endured three weeks of the Siege of Cawnpore with little water or food, suffering continuous casualties to men, women and children. On 25 June Nana Sahib made an offer of safe passage to Allahabad. With barely three days' food rations remaining, the British agreed provided they could keep their small arms and that the evacuation should take place in daylight on the morning of the 27th (the Nana Sahib wanted the evacuation to take place on the night of the 26th). Early in the morning of 27 June, the European party left their entrenchment and made their way to the river where boats provided by the

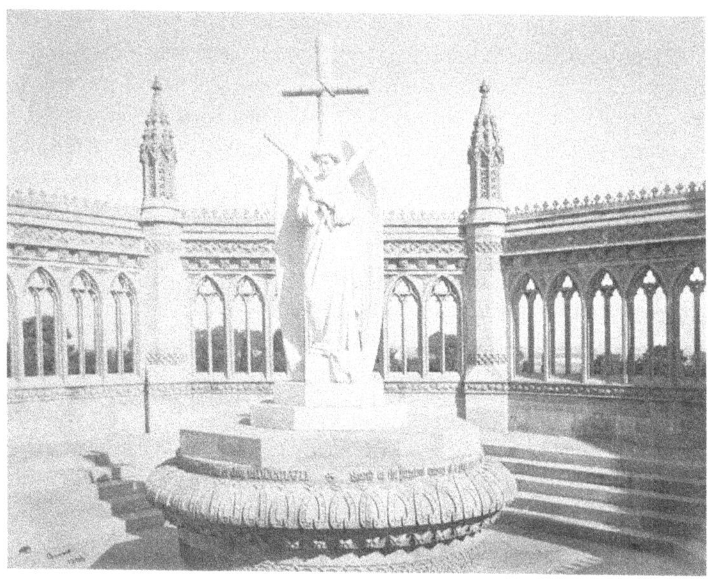

Figure 26: *A memorial erected (circa 1860) by the British after the Mutiny at the Bibighar Well. After India's Independence the statue was moved to the All Souls Memorial Church, Cawnpore. Albumen silver print by Samuel Bourne, 1860*

Nana Sahib were waiting to take them to Allahabad.[56] Several sepoys who had stayed loyal to the Company were removed by the mutineers and killed, either because of their loyalty or because "they had become Christian." A few injured British officers trailing the column were also apparently hacked to death by angry sepoys. After the European party had largely arrived at the dock, which was surrounded by sepoys positioned on both banks of the Ganges,[57] with clear lines of fire, firing broke out and the boats were abandoned by their crew, and caught or were set[58] on fire using pieces of red hot charcoal. The British party tried to push the boats off but all except three remained stuck. One boat with over a dozen wounded men initially escaped, but later grounded, was caught by mutineers and pushed back down the river towards the carnage at Cawnpore. Towards the end rebel cavalry rode into the water to finish off any survivors. After the firing ceased the survivors were rounded up and the men shot. By the time the massacre was over, most of the male members of the party were dead while the surviving women and children were removed and held hostage to be later killed in the Bibighar massacre.[59] Only four men eventually escaped alive from Cawnpore on one of the boats: two private soldiers, a lieutenant, and Captain Mowbray Thomson, who wrote a first-hand account of his experiences entitled *The Story of Cawnpore* (London, 1859).

During his trial, Tatya Tope denied the existence of any such plan and described the incident in the following terms: the Europeans had already boarded the boats and Tatya Tope raised his right hand to signal their departure. That very moment someone from the crowd blew a loud bugle, which created disorder and in the ongoing bewilderment, the boatmen jumped off the boats. The rebels started shooting indiscriminately. Nana Sahib, who was staying in Savada Kothi (Bungalow) nearby, was informed about what was happening and immediately came to stop it.[60] Some British histories allow that it might well have been the result of accident or error; someone accidentally or maliciously fired a shot, the panic-stricken British opened fire, and it became impossible to stop the massacre.[61]

The surviving women and children were taken to the Nana Sahib and then confined first to the Savada Kothi and then to the home of the local magistrate's clerk (the Bibighar) where they were joined by refugees from Fatehgarh. Overall five men and two hundred and six women and children were confined in The Bibigarh for about two weeks. In one week 25 were brought out dead, from dysentery and cholera. Meanwhile, a Company relief force that had advanced from Allahabad defeated the Indians and by 15 July it was clear that the Nana Sahib would not be able to hold Cawnpore and a decision was made by the Nana Sahib and other leading rebels that the hostages must be killed. After the sepoys refused to carry out this order, two Muslim butchers, two Hindu peasants and one of Nana's bodyguards went into The Bibigarh. Armed with knives and hatchets they murdered the women and children. After the massacre the walls were covered in bloody hand prints, and the floor littered with fragments of human limbs. The dead and the dying were thrown down a nearby well. When the 50-foot (15 m) deep well was filled with remains to within 6 feet (1.8 m) of the top,[62] the remainder were thrown into the Ganges.[63]

Historians have given many reasons for this act of cruelty. With Company forces approaching Cawnpore and some believing that they would not advance if there were no hostages to save, their murders were ordered. Or perhaps it was to ensure that no information was leaked after the fall of Cawnpore. Other historians have suggested that the killings were an attempt to undermine Nana Sahib's relationship with the British.[64] Perhaps it was due to fear, the fear of being recognised by some of the prisoners for having taken part in the earlier firings.

Figure 27: *Photograph entitled, 'The Hospital in General Wheeler's entrenchment, Cawnpore." (1858) The hospital was the site of the first major loss of European lives in Cawnpore*

Figure 28: *1858 picture of Sati Chaura Ghat on the banks of the Ganges River, where on 27 June 1857 many British men lost their lives and the surviving women and children were taken prisoner by the rebels.*

Figure 29: *Bibigarh house where European women and children were killed and the well where their bodies were found, 1858.*

Figure 30: *The Bibighar Well site where a memorial had been built. Samuel Bourne, 1860.*

Figure 31: *A contemporary image of the massacre at the Satichaura Ghat*

The killing of the women and children hardened British attitudes against the sepoys. The British public was aghast and the anti-Imperial and pro-Indian proponents lost all their support. Cawnpore became a war cry for the British and their allies for the rest of the conflict. Nana Sahib disappeared near the end of the Rebellion and it is not known what happened to him.

Other British accounts[65,66,67] state that indiscriminate punitive measures were taken in early June, two weeks before the murders at the Bibighar (but after those at both Meerut and Delhi), specifically by Lieutenant Colonel James George Smith Neill of the Madras Fusiliers, commanding at Allahabad while moving towards Cawnpore. At the nearby town of Fatehpur, a mob had attacked and murdered the local European population. On this pretext, Neill ordered all villages beside the Grand Trunk Road to be burned and their inhabitants to be killed by hanging. Neill's methods were "ruthless and horrible"[68] and far from intimidating the population, may well have induced previously undecided sepoys and communities to revolt.

Neill was killed in action at Lucknow on 26 September and was never called to account for his punitive measures, though contemporary British sources lionised him and his "gallant blue caps".[69] When the British retook Cawnpore, the soldiers took their sepoy prisoners to the Bibighar and forced them to lick the bloodstains from the walls and floor. They then hanged or "blew from the cannon", the traditional Mughal punishment for mutiny, the majority of the sepoy prisoners. Although some claimed the sepoys took no actual part in the

Figure 32: *The interior of the Secundra Bagh, several months after its storming during the second relief of Lucknow. Albumen silver print by Felice Beato, 1858*

killings themselves, they did not act to stop it and this was acknowledged by Captain Thompson after the British departed Cawnpore for a second time.

Lucknow

Very soon after the events at Meerut, rebellion erupted in the state of Awadh (also known as Oudh, in modern-day Uttar Pradesh), which had been annexed barely a year before. The British Commissioner resident at Lucknow, Sir Henry Lawrence, had enough time to fortify his position inside the Residency compound. The Company forces numbered some 1700 men, including loyal sepoys. The rebels' assaults were unsuccessful, and so they began a barrage of artillery and musket fire into the compound. Lawrence was one of the first casualties. The rebels tried to breach the walls with explosives and bypass them via underground tunnels that led to underground close combat.:[486] After 90 days of siege, defended by John Eardley Inglis, numbers of Company forces were reduced to 300 loyal sepoys, 350 British soldiers and 550 non-combatants.

On 25 September, a relief column under the command of Sir Henry Havelock and accompanied by Sir James Outram (who in theory was his superior) fought its way from Cawnpore to Lucknow in a brief campaign, in which the numerically small column defeated rebel forces in a series of increasingly large battles. This became known as 'The First Relief of Lucknow', as this force was not strong enough to break the siege or extricate themselves, and so was forced to join the garrison. In October another, larger, army under the new Commander-in-Chief, Sir Colin Campbell, was finally able to relieve the garrison and on 18 November, they evacuated the defended enclave within the city, the women and children leaving first. They then conducted an orderly withdrawal, firstly to Alambagh 4 miles (6.4 km) north where a force of 4,000 were left to construct a fort, then to Cawnpore, where they defeated an attempt by Tatya Tope to recapture the city in the Second Battle of Cawnpore.

In March 1858, Campbell once again advanced on Lucknow with a large army, meeting up with the force at Alambagh, this time seeking to suppress the rebellion in Awadh. He was aided by a large Nepalese contingent advancing from the north under Jang Bahadur. Campbell's advance was slow and methodical, with a force under General Outram crossing the river on cask bridges on 4 March to enable them to fire artillery in flank, the forces drove the large but disorganised rebel army from Lucknow with the final fighting shooting on 21 March,[:491] there were few casualties to his own troops. This nevertheless allowed large numbers of the rebels to disperse into Awadh, and Campbell was forced to spend the summer and autumn dealing with scattered pockets of resistance while losing men to heat, disease and guerrilla actions.

Jhansi

Jhansi was a Maratha-ruled princely state in Bundelkhand. When the Raja of Jhansi died without a biological male heir in 1853, it was annexed to the British Raj by the Governor-General of India under the doctrine of lapse. His widow, Rani Lakshmi Bai, the Rani of Jhansi protested against the denial of rights of their adopted son. When war broke out, Jhansi quickly became a centre of the rebellion. A small group of Company officials and their families took refuge in Jhansi Fort, and the Rani negotiated their evacuation. However, when they left the fort they were massacred by the rebels over whom the Rani had no control; the Europeans suspected the Rani of complicity, despite her repeated denials.

By the end of June 1857, the Company had lost control of much of Bundelkhand and eastern Rajasthan. The Bengal Army units in the area, having rebelled, marched to take part in the battles for Delhi and Cawnpore. The many princely states that made up this area began warring amongst themselves. In September and October 1857, the Rani led the successful defence of Jhansi against the invading armies of the neighbouring rajas of Datia and Orchha.

On 3 February, Sir Hugh Rose broke the 3-month siege of Saugor. Thousands of local villagers welcomed him as a liberator, freeing them from rebel occupation.[70]

Figure 33: *Jhansi Fort, which was taken over by rebel forces, and subsequently defended against British recapture by the Rani of Jhansi*

In March 1858, the Central India Field Force, led by Sir Hugh Rose, advanced on and laid siege to Jhansi. The Company forces captured the city, but the Rani fled in disguise.

After being driven from Jhansi and Kalpi, on 1 June 1858 Rani Lakshmi Bai and a group of Maratha rebels captured the fortress city of Gwalior from the Scindia rulers, who were British allies. This might have reinvigorated the rebellion but the Central India Field Force very quickly advanced against the city. The Rani died on 17 June, the second day of the Battle of Gwalior, probably killed by a carbine shot from the 8th King's Royal Irish Hussars according to the account of three independent Indian representatives. The Company forces recaptured Gwalior within the next three days. In descriptions of the scene of her last battle, she was compared to Joan of Arc by some commentators.[71]

Indore

Colonel Henry Marion Durand, the then-Company resident at Indore, had brushed away any possibility of uprising in Indore. However, on 1 July, sepoys in Holkar's army revolted and opened fire on the cavalry pickets of the Bhopal Contingent (a locally raised force with British officers). When Colonel Travers rode forward to charge, the Bhopal Cavalry refused to follow. The Bhopal Infantry also refused orders and instead levelled their guns at European sergeants and officers. Since all possibility of mounting an effective deterrent was lost,

Figure 34: *Execution of mutineers at Peshawar*

Durand decided to gather up all the European residents and escape, although 39 European residents of Indore were killed.

Other regions

Punjab

What was then referred to by the British as the Punjab was a very large administrative division, centered on Lahore. It included not only the present-day Indian and Pakistani Punjabi regions but also the North West Frontier districts bordering Afghanistan

Much of the region had been the Sikh Empire, ruled by Ranjit Singh until his death in 1839. The kingdom had then fallen into disorder, with court factions and the Khalsa (the Sikh army) contending for power at the Lahore Durbar (court). After two Anglo-Sikh Wars, the entire region was annexed by the East India Company in 1849. In 1857, the region still contained the highest numbers of both European and Indian troops.

The inhabitants of the Punjab were not as sympathetic to the sepoys as they were elsewhere in India, which limited many of the outbreaks in the Punjab to disjointed uprisings by regiments of sepoys isolated from each other. In some garrisons, notably Ferozepore, indecision on the part of the senior European officers allowed the sepoys to rebel, but the sepoys then left the area, mostly

Figure 35: *Marble Lectern in memory of 35 British soldiers in Jhelum*

heading for Delhi. At the most important garrison, that of Peshawar close to the Afghan frontier, many comparatively junior officers ignored their nominal commander, General Reed, and took decisive action. They intercepted the sepoys' mail, thus preventing their coordinating an uprising, and formed a force known as the "Punjab Movable Column" to move rapidly to suppress any revolts as they occurred. When it became clear from the intercepted correspondence that some of the sepoys at Peshawar were on the point of open revolt, the four most disaffected Bengal Native regiments were disarmed by the two British infantry regiments in the cantonment, backed by artillery, on 22 May. This decisive act induced many local chieftains to side with the British.[72]

Jhelum in Punjab saw a mutiny of native troops against the British. Here 35 British soldiers of Her Majesty's 24th Regiment of Foot (South Wales Borderers) were killed by mutineers on 7 July 1857. Among the dead was Captain Francis Spring, the eldest son of Colonel William Spring. To commemorate this event St. John's Church Jhelum was built and the names of those 35 British soldiers are carved on a marble lectern present in that church.

The final large-scale military uprising in the Punjab took place on 9 July, when most of a brigade of sepoys at Sialkot rebelled and began to move to Delhi. They were intercepted by John Nicholson with an equal British force as they tried to cross the Ravi River. After fighting steadily but unsuccessfully for

Figure 36: *Lieutenant William Alexander Kerr, 24th Bombay Native Infantry, near Kolapore, July 1857*

several hours, the sepoys tried to fall back across the river but became trapped on an island. Three days later, Nicholson annihilated the 1,100 trapped sepoys in the Battle of Trimmu Ghat.[73]

The British had been recruiting irregular units from Sikh and Pakhtun communities even before the first unrest among the Bengal units, and the numbers of these were greatly increased during the Rebellion, 34,000 fresh levies eventually being raised.[74]

At one stage, faced with the need to send troops to reinforce the besiegers of Delhi, the Commissioner of the Punjab (Sir John Lawrence) suggested handing the coveted prize of Peshawar to Dost Mohammed Khan of Afghanistan in return for a pledge of friendship. The British Agents in Peshawar and the adjacent districts were horrified. Referring to the massacre of a retreating British army in 1842, Herbert Edwardes wrote, "Dost Mahomed would not be a mortal Afghan ... if he did not assume our day to be gone in India and follow after us as an enemy. Europeans cannot retreat – Kabul would come again."[75] In the event Lord Canning insisted on Peshawar being held, and Dost Mohammed, whose relations with Britain had been equivocal for over 20 years, remained neutral.

In September 1858 Rae Ahmed Nawaz Khan Kharal, head of the Khurrul tribe, led an insurrection in the Neeli Bar district, between the Sutlej, Ravi and Chenab rivers. The rebels held the jungles of Gogaira and had some initial successes against the British forces in the area, besieging Major Crawford Chamberlain at Chichawatni. A squadron of Punjabi cavalry sent by Sir John Lawrence raised the siege. Ahmed Khan was killed but the insurgents found a new leader in Mahr Bahawal Fatyana, who maintained the uprising for three months until Government forces penetrated the jungle and scattered the rebel tribesmen.[76]

Bihar

Kunwar Singh, the 80-year-old Rajput Zamindar of Jagdispur, whose estate was in the process of being sequestrated by the Revenue Board, instigated and assumed the leadership of revolt in Bihar.

On 25 July, mutiny erupted in the garrisons of Dinapur. Mutinying sepoys from the 7th, 8th and 40th regiments of Bengal Native Infantry quickly moved towards the city of Arrah and were joined by Kunwar Singh and his men. Mr. Boyle, a British railway engineer in Arrah, had already prepared an outbuilding on his property for defence against such attacks.[77] As the rebels approached Arrah, all European residents took refuge at Mr. Boyle's house. A siege soon ensued – eighteen civilians and 50 loyal sepoys from the Bengal Military Police Battalion under the command of Herwald Wake, the local magistrate, defended the house against artillery and musketry fire from an estimated 2000 to 3000 mutineers and rebels.

On 29 July 400 men were sent out from Dinapore to relieve Arrah, but this force was ambushed by the rebels around a mile away from the siege house, severely defeated, and driven back. On 30 July, Major Vincent Eyre, who was going up the river with his troops and guns, reached Buxar and heard about the siege. He immediately disembarked his guns and troops (the 5th Fusiliers) and started marching towards Arrah, disregarding direct orders not to do so. On 2 August, some 6 miles (9.7 km) short of Arrah, the Major was ambushed by the mutineers and rebels. After an intense fight, the 5th Fusiliers charged and stormed the rebel positions successfully. On 3 August, Major Eyre and his men reached the siege house and successfully ended the siege.

After receiving reinforcements Major Eyre pursued Kunwar Singh to his palace in Jagdispur, however Singh had left by the time Eyre's forces arrived. Eyre then proceeded to destroy the palace and the homes of Singh's brothers.

Bengal and Tripura

In September 1857, sepoys took control of the treasury in Chittagong. The treasury remained under rebel control for several days. Further mutinies on 18 November saw the 2nd, 3rd and 4th companies of the 34th Bengal Infantry Regiment storming the Chittagong Jail and releasing all prisoners. The mutineers were eventually suppressed by the Gurkha regiments. The mutiny also spread to Dacca, the former Mughal capital of Bengal. Residents in the city's Lalbagh area were kept awake at night by the rebellion. Sepoys joined hands with the common populace in Jalpaiguri to take control of the city's cantonment. In January 1858, many sepoys received shelter from the royal family of the princely state of Hill Tippera.

The interior areas of Bengal proper were already experiencing growing resistance to Company rule due to the Muslim Faraizi movement.

Gujarat

In central and north Gujarat, the rebellion was sustained by land owner Jagirdars, Talukdars and Thakors with the support of armed communities of Bhil, Koli, Pathans and Arabs, unlike the mutiny by sepoys in north India. Their main opposition of British was due to Inam commission. The Bet Dwarka island, along with Okhamandal region of Kathiawar peninsula which was under Gaekwad of Baroda State, saw a revolt by the Vaghers in January 1858 who, by July 1859, controlled that region. In October 1859, a joint offensive by British, Gaekwad and other princely states troops ousted the rebels and recaptured the region.

British Empire

The authorities in British colonies with an Indian population, sepoy or civilian, took measures to secure themselves against copycat uprisings. In the Straits Settlements, and Trinidad the annual Hosay processions were banned,[78] riots broke out in penal settlements in Burma, and the Settlements, in Penang the loss of a musket provoked a near riot,[79] and security was boosted especially in locations with an Indian convict population.[80]

Figure 37: *'The Relief of Lucknow" by Thomas Jones Barker*

Aftermath

Death toll and atrocities

Both combatant sides committed atrocities against civilians.[81]

In Oudh alone, 150,000 Indians were estimated to have been killed during the war, with 100,000 of them being civilians. The general population in places such as such as Delhi, Allahabad, Kanpur and Lucknow was massacred after being recaptured by British forces.

Another notable atrocity was carried out by General Neill who massacred thousands of Indian mutineers and Indian civilians suspected of supporting the rebellion.

The rebels' murder of women, children and wounded British soldiers at Cawnpore, and the subsequent printing of the events in the British papers, left many British soldiers outraged and seeking revenge. As well as hanging mutineers, the British had some "blown from cannon," (an old Mughal punishment adopted many years before in India), in which sentenced rebels were tied over the mouths of cannons and blown to pieces when the cannons were fired.[82] A particular act of cruelty on behalf of the British troops at Cawnpore included forcing many Muslim or Hindu rebels to eat pork or beef, as well as licking buildings freshly stained with blood of the dead before subsequent public hangings.

Most of the British press, outraged by the stories of rape and the killings of civilians and wounded British soldiers, did not advocate clemency of any kind.

Figure 38: *British soldiers looting Qaisar Bagh, Lucknow, after its recapture (steel engraving, late 1850s)*

Governor General Canning ordered moderation in dealing with native sensibilities and earned the scornful sobriquet "Clemency Canning" from the press[83] and later parts of the British public.

In terms of sheer numbers, the casualties were much higher on the Indian side. A letter published after the fall of Delhi in the *Bombay Telegraph* and reproduced in the British press testified to the scale of the Indian casualties:

> .... *All the city's people found within the walls of the city of Delhi when our troops entered were bayoneted on the spot, and the number was considerable, as you may suppose, when I tell you that in some houses forty and fifty people were hiding. These were not mutineers but residents of the city, who trusted to our well-known mild rule for pardon. I am glad to say they were disappointed.*

From the end of 1857, the British had begun to gain ground again. Lucknow was retaken in March 1858. On 8 July 1858, a peace treaty was signed and the rebellion ended. The last rebels were defeated in Gwalior on 20 June 1858. By 1859, rebel leaders Bakht Khan and Nana Sahib had either been slain or had fled.

Edward Vibart, a 19-year-old officer whose parents, younger brothers, and two of his sisters had died in the Cawnpore massacre,[84] recorded his experience:

Figure 39: *Blowing from a gun, 8 September 1857*

> *The orders went out to shoot every soul.... It was literally murder... I have seen many bloody and awful sights lately but such a one as I witnessed yesterday I pray I never see again. The women were all spared but their screams on seeing their husbands and sons butchered, were most painful... Heaven knows I feel no pity, but when some old grey bearded man is brought and shot before your very eyes, hard must be that man's heart I think who can look on with indifference...*

Some British troops adopted a policy of "no prisoners". One officer, Thomas Lowe, remembered how on one occasion his unit had taken 76 prisoners – they were just too tired to carry on killing and needed a rest, he recalled. Later, after a quick trial, the prisoners were lined up with a British soldier standing a couple of yards in front of them. On the order "fire", they were all simultaneously shot, "swept... from their earthly existence".

The aftermath of the rebellion has been the focus of new work using Indian sources and population studies. In *The Last Mughal*, historian William Dalrymple examines the effects on the Muslim population of Delhi after the city was retaken by the British and finds that intellectual and economic control of the city shifted from Muslim to Hindu hands because the British, at that time, saw an Islamic hand behind the mutiny.

Figure 40: *Justice, a print by Sir John Tenniel in a September 1857 issue of Punch*

Reaction in Britain

The scale of the punishments handed out by the British "Army of Retribution" were considered largely appropriate and justified in a Britain shocked by embellished reports of atrocities carried out against British and European civilians by the rebels. Accounts of the time frequently reach the "hyperbolic register", according to Christopher Herbert, especially in the often-repeated claim that the "Red Year" of 1857 marked "a terrible break" in British experience. Such was the atmosphere – a national "mood of retribution and despair" that led to "almost universal approval" of the measures taken to pacify the revolt.

Incidents of rape allegedly committed by Indian rebels against European women and girls appalled the British public. These atrocities were often used to justify the British reaction to the rebellion. British newspapers printed various eyewitness accounts of the rape of English women and girls. One such account was published by *The Times*, regarding an incident where 48 English girls as young as 10 had been raped by Indian rebels in Delhi. Karl Marx criticized this story as false propaganda, and pointed out that the story was written by a clergyman in Bangalore, far from the events of the rebellion, with no evidence to support his allegation. Individual incidents captured the public's interest and were heavily reported by the press. One such incident was that of

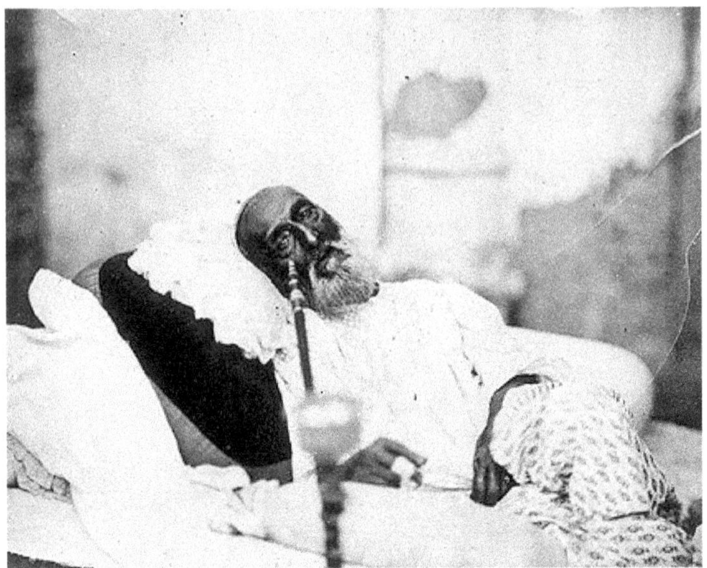

Figure 41: *Bahadur Shah Zafar (the last Mughal emperor) in Delhi, awaiting trial by the British for his role in the Uprising. Photograph by Robert Tytler and Charles Shepherd, May 1858*

General Wheeler's daughter Margaret being forced to live as her captor's concubine, though this was reported to the Victorian public as Margaret killing her rapist then herself. Another version of the story suggested that Margaret had been killed after her abductor had argued with his wife over her.[85]

During the aftermath of the rebellion, a series of exhaustive investigations were carried out by British police and intelligence officials into reports that British women prisoners had been "dishonored" at the Bibighar and elsewhere. One such detailed enquiry was at the direction of Lord Canning. The consensus was that there was no convincing evidence of such crimes having been committed, although numbers of European women and children had been killed outright.

The term 'Sepoy' or 'Sepoyism' became a derogatory term for nationalists, especially in Ireland.

Reorganisation

Bahadur Shah was tried for treason by a military commission assembled at Delhi, and exiled to Rangoon where he died in 1862, bringing the Mughal dynasty to an end. In 1877 Queen Victoria took the title of Empress of India on the advice of Prime Minister, Benjamin Disraeli.

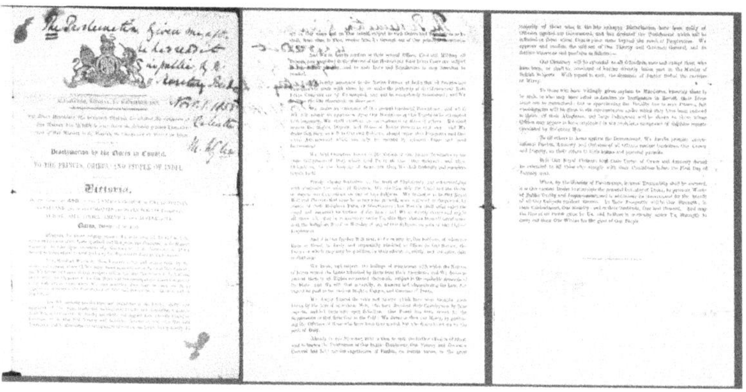
Proclamation by the Queen in Council.

TO THE PRINCES, CHIEFS, AND PEOPLE OF INDIA.

Victoria,

Figure 42: *The proclamation to the "Princes, Chiefs, and People of India," issued by Queen Victoria on November 1, 1858. "We hold ourselves bound to the natives of our Indian territories by the same obligation of duty which bind us to all our other subjects." (p. 2)*

The rebellion saw the end of the East India Company's rule in India. In August, by the Government of India Act 1858, the company was formally dissolved and its ruling powers over India were transferred to the British Crown. A new British government department, the India Office, was created to handle the governance of India, and its head, the Secretary of State for India, was entrusted with formulating Indian policy. The Governor-General of India gained a new title, Viceroy of India, and implemented the policies devised by the India Office. Some former East India Company territories, such as the Straits Settlements, became colonies in their own right. The British colonial administration embarked on a program of reform, trying to integrate Indian higher castes and rulers into the government and abolishing attempts at Westernization. The Viceroy stopped land grabs, decreed religious tolerance and admitted Indians into civil service, albeit mainly as subordinates.

Essentially the old East India Company bureaucracy remained, though there was a major shift in attitudes. In looking for the causes of the Rebellion the authorities alighted on two things: religion and the economy. On religion it was felt that there had been too much interference with indigenous traditions, both Hindu and Muslim. On the economy it was now believed that the previous attempts by the Company to introduce free market competition had undermined traditional power structures and bonds of loyalty placing the peasantry at the mercy of merchants and money-lenders. In consequence the new British Raj was constructed in part around a conservative agenda, based on a preservation of tradition and hierarchy.

On a political level it was also felt that the previous lack of consultation between rulers and ruled had been another significant factor in contributing to the uprising. In consequence, Indians were drawn into government at a local level. Though this was on a limited scale a crucial precedent had been set, with the creation of a new 'white collar' Indian elite, further stimulated by the opening of universities at Calcutta, Bombay and Madras, a result of the Indian Universities Act. So, alongside the values of traditional and ancient India, a new professional middle class was starting to arise, in no way bound by the values of the past. Their ambition can only have been stimulated by Queen Victoria's Proclamation of November 1858, in which it is expressly stated, "We hold ourselves bound to the natives of our Indian territories by the same obligations of duty which bind us to our other subjects...it is our further will that... our subjects of whatever race or creed, be freely and impartially admitted to offices in our service, the duties of which they may be qualified by their education, ability and integrity, duly to discharge."

Acting on these sentiments, Lord Ripon, viceroy from 1880 to 1885, extended the powers of local self-government and sought to remove racial practices in the law courts by the Ilbert Bill. But a policy at once liberal and progressive at one turn was reactionary and backward at the next, creating new elites and confirming old attitudes. The Ilbert Bill had the effect only of causing a white mutiny and the end of the prospect of perfect equality before the law. In 1886 measures were adopted to restrict Indian entry into the civil service.

Military reorganisation

The Bengal army dominated the Indian army before 1857 and a direct result after the rebellion was the scaling back of the size of the Bengali contingent in the army.[86] The Brahmin presence in the Bengal Army was reduced because of their perceived primary role as mutineers. The British looked for increased recruitment in the Punjab for the Bengal army as a result of the apparent discontent that resulted in the Sepoy conflict.

The rebellion transformed both the native and European armies of British India. Of the 74 regular Bengal Native Infantry regiments in existence at the beginning of 1857, only twelve escaped mutiny or disbandment.[87] All ten of the Bengal Light Cavalry regiments were lost. The old Bengal Army had accordingly almost completely vanished from the order of battle. These troops were replaced by new units recruited from castes hitherto under-utilised by the British and from the minority so-called "Martial Races", such as the Sikhs and the Gurkhas.

The inefficiencies of the old organisation, which had estranged sepoys from their British officers, were addressed, and the post-1857 units were mainly

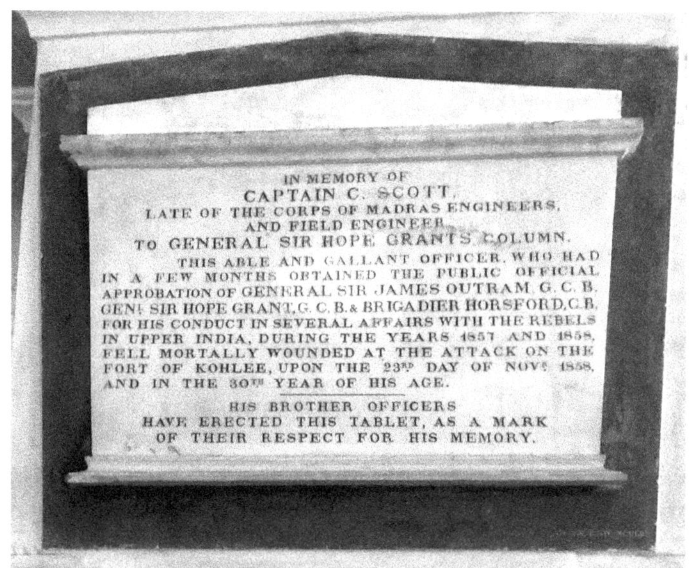

Figure 43: *Captain C Scott of the Gen. Sir. Hope Grant's Column, Madras Regiment, who fell on the attack of Fort of Kohlee, 1858. Memorial at the St. Mary's Church, Madras*

Figure 44: *Memorial inside the York Minster*

organised on the "irregular" system. From 1797 until the rebellion of 1857, each regular Bengal Native Infantry regiment had had 22 or 23 British officers,[88] who held every position of authority down to the second-in-command of each company. In irregular units there were fewer European officers, but they associated themselves far more closely with their soldiers, while more responsibility was given to the Indian officers.

The British increased the ratio of British to Indian soldiers within India. From 1861 Indian artillery was replaced by British units, except for a few mountain batteries.[89] The post-rebellion changes formed the basis of the military organisation of British India until the early 20th century.

Awards

Victoria Cross

Medals were awarded to members of the British Armed Forces and the British Indian Army during the rebellion. The 182 recipients of the Victoria Cross are listed here.

Indian Mutiny Medal

290,000 Indian Mutiny Medals were awarded. Clasps were awarded for the siege of Delhi and the siege and relief of Lucknow.[90]

Indian Order of Merit

A military and civilian decoration of British India, the Indian Order of Merit was first introduced by the East India Company in 1837, and was taken over by the Crown in 1858, following the Indian Mutiny of 1857. The Indian Order of Merit was the only gallantry medal available to Native soldiers between 1837 and 1907.

Nomenclature

There is no universally agreed name for the events of this period.

In India and Pakistan it has been termed as the "War of Independence of 1857" or "First War of Indian Independence"[91] but it is not uncommon to use terms such as the "Revolt of 1857". The classification of the Rebellion being "First War of Independence" is not without its critics in India.[92,93] The use of the term "Indian Mutiny" is considered by some Indian politicians as belittling the importance of what happened and therefore reflecting an imperialistic attitude. Others dispute this interpretation.

In the UK and parts of the Commonwealth it is commonly called the "Indian Mutiny", but terms such as "Great Indian Mutiny", the "Sepoy Mutiny", the

Figure 45: *The Mutiny Memorial in Delhi, a monument to those killed on the British side during the fighting*

"Sepoy Rebellion", the "Sepoy War", the "Great Mutiny", the "Rebellion of 1857", "the Uprising", the "Mahomedan Rebellion", and the "Revolt of 1857" have also been used.[94] "The Indian Insurrection" was a name used in the press of the UK and British colonies at the time.[95]

Historiography

Adas (1971) examines the historiography with emphasis on the four major approaches: the Indian nationalist view; the Marxist analysis; the view of the Rebellion as a traditionalist rebellion; and intensive studies of local uprisings.[96] Many of the key primary and secondary sources appear in Biswamoy Pati, ed. *1857 Rebellion*.[97,98]

Thomas Metcalf has stressed the importance of the work by Cambridge professor Eric Stokes (1924–1981), especially Stokes' *The Peasant and the Raj: Studies in Agrarian Society and Peasant Rebellion in Colonial India* (1978). Metcalf says Stokes undermines the assumption that 1857 was a response to general causes emanating from entire classes of people. Instead, Stokes argues that 1) those Indians who suffered the greatest relative deprivation rebelled and that 2) the decisive factor in precipitating a revolt was the presence of prosperous magnates who supported British rule. Stokes also explores issues of

Figure 46: *Vasily Vereshchagin. Suppression of the Indian Revolt by the English (1884).*

economic development, the nature of privileged landholding, the role of moneylenders, the usefulness of classical rent theory, and, especially, the notion of the "rich peasant."[99]

To Professor Kim Wagner, who has the most recent survey of the historiography, modern Indian historiography is yet to move beyond responding to the "prejudice" of colonial accounts. Wagner sees no reason why atrocities committed by Indians should be understated or inflated merely because these things "offend our post-colonial sensibilities."

Wagner also stresses the importance of William Dalrymple's *The Last Mughal: The Fall of a Dynasty, Delhi 1857*. Dalrymple was assisted by Mahmood Farooqui, who translated key Urdu and Shikastah sources and published a selection in *Besieged: Voices from Delhi 1857*.[100] Dalrymple emphasized the role of religion, and explored in detail the internal divisions and politico-religious discord amongst the rebels. He did not discover much in the way of proto-nationalism or any of the roots of modern India in the rebellion.[101,102] Sabbaq Ahmed has looked at the ways in which ideologies of royalism, militarism, and Jihad influenced the behaviour of contending Muslim factions.[103]

Almost from the moment the first sepoys mutinied in Meerut, the nature and the scope of the Indian Rebellion of 1857 has been contested and argued over. Speaking in the House of Commons in July 1857, Benjamin Disraeli labelled it a 'national revolt' while Lord Palmerston, the Prime Minister, tried to downplay the scope and the significance of the event as a 'mere military mutiny'.[104] Reflecting this debate, an early historian of the rebellion, Charles Ball, used the word mutiny in his title, but labelled it a 'struggle for liberty and independence

Figure 47: *The hanging of two participants in the Indian Rebellion, Sepoys of the 31st Native Infantry. Albumen silver print by Felice Beato, 1857*

as a people' in the text.[105] Historians remain divided on whether the rebellion can properly be considered a war of Indian independence or not,[106] although it is popularly considered to be one in India. Arguments against include:

- A united India did not exist at that time in political, cultural, or ethnic terms;
- The rebellion was put down with the help of other Indian soldiers drawn from the Madras Army, the Bombay Army and the Sikh regiments; 80% of the East India Company forces were Indian;[107]
- Many of the local rulers fought amongst themselves rather than uniting against the British;
- Many rebel Sepoy regiments disbanded and went home rather than fight;
- Not all of the rebels accepted the return of the Mughals;
- The King of Delhi had no real control over the mutineers;[108]
- The revolt was largely limited to north and central India. Whilst risings occurred elsewhere they had little impact because of their limited nature;
- A number of revolts occurred in areas not under British rule, and against native rulers, often as a result of local internal politics;
- The revolt was fractured along religious, ethnic and regional lines.[109]

A second school of thought while acknowledging the validity of the above-mentioned arguments opines that this rebellion may indeed be called a war of India's independence. The reasons advanced are:

- Even though the rebellion had various causes, most of the rebel sepoys who were able to do so, made their way to Delhi to revive the old Mughal empire that signified national unity for even the Hindus amongst them;
- There was a widespread popular revolt in many areas such as Awadh, Bundelkhand and Rohilkhand. The rebellion was therefore more than just a military rebellion, and it spanned more than one region;
- The sepoys did not seek to revive small kingdoms in their regions, instead they repeatedly proclaimed a "country-wide rule" of the Mughals and vowed to drive out the British from "India", as they knew it then. (The sepoys ignored local princes and proclaimed in cities they took over: *Khalq Khuda Ki, Mulk Badshah Ka, Hukm Subahdar Sipahi Bahadur Ka* – "the people belong to God, the country to the Emperor and authority to the Sepoy Commandant"). The objective of driving out "foreigners" from not only one's own area but from their conception of the entirety of "India", signifies a nationalist sentiment;
- The mutineers, although some were recruited from outside Oudah, displayed a common purpose.[110]

150th anniversary

The Government of India celebrated the year 2007 as the 150th anniversary of "India's First War of Independence". Several books written by Indian authors were released in the anniversary year including Amresh Mishra's "War of Civilizations", a controversial history of the Rebellion of 1857, and "Recalcitrance" by Anurag Kumar, one of the few novels written in English by an Indian based on the events of 1857.

In 2007, a group of retired British soldiers and civilians, some of them descendants of British soldiers who died in the conflict, attempted to visit the site of the Siege of Lucknow. However, fears of violence by Indian demonstrators, supported by the Hindu nationalist Bharatiya Janata Party, prevented the British visitors from visiting the site. Despite the protests, Sir Mark Havelock was able to make his way past police to visit the grave of his ancestor, General Henry Havelock.

Figure 48: *Henry Nelson O'Neil's 1857 painting Eastward Ho! depicting British soldiers say farewell to their loved ones as they embark on a deployment to India.*

In popular culture

Films

- *Bengal Brigade* – A 1954 film: at the outbreak of the Indian Mutiny. A British officer, Captain Claybourne (Hudson), is cashiered from his regiment over a charge of disobeying orders, but finds that his duty to his men is far from over
- *Shatranj Ke Khilari* – A 1977 Indian film directed by Satyajit Ray, chronicling the events just before the onset of the Revolt of 1857. The focus is on the British annexation of Oudh, and the detachment of the nobility from the political sphere in 19th-century India.
- *Junoon (1978 film)* – Directed by Shyam Benegal, it is a critically acclaimed film about the love affair between a Pathan feudal chief and a British girl sheltered by his family during the revolt.
- *Mangal Pandey: The Rising* (2005) – Ketan Mehta's Hindi film chronicles the life of Mangal Pandey.
- *The Charge of the Light Brigade* (1936) features a sequence inspired by the massacre at Cawnpore.
- *Indiana Jones and the Temple of Doom* – During the dinner scene at the fictional Pankot Palace, Indiana Jones mentions that Captain Blumburtt

was telling him about the role which the palace played in "the mutiny" and Chattar Lal complains, "It seems the British never forget the Mutiny of 1857".

- *The Last Cartridge, an Incident of the Sepoy Rebellion in India* (1908) – A fictionalized account of a British fort besieged during the Rebellion.

Theatre

- *1857: Ek Safarnama* – A play by Javed Siddiqui, set during the Rebellion of 1857 and staged at Purana Qila, Delhi.

Literature

- Malcolm X's autobiography *The Autobiography of Malcolm X* details his first encounters with atrocities in the non-European world and his reaction to the rebellion and massacres in 1857.
- John Masters's novel *Nightrunners of Bengal*, first published by Michael Joseph in 1951 and dedicated to the Sepoy of India, is a fictionalised account of the Rebellion as seen through the eyes of a British Captain in the Bengal Native Infantry who was based in Bhowani, itself a fictionalised version of the town of Jhansi. Captain Savage and his turbulent relationship with the Rani of Kishanpur form an analogous interrelationship of the Indian people and the British and sepoy regiments at that time.
- J. G. Farrell's 1973 novel *The Siege of Krishnapur* details the siege of the fictional Indian town of Krishnapur during the Rebellion.
- George MacDonald Fraser's 1975 novel *Flashman in the Great Game* deals with the events leading up to and during the Rebellion.
- Two of Sir Arthur Conan Doyle's Sherlock Holmes stories, *The Sign of the Four* and "The Adventure of the Crooked Man," feature events that took place during the Rebellion.
- Michael Crichton's 1975 novel *The Great Train Robbery* mentions the Rebellion and briefly details the events of the Siege of Cawnpore, as the Rebellion was happening in tandem with the trial of Edward Pierce.
- The majority of M. M. Kaye's novel *Shadow of the Moon* is set between 1856–58, and the Rebellion is shown to greatly affect the lives of the main characters, who were inhabitants of the Residency at Lunjore (a fictional town in north India). The early chapters of her novel *The Far Pavilions* take place during the Rebellion, which leads to the protagonist, a child of British ancestry, being raised as a Hindu.
- Indian writer Ruskin Bond's fictional novella *A Flight of Pigeons* is set around the Indian Rebellion of 1857. It is from this story that the film *Junoon* was later adapted in 1978 by Shyam Benegal.

- The 1880 novel *The Steam House* by Jules Verne takes place in the aftermath of the Indian Rebellion of 1857.
- Jules Verne's famous character Captain Nemo, originally an Indian prince, fought on the side of the rebels during the rebellion (as stated in Verne's later novel The Mysterious Island).
- E. M. Forster's 1924 novel *A Passage to India* alludes several times to the Mutiny.
- Flora Annie Steel's novel *On the Face of the Waters* (1896) describes incidents of the Mutiny.
- The plot of H. Beam Piper's science fiction novel Uller Uprising is based on the events of the Indian Rebellion of 1857.
- *Rujub, the juggler* and *In Times of Peril: A tale of India* by G.A. Henty are each based on the Indian Rebellion of 1857

References

Text-books and academic monographs

<templatestyles src="Template:Refbegin/styles.css" />

- Alavi, Seema (1996), *The Sepoys and the Company: Tradition and Transition 1770–1830*, Oxford University Press, p. 340, ISBN 0-19-563484-5.
- Anderson, Clare (2007), *Indian Uprising of 1857–8: Prisons, Prisoners and Rebellion*, New York: Anthem Press, p. 217, ISBN 978-1-84331-249-9.
- Bandyopadhyay, Sekhara (2004), *From Plassey to Partition: A History of Modern India*, New Delhi: Orient Longman, p. 523, ISBN 81-250-2596-0.
- Bayly, Christopher Alan (1988), *Indian Society and the Making of the British Empire*, Cambridge University Press, p. 230, ISBN 0-521-25092-7.
- Bayly, Christopher Alan (2000), *Empire and Information: Intelligence Gathering and Social Communication in India, c 1780–1870*, Cambridge University Press, p. 412, ISBN 0-521-57085-9.
- Bose, Sugata; Jalal, Ayesha (2004), *Modern South Asia: History, Culture, Political Economy* (2nd ed.), London: Routledge, p. 253, ISBN 0-415-30787-2.
- Brown, Judith M. (1994), *Modern India: The Origins of an Asian Democracy*[111] (2nd ed.), Oxford University Press, p. 480, ISBN 0-19-873113-2.
- Greenwood, Adrian (2015), *Victoria's Scottish Lion: The Life of Colin Campbell, Lord Clyde*[112], UK: History Press, p. 496, ISBN 0-75095-685-2.

- Harris, John (2001), *The Indian Mutiny*, Ware: Wordsworth Editions, p. 205, ISBN 1-84022-232-8.
- Hibbert, Christopher (1980), *The Great Mutiny: India 1857*, London: Allen Lane, p. 472, ISBN 0-14-004752-2.
- Jain, Meenakshi (2010), *Parallel Pathways: Essays On Hindu-Muslim Relations (1707-1857)*, Delhi: Konark, ISBN 978-8122007831.
- Judd, Denis (2004), *The Lion and the Tiger: The Rise and Fall of the British Raj, 1600–1947*, Oxford University Press, xiii, 280, ISBN 0-19-280358-1.
- Keene, Henry George (1883), *Fifty-Seven. Some account of the administration of Indian Districts during the revolt of the Bengal Army*, London: W.H. Allen, p. 145.
- Kulke, Hermann; Rothermund, Dietmar (2004), *A History of India* (4th ed.), London: Routledge, xii, 448, ISBN 0-415-32920-5.
- Leasor, James (1956), *The Red Fort*[113], London: W. Lawrie, p. 377, ISBN 0-02-034200-4.
- Ludden, David (2002), *India And South Asia: A Short History*, Oxford: Oneworld, xii, 306, ISBN 1-85168-237-6.
- Majumdar, R.C.; Raychaudhuri, H.C.; Datta, Kalikinkar (1967), *An Advanced History of India* (3rd ed.), London: Macmillan, p. 1126.
- Markovits, Claude, ed. (2004), *A History of Modern India 1480–1950*, London: Anthem, p. 607, ISBN 1-84331-152-6.
- Marshall, P. J. (2007), *The Making and Unmaking of Empires: Britain, India, and America c.1750–1783*, Oxford and New York: Oxford University Press. Pp. 400, ISBN 0-19-922666-0
- Metcalf, Barbara D.; Metcalf, Thomas R. (2006), *A Concise History of Modern India* (2nd ed.), Cambridge University Press, p. 337, ISBN 0-521-68225-8.
- Metcalf, Thomas R. (1990), *The Aftermath of Revolt: India, 1857–1870*, New Delhi: Manohar, p. 352, ISBN 81-85054-99-1.
- Metcalf, Thomas R. (1997), *Ideologies of the Raj*, Cambridge University Press, p. 256, ISBN 0-521-58937-1.
- Mukherjee, Rudrangshu (2002), *Awadh in Revolt 1857–1858: A Study of Popular Resistance* (2nd ed.), London: Anthem, ISBN 1-84331-075-9.
- Palmer, Julian A.B. (1966), *The Mutiny Outbreak at Meerut in 1857*, Cambridge University Press, p. 175, ISBN 0-521-05901-1.
- Peers, Douglas M. (2013), *India Under Colonial Rule: 1700–1885*[114], Routledge, ISBN 978-1-317-88286-2
- Ray, Rajat Kanta (2002), *The Felt Community: Commonality and Mentality before the Emergence of Indian Nationalism*, Oxford University Press, p. 596, ISBN 0-19-565863-9.

- Robb, Peter (2002), *A History of India*, Basingstoke: Palgrave, p. 344, ISBN 0-333-69129-6.
- Roy, Tapti (1994), *The politics of a popular uprising: Bundelkhand 1857*, Delhi: Oxford University Press, p. 291, ISBN 0-19-563612-0.
- Spear, Percival (1990) [First published 1965], *A History of India*, Volume 2, New Delhi and London: Penguin Books, ISBN 978-0-14-013836-8.
- Stanley, Peter (1998), *White Mutiny: British Military Culture in India, 1825–1875*, London: Hurst, p. 314, ISBN 1-85065-330-5.
- Stein, Burton (2001), *A History of India*, New Delhi: Oxford University Press, p. 432, ISBN 0-19-565446-3.
- Stokes, Eric (1980), *The Peasant and the Raj: Studies in Agrarian Society and Peasant Rebellion in Colonial India*, Cambridge University Press, p. 316, ISBN 0-521-29770-2.
- Stokes, Eric; Bayly, C.A. (1986), *The Peasant Armed: The Indian Revolt of 1857*, Oxford: Clarendon, p. 280, ISBN 0-19-821570-3.
- Taylor, P.J.O. (1997), *What really happened during the mutiny: a day-by-day account of the major events of 1857–1859 in India*, Delhi: Oxford University Press, p. 323, ISBN 0-19-564182-5.
- Wolpert, Stanley (2004), *A New History of India* (7th ed.), Oxford University Press, p. 530, ISBN 0-19-516678-7.

Articles in journals and collections

- Alam Khan, Iqtidar (May–June 2013), "The Wahabis in the 1857 Revolt: A Brief Reappraisal of Their Role", *Social Scientist*, **41** (5/6): 15–23, JSTOR 23611115[115]
- Alavi, Seema (February 1993), "The Company Army and Rural Society: The Invalid *Thanah* 1780–1830", *Modern Asian Studies*, Cambridge University Press, **27** (1): 147–178, doi: 10.1017/S0026749X00016097[116], JSTOR 312880[117]
- Baker, David (1991), "Colonial Beginnings and the Indian Response: The Revolt of 1857–58 in Madhya Pradesh", *Modern Asian Studies*, **25** (3): 511–543, doi: 10.1017/S0026749X00013913[118], JSTOR 312615[119]
- Blunt, Alison (July 2000), "Embodying war: British women and domestic defilement in the Indian "Mutiny", 1857–8", *Journal of Historical Geography*, **26** (3): 403–428, doi: 10.1006/jhge.2000.0236[120]
- English, Barbara (February 1994), "The Kanpur Massacres in India in the Revolt of 1857", *Past & Present*, Oxford University Press, **142**: 169–178, doi: 10.1093/past/142.1.169[121], JSTOR 651200[122]
- Hasan, Farhat; Roy, Tapti (1998), "Review of Tapti Roy, The Politics of a Popular Uprising, OUP, 1994", *Social Scientist*, **26** (1): 148–151, doi: 10.2307/3517586[123]

- Klein, Ira (July 2000), "Materialism, Mutiny and Modernization in British India", *Modern Asian Studies*, Cambridge University Press, **34** (3): 545–580, JSTOR 313141[124]
- Lahiri, Nayanjot (June 2003), "Commemorating and Remembering 1857: The Revolt in Delhi and Its Afterlife", *World Archaeology*, Taylor & Francis, **35** (1): 35–60, doi: 10.1080/0043824032000078072[125], JSTOR 3560211[126]
- Mukherjee, Rudrangshu (August 1990), "'Satan Let Loose upon Earth': The Kanpur Massacres in India in the Revolt of 1857", *Past & Present*, Oxford University Press, **128**: 92–116, doi: 10.1093/past/128.1.92[127], JSTOR 651010[128]
- Mukherjee, Rudrangshu (February 1994), "The Kanpur Massacres in India in the Revolt of 1857: Reply", *Past & Present*, Oxford University Press, **142**: 178–189, doi: 10.1093/past/142.1.178[129], JSTOR 651201[130]
- Nanda, Krishan (September 1965), *The Western Political Quarterly*, **18** (3), University of Utah on behalf of the Western Political Science Association, pp. 700–701.
- Roy, Tapti (February 1993), "Visions of the Rebels: A Study of 1857 in Bundelkhand", *Modern Asian Studies*, Cambridge University Press, **27** (1): 205–228 (Special Issue: How Social, Political and Cultural Information Is Collected, Defined, Used and Analyzed), doi: 10.1017/S0026749X00016115[131], JSTOR 312882[132]
- Stokes, Eric (December 1969), "Rural Revolt in the Great Rebellion of 1857 in India: A Study of the Saharanpur and Muzaffarnagar Districts", *The Historical Journal*, Cambridge University Press, **12** (4): 606–627, doi: 10.1017/s0018246x00010554[133], JSTOR 2638016[134]
- Washbrook, D. A. (2001), "India, 1818–1860: The Two Faces of Colonialism", in Porter, Andrew, *Oxford History of the British Empire: The Nineteenth Century*, Oxford and New York: Oxford University Press, pp. 395–421, ISBN 0-19-924678-5
- Hakim Syed Zillur Rahman (2008), "1857 ki Jung-e Azadi main Khandan ka hissa", *Hayat Karam Husain* (2nd ed.), Aligarh/India: Ibn Sina Academy of Medieval Medicine and Sciences, pp. 253–258, OCLC 852404214[135]

Historiography and memory

- Bates, Crispin, ed. *Mutiny at the Margins: New Perspectives on the Indian Uprising of 1857* (5 vol. SAGE Publications India, 2013–14). online guide[136]; With illustrations, maps, selected text and more.
- Chakravarty, Gautam. *The Indian Mutiny and the British Imagination* (Cambridge University Press, 2005).

- Deshpande, Prachi. "The Making of an Indian Nationalist Archive: Lakshmibai, Jhansi, and 1857." *journal of Asian studies* 67#3 (2008): 855–879.
- Erll, Astrid. "Re-writing as re-visioning: Modes of representing the 'Indian Mutiny'in British novels, 1857 to 2000." *European Journal of English Studies* 10.2 (2006): 163–185. online[137]
- Frykenberg, Robert E. (2001), "India to 1858", in Winks, Robin, *Oxford History of the British Empire: Historiography*, Oxford and New York: Oxford University Press, pp. 194–213, ISBN 0-19-924680-7
- Pati, Biswamoy (12–18 May 2007). "Historians and Historiography: Situating 1857". *Economic and Political Weekly*. **42** (19): 1686–1691. JSTOR 4419570[138].
- Perusek, Darshan (Spring 1992). "Subaltern Consciousness and the Historiography of the Indian Rebellion of 1857". *NOVEL: A Forum on Fiction*. Duke University Press. **25** (3): 286–301. doi: 10.2307/1345889[139]. JSTOR 1345889[140].
- Wagner, Kim A. (October 2011). "The Marginal Mutiny: The New Historiography of the Indian Uprising of 1857". *History Compass*. **9** (10): 760–766. doi: 10.1111/j.1478-0542.2011.00799.x[141].

Other histories

- Dalrymple, William (2006), *The Last Mughal*, Viking Penguin, ISBN 0-670-99925-3
- David, Saul (2003), *The Indian Mutiny: 1857*, London: Penguin Books, Pp. 528, ISBN 0-14-100554-8
- David, Saul (2007), *Victoria's Wars*, London: Penguin Books, ISBN 978-0-141-00555-3
- Mishra, Amaresh. 2007. *War of Civilisations: The Long Revolution (India AD 1857, 2 Vols.)*, ISBN 978-81-291-1282-8
- Ward, Andrew. *Our Bones Are Scattered*. New York: Holt & Co., 1996.

First person accounts and classic histories

- Parag Tope , "Tatya Tope's Operation Red Lotus" , Publisher: Rupa Publications India
- Anderson, Clare. The Indian Uprising of 1857–8: Prisons, Prisoners, and Rebellion. London, 2007.
- Barter, Captain Richard *The Siege of Delhi. Mutiny memories of an old officer*, London, The Folio Society, 1984.
- Campbell, Sir Colin. *Narrative of the Indian Revolt*. London: George Vickers, 1858.
- Collier, Richard. *The Great Indian Mutiny*. New York: Dutton, 1964.

- Forrest, George W. *A History of the Indian Mutiny*, William Blackwood and Sons, London, 1904. (4 vols)
- Fitchett, W.H., B.A., LL.D., *A Tale of the Great Mutiny*, Smith, Elder & Co., London, 1911.
- Inglis, Julia Selina, Lady, 1833–1904, *The Siege of Lucknow: a Diary*[142], London: James R. Osgood, McIlvaine & Co., 1892. Online at A Celebration of Women Writers.[143]
- Innes, Lt. General McLeod: *The Sepoy Revolt*, A.D. Innes & Co., London, 1897.
- Kaye, John William. *A History of the Sepoy War In India* (3 vols). London: W.H. Allen & Co., 1878.
- Kaye, Sir John & Malleson, G.B.: *The Indian Mutiny of 1857*, Rupa & Co., Delhi, (1st edition 1890) reprint 2005.
- Khan, Syed Ahmed (1859), Asbab-e Baghawat-e Hind, Translated as *The Causes of the Indian Revolt*, Allahabad, 1873
- Malleson, Colonel G.B. *The Indian Mutiny of 1857*. New York: Scribner & Sons, 1891.
- Marx, Karl & Freidrich Engels. *The First Indian War of Independence 1857–1859*. Moscow: Foreign Languages Publishing House, 1959.
- Pandey, Sita Ram, *From Sepoy to Subedar, Being the Life and Adventures of Subedar Sita Ram, a Native Officer of the Bengal Native Army, Written and Related by Himself*, trans. Lt. Col. Norgate, (Lahore: Bengal Staff Corps, 1873), ed. James Lunt, (Delhi: Vikas Publications, 1970).
- Raikes, Charles: *Notes on the Revolt in the North-Western Provinces of India*, Longman, London, 1858.
- Roberts, Field Marshal Lord, *Forty-one Years in India*, Richard Bentley, London, 1897
- *Forty-one years in India* at Project Gutenberg
- Russell, William Howard, *My Diary in India in the years 1858-9*, Routledge, London, 1860, (2 vols.)
- Sen, Surendra Nath, *Eighteen fifty-seven*, (with a foreword by Maulana Abul Kalam Azad), Indian Ministry of Information & Broadcasting, Delhi, 1957.
- Thomson, Mowbray (Capt.), *The Story of Cawnpore*, Richard Bentley, London, 1859.
- Trevelyan, Sir George Otto, *Cawnpore*, Indus, Delhi, (first edition 1865), reprint 2002.
- Wilberforce, Reginald G, *An Unrecorded Chapter of the Indian Mutiny, Being the Personal Reminiscences of Reginald G. WIlberforce, Late 52nd Infantry, Compiled from a Diary and Letters Written on the Spot* London: John Murray 1884, facsimile reprint: Gurgaon: The Academic Press, 1976.

Tertiary sources

- "Indian Mutiny." Encyclopædia Britannica Online. Online. https://www.britannica.com/event/Indian-Mutiny. 23 March 1998.
- " Lee-Enfield Rifle[144]." Encyclopædia Britannica Online. 23 March 1998.

Fictional and narrative literature

- Conan Doyle, Arthur. *The Sign of the Four*, featuring Sherlock Holmes, originally appearing in *Lippincott's Monthly Magazine* 1890.
- Farrell, J.G. *The Siege of Krishnapur*. New York: Carroll & Graf, 1985 (orig. 1973; Booker Prize winner).
- Fenn, Clive Robert. *For the Old Flag: A Tale of the Mutiny*. London: Sampson Low, 1899.
- Fraser, George MacDonald. *Flashman in the Great Game*. London: Barrie & Jenkins, 1975.
- Grant, James. *First Love and Last Love: A Tale of the Mutiny*. New York: G. Routledge & Sons, 1869.
- Kaye, Mary Margaret. *Shadow of the Moon*. New York: St. Martin's Press, 1979.
- Kilworth, Garry Douglas. *Brothers of the Blade*: Constable & Robinson, 2004.
- Leasor, James. *Follow the Drum*[145]. London: Heinemann, 1972, reissued James Leasor Ltd, 2011.
- Masters, John. *Nightrunners of Bengal*. New York: Viking Press, 1951.
- Raikes, William Stephen. *12 Years of a Soldier's Life In India*. Boston: Ticknor and Fields, 1860.
- Julian Rathbone, *The Mutiny*.
- Rossetti, Christina Georgina. "In the Round Tower at Jhansi, 8 June 1857." *Goblin Market and Other Poems*. 1862.
- Anurag Kumar. *Recalcitrance: a novel based on events of 1857–58 in Lucknow*. Lucknow: AIP Books, Lucknow 2008.
- Stuart, V.A. The Alexander Sheridan Series: # 2: 1964. *The Sepoy Mutiny*; # 3: 1974. *Massacre at Cawnpore*; # 4: 1974. *The Cannons of Lucknow*; 1975. # 5: *The Heroic Garrison*. Reprinted 2003 by McBooks Press. (Note: # 1 – *Victors & Lords* deals with the Crimean War.)
- Valerie Fitzgerald "Zemindar": 1981 Bodley Head. historic novel.
- Frédéric Cathala, *1857*, KDP, 2017, historical novel.

External links

	Wikimedia Commons has media related to ***Indian Rebellion of 1857***.

Library resources about **Indian Rebellion of 1857**
• Online books[146] • Resources in your library[147] • Resources in other libraries[148]

- Detailed Map: The revolt of 1857–1859, Historical Atlas of South Asia, Digital South Asia Library, hosted by the University of Chicago[149]
- Development of Situation-January to July 1857 – Maj (Retd) AGHA HUMAYUN AMIN from WASHINGTON DC defencejounal.com[150]
- The Indian Mutiny BritishEmpire.co.uk[151]
- Karl Marx, *New York Tribune*, 1853–1858, The Revolt in India marxists.org[152]

Preceded by **Second Anglo-Sikh War**	**Indo-British conflicts**	Succeeded by **Hindu German Conspiracy**

Company Rule in India

Company rule in India

Company rule in India		
Joint-stock colony established by the East India Company and regulated by the British Parliament.		
1757–1858		
Flag		
Coat of arms		
Motto *Auspicio Regis et Senatus Angliae* "By command of the King and Parliament of England"		
Capital		Calcutta (1757–1858)
Languages		English, and others
Government		Corporatocracy
Governor-General		
•	1774–75	Warren Hastings (first)
•	1857–58	Charles Canning (last)
History		
•	Battle of Plassey	23 June 1757
•	Treaty of Allahabad	16 August 1765

•	Treaty of Seringapatam	18 March 1792
•	Treaty of Bassein	31 December 1802
•	Treaty of Yandabo	24 February 1826
•	Treaty of Lahore	9 March 1846
•	Treaty of Lahore	29 March 1849
•	Government of India Act	2 August 1858
Area		
•	1858	1,942,481 km^2 (749,996 sq mi)
Currency		Rupee

Preceded by	Succeeded by
Maratha Empire	
Mughal Empire	British Raj
Kingdom of Mysore	Straits Settlements
Sikh Empire	

Today part of

- Bahrain
- Bangladesh
- China
- Christmas Island
- Cocos (Keeling) Islands
- India
- Kuwait
- Malaysia
- Maldives
- Myanmar
- Nepal (Banke, Bardiya, Kailali and Kanchanpur)[153]
- Oman
- Pakistan
- Qatar
- Saudi Arabia (nominal)
- Singapore
- Somalia
- Sri Lanka
- United Arab Emirates
- Yemen

Part of **a series** on the

History of India

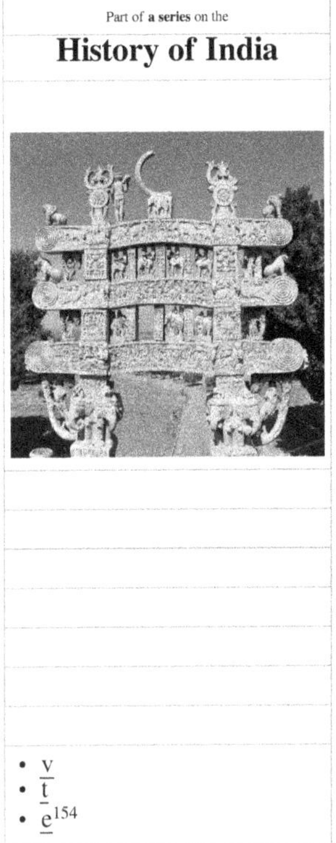

- v
- t
- e[154]

Colonial India

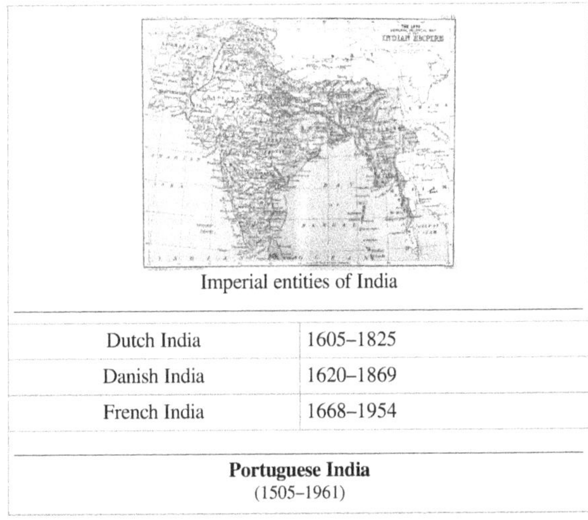

Imperial entities of India

Dutch India	1605–1825
Danish India	1620–1869
French India	1668–1954

Portuguese India
(1505–1961)

Casa da Índia	1434–1833
Portuguese East India Company	1628–1633
British India (1612–1947)	
East India Company	1612–1757
Company rule in India	1757–1858
British Raj	1858–1947
British rule in Burma	1824–1948
Princely states	1721–1949
Partition of India	1947

- v
- t
- e[155]

Company rule in India (sometimes, **Company *Raj***,[156] "*raj*", lit. "rule" in Hindi[157]) refers to the rule or dominion of the British East India Company over parts of the Indian subcontinent. This is variously taken to have commenced in 1757, after the Battle of Plassey, when Mir Jafar, the new Nawab of Bengal enthroned by Robert Clive, became a puppet in the Company's hands;[158,159] in 1765, when the Company was granted the *diwani*, or the right to collect revenue, in Bengal and Bihar; or in 1773, when the Company established a capital in Calcutta, appointed its first Governor-General, Warren Hastings, and became directly involved in governance, By 1818, with the defeat of the Marathas, followed by the pensioning of the Peshwa and the annexation of his territories, British supremacy in India was complete.

The East India Company was a private company owned by stockholders and reporting to a board of directors in London. Originally formed as a monopoly on trade, it increasingly took on governmental powers with its own army and judiciary. It seldom turned a profit, as employees diverted funds into their own pockets. The British government had little control, and there was increasing anger at the corruption and irresponsibility of Company officials or "nabobs" who made vast fortunes in a few years. Pitt's India Act of 1784 gave the British government effective control of the private company for the first time. The new policies were designed for an elite civil service career that minimized temptations for corruption. Increasingly Company officials lived in separate compounds according to British standards. The Company's rule lasted until 1858, when, after the Indian rebellion of 1857, it was abolished. With the Government of India Act 1858, the British government assumed the task of directly administering India in the new British Raj.

Origins

The English East India Company ("the Company") was founded in 1600, as *The Company of Merchants of London Trading into the East Indies*. It gained a foothold in India with the establishment of a factory in Masulipatnam on the Eastern coast of India in 1611 and the grant of the rights to establish a factory in Surat in 1612 by the Mughal emperor Jahangir. In 1640, after receiving similar permission from the Vijayanagara ruler farther south, a second factory was established in Madras on the southeastern coast. Bombay island, not far from Surat, a former Portuguese outpost gifted to England as dowry in the marriage of Catherine of Braganza to Charles II, was leased by the Company in 1668. Two decades later, the Company established a presence on the eastern coast as well; far up that coast, in the Ganges river delta, a factory was set up in Calcutta. Since, during this time other *companies*—established by the Portuguese, Dutch, French, and Danish—were similarly expanding in the region, the English Company's unremarkable beginnings on coastal India offered no clues to what would become a lengthy presence on the Indian subcontinent.

The Company's victory under Robert Clive in the 1757 Battle of Plassey and another victory in the 1764 Battle of Buxar (in Bihar), consolidated the Company's power, and forced emperor Shah Alam II to appoint it the *diwan*, or revenue collector, of Bengal, Bihar, and Orissa. The Company thus became the de facto ruler of large areas of the lower Gangetic plain by 1773. It also proceeded by degrees to expand its dominions around Bombay and Madras. The Anglo-Mysore Wars (1766–99) and the Anglo-Maratha Wars (1772–1818) left it in control of large areas of India south of the Sutlej River. With the defeat of the Marathas, no native power represented a threat for the Company any longer.

The expansion of the Company's power chiefly took two forms. The first of these was the outright annexation of Indian states and subsequent direct governance of the underlying regions, which collectively came to comprise British India. The annexed regions included the North-Western Provinces (comprising Rohilkhand, Gorakhpur, and the Doab) (1801), Delhi (1803), Assam (Ahom Kingdom 1828), and Sindh (1843). Punjab, North-West Frontier Province, and Kashmir, were annexed after the Anglo-Sikh Wars in 1849–56 (Period of tenure of Marquess of Dalhousie Governor General); however, Kashmir was immediately sold under the Treaty of Amritsar (1850) to the Dogra Dynasty of Jammu, and thereby became a princely state. In 1854 Berar was annexed, and the state of Oudh two years later.

The second form of asserting power involved treaties in which Indian rulers acknowledged the Company's hegemony in return for limited internal autonomy. Since the Company operated under financial constraints, it had to set up *political* underpinnings for its rule. The most important such support came from the *subsidiary alliances* with Indian princes during the first 75 years of Company rule. In the early 19th century, the territories of these princes accounted for two-thirds of India. When an Indian ruler, who was able to secure his territory, wanted to enter such an alliance, the Company welcomed it as an economical method of indirect rule, which did not involve the economic costs of direct administration or the political costs of gaining the support of alien subjects.

In return, the Company undertook the "defense of these subordinate allies and treated them with traditional respect and marks of honor." Subsidiary alliances created the princely states, of the Hindu maharajas and the Muslim nawabs. Prominent among the princely states were: Cochin (1791), Jaipur (1794), Travancore (1795), Hyderabad (1798), Mysore (1799), Cis-Sutlej Hill States (1815), Central India Agency (1819), Cutch and Gujarat Gaikwad territories (1819), Rajputana (1818), and Bahawalpur (1833).

Expansion

The area encompassed by modern India was significantly fractured following the decline of the Mughal Empire in the first half of the 18th century[160]

Chronology

- 1757: 24 Parganas of the Sundarbans annexed to Clive after the Battle of Plassey.
- 1760: Northern Circars annexed.
- 1765: Nawabs of Bengal and Murshidabad (and Bihar) annexed after the Battle of Buxar.
- 1773: Raja of Banares annexed.
- 1775: Nawab of Ghazipur annexed.
- 1795: Asaf Jah II the Nizam of Hyderabad was defeated at the Battle of Kharda,[161] after the Maratha-Mysore War.
- 1799: Fall of Mysore after Siege of Seringapatam (1799); Nawab of Kadapa and Nawab of Kurnool annexed.
- 1801: Nawab of the Carnatic (of Arcot and Nellore), Nawab of Junagarh, and Rohilkhand of Lower Doab annexed.
- 1803: Rohilkhand of Upper Doab annexed; nonresistance from the Emperor; Nawab of Bhawalpur accepts borders with British India.

India in 1765 and 1805 showing East India Company Territories in pink.

India in 1837 and 1857 showing East India Company (pink) and other territories

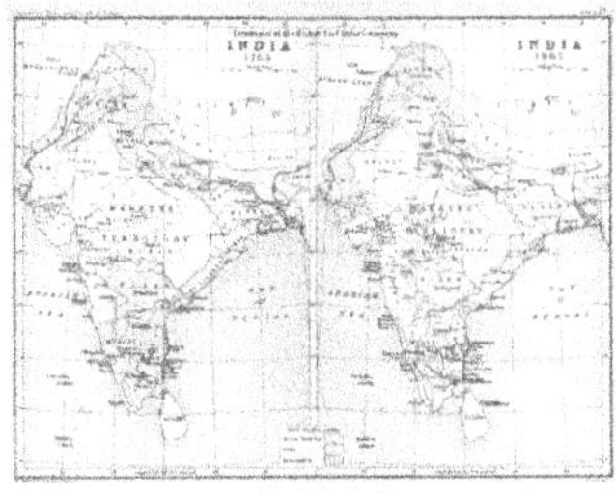

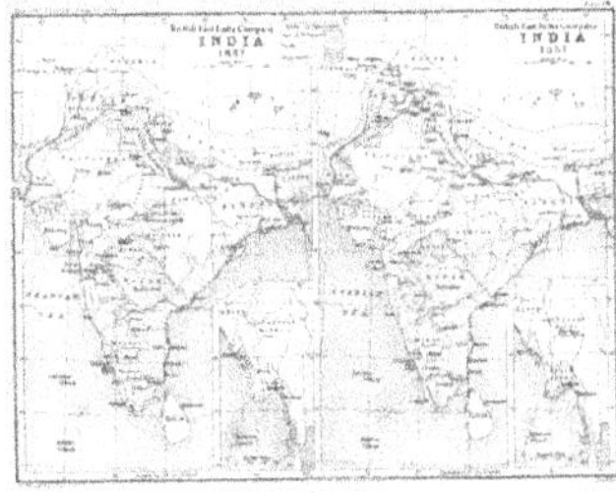

The Governors-General

(The Governors-General (locum tenens) are not included in this table unless a major event occurred during their tenure.)

Governor-General	Period of Tenure	Events
Warren Hastings	20 October 1773 – 1 February 1785	Bengal famine of 1770 (1769–73) Rohilla War (1773–74) First Anglo-Maratha War (1777–83) *Chalisa* famine (1783–84) Second Anglo-Mysore War (1780–1784)
Charles Cornwallis	12 September 1786 – 28 October 1793	Cornwallis Code (1793) Permanent Settlement Cochin become semi-protected States under British (1791) Third Anglo-Mysore War (1789–92) *Doji bara* famine (1791–92)
John Shore	28 October 1793 – March 1798	East India Company Army re-organised and down-sized. First Pazhassi Revolt in Malabar(1793–97) Jaipur (1794) & Travancore (1795) come under British protection. Andaman Islands occupied (1796) Company took control of coastal region Ceylon from Dutch (1796).

Richard Wellesley	18 May 1798 – 30 July 1805	Nizam of Hyderabad becomes first State to sign Subsidiary alliance introduced by Wellesley (1798). Fourth Anglo-Mysore War (1798–99) Second Pazhassi Revolt in Malabar(1800–1805) Nawab of Oudh cedes Gorakhpur and Rohilkhand divisions; Allahabad, Fatehpur, Cawnpore, Etawah, Mainpuri, Etah districts; part of Mirzapur; and *terai* of Kumaun (*Ceded Provinces*, 1801) Treaty of Bassein signed by Peshwa Baji Rao II accepting Subsidiary Alliance Battle of Delhi (1803). Second Anglo-Maratha War (1803–05) Remainder of Doab, Delhi and Agra division, parts of Bundelkhand annexed from Maratha Empire (1805). Ceded and Conquered Provinces established (1805)
Charles Cornwallis (second term)	30 July 1805 – 5 October 1805	Financial strain in East India Company after costly campaigns. Cornwallis reappointed to bring peace, but dies in Ghazipur.
George Hilario Barlow (locum tenens)	10 October 1805 – 31 July 1807	Vellore Mutiny (10 July 1806)
Lord Minto	31 July 1807 – 4 October 1813	Invasion of Java Occupation of Mauritius
Marquess of Hastings	4 October 1813 – 9 January 1823	Anglo-Nepal War of 1814 Annexation of Kumaon, Garhwal, and east Sikkim. Cis-Sutlej states (1815). Third Anglo-Maratha War (1817–18) States of Rajputana accept British suzerainty (1817). Singapore was founded (1818). Cutch accepts British suzerainty (1818). Gaikwads of Baroda accept British suzerainty (1819). Central India Agency (1819).
Lord Amherst	1 August 1823 – 13 March 1828	First Anglo–Burmese War (1823–26) Annexation of Assam, Manipur, Arakan, and Tenasserim from Burma
William Bentinck	4 July 1828 – 20 March 1835	Bengal Sati Regulation, 1829 Thuggee and Dacoity Suppression Acts, 1836–48 Mysore State goes under British administration (1831–81) Bahawalpur accepts British Suzerainty (1833) Coorg annexed (1834).
Lord Auckland	4 March 1836 – 28 February 1842	North-Western Provinces established (1836) Post Offices were established (1837) Agra famine of 1837–38 Aden is captured by Company (1839) First Anglo-Afghan War (1839–1842) Massacre of Elphinstone's army (1842).
Lord Ellenborough	28 February 1842 – June 1844	First Anglo-Afghan War (1839–42) Annexation of Sindh (1843) Indian Slavery Act, 1843

Henry Hardinge	23 July 1844 – 12 January 1848	First Anglo-Sikh War (1845–46) Sikhs cede Jullundur Doab, Hazara, and Kashmir to the British under Treaty of Lahore (1846) Sale of Kashmir to Gulab Singh of Jammu under Treaty of Amritsar (1846).
Marquess of Dalhousie	12 January 1848 – 28 February 1856	Second Anglo-Sikh War (1848–1849) Annexation of Punjab and North-West Frontier Province (1849–56) Construction begins on Indian Railways (1850) Caste Disabilities Removal Act, 1850 First telegraph line laid in India (1851) Second Anglo-Burmese War (1852–53) Annexation of Lower Burma Ganges Canal opened (1854) Annexation of Satara (1848), Jaipur and Sambalpur (1849), Nagpur and Jhansi (1854) under Doctrine of Lapse. Annexation of Berar (1853) and Awadh (1856). Postage Stamps for India were introduced. (1854). Public Telegram services starts operation (1855).
Charles Canning	28 February 1856 – 1 November 1858	Hindu Widows Remarriage Act (25 July 1856) First Indian universities founded (January–September 1857) Indian Rebellion of 1857 (10 May 1857 – 20 June 1858) largely in North-Western Provinces and Oudh Liquidation of the English East India Company under Government of India Act 1858

Regulation of Company rule

A view of Calcutta from Fort William, 1807.

Government House, Fort St. George, Madras, the headquarters of the Madras Presidency.

Warren Hastings, the first Governor-General of Fort William (Bengal) who oversaw the Company's territories in India.

The trial of Warren Hastings in the Court of Westminster Hall, 1789.

Until Clive's victory at Plassey, the East India Company territories in India, which consisted largely of the presidency towns of Calcutta, Madras, and Bombay, were governed by the mostly autonomous—and sporadically unmanageable—*town councils*, all composed of merchants. The councils barely had enough powers for the effective management of their local affairs, and the ensuing lack of oversight of the overall Company operations in India led to some grave abuses by Company officers or their allies. Clive's victory, and the award of the *diwani* of the rich region of Bengal, brought India into the public spotlight in Britain. The Company's money management practices came to be questioned, especially as it began to post net losses even as some Company servants, the "Nabobs," returned to Britain with large fortunes, which—according to rumours then current—were acquired unscrupulously.[162] By 1772, the

Company needed British government loans to stay afloat, and there was fear in London that the Company's corrupt practices could soon seep into British business and public life. The rights and duties of the British government with regards the Company's new territories came also to be examined. The British parliament then held several inquiries and in 1773, during the premiership of Lord North, enacted the *Regulating Act*, which established regulations, its long title stated, "for the better Management of the Affairs of the *East India Company*, as well in *India* as in *Europe*"

Although Lord North himself wanted the Company's territories to be taken over by the British state, he faced determined political opposition from many quarters, including some in the City of London and the British parliament. The result was a compromise in which the Regulating Act—although implying the ultimate sovereignty of the British Crown over these new territories—asserted that the Company could act as a sovereign power on behalf of the Crown. It could do this while concurrently being subject to oversight and regulation by

Figure 49: *Robert Clive*

the British government and parliament. The Court of Directors of the Company were required under the Act to submit all communications regarding civil, military, and revenue matters in India for scrutiny by the British government. For the governance of the Indian territories, the act asserted the supremacy of the Presidency of Fort William (Bengal) over those of Fort St. George (Madras) and Bombay. It also nominated a Governor-General (Warren Hastings) and four councillors for administering the Bengal Presidency (and for overseeing the Company's operations in India). "The subordinate Presidencies were forbidden to wage war or make treaties without the previous consent of the Governor-General of Bengal in Council,[163] except in case of imminent necessity. The Governors of these Presidencies were directed in general terms to obey the orders of the Governor-General-in-Council, and to transmit to him intelligence of all important matters." However, the imprecise wording of the Act, left it open to be variously interpreted; consequently, the administration in India continued to be hobbled by disunity between the provincial governors, between members of the Council, and between the Governor-General himself and his Council. The *Regulating Act* also attempted to address the prevalent corruption in India: Company servants were henceforth forbidden to engage in private trade in India or to receive "presents" from Indian nationals.

William Pitt's India Act of 1784 established a Board of Control in England both to supervise the East India Company's affairs and to prevent the Company's shareholders from interfering in the governance of India. The Board of Control consisted of six members, which included one Secretary of State from the British cabinet, as well as the Chancellor of the Exchequer. Around this time, there was also extensive debate in the British Parliament on the issue of landed rights in Bengal, with a consensus developing in support of the view advocated by Philip Francis, a member of the Bengal council and political adversary of Warren Hastings, that all lands in Bengal should be considered the "estate and inheritance of native land-holders and families ..."[164]

Mindful of the reports of abuse and corruption in Bengal by Company servants, the India Act itself noted numerous complaints that "'divers Rajahs, Zemindars, Polygars, Talookdars, and landholders"' had been unjustly deprived of 'their lands, jurisdictions, rights, and privileges'." At the same time the Company's directors were now leaning towards Francis's view that the land-tax in Bengal should be made fixed and permanent, setting the stage for the Permanent Settlement (see section Revenue settlements under the Company below). The India Act also created in each of the three presidencies a number of administrative and military posts, which included: a Governor and three Councilors, one of which was the Commander in Chief of the Presidency army. Although the supervisory powers of the Governor-General-in-Council in Bengal (over Madras and Bombay) were extended—as they were again in the Charter Act of 1793—the subordinate presidencies continued to exercise some autonomy until both the extension of British possessions into becoming contiguous and the advent of faster communications in the next century.

Still, the new Governor-General appointed in 1786, Lord Cornwallis, not only had more power than Hastings, but also had the support of a powerful British cabinet minister, Henry Dundas, who, as Secretary of State for the Home Office, was in charge of the overall India policy. From 1784 onwards, the British government had the final word on all major appointments in India; a candidate's suitability for a senior position was often decided by the strength of his political connections rather than that of his administrative ability. Although this practice resulted in many Governor-General nominees being chosen from Britain's conservative landed gentry, there were some liberals as well, such as Lord William Bentinck and Lord Dalhousie.

British political opinion was also shaped by the attempted Impeachment of Warren Hastings; the trial, whose proceedings began in 1788, ended with Hastings' acquittal, in 1795. Although the effort was chiefly coordinated by Edmund Burke, it also drew support from within the British government. Burke accused Hastings not only of corruption, but—appealing to universal standards of justice—also of acting solely upon his own discretion, without concern for law, and of wilfully causing distress to others in India. Hastings' defenders countered that his actions were consistent with Indian customs and traditions. Although Burke's speeches at the trial drew applause and focused attention on India, Hastings was eventually acquitted, due in part to the revival of nationalism in Britain in the wake of the French Revolution. Nonetheless, Burke's effort had the effect of creating a sense of responsibility in British public life for the Company's dominion in India.

Soon rumblings appeared amongst merchants in London that the monopoly granted to the East India Company in 1600, intended to facilitate its competition against Dutch and French in a distant region, was no longer needed. In response, in the Charter Act of 1813, the British Parliament renewed the Company's charter but terminated its monopoly except with regard to tea and trade with China, opening India both to private investment and missionaries. With increased British power in India, supervision of Indian affairs by the British Crown and Parliament increased as well. By the 1820s British nationals could transact business or engage in missionary work under the protection of the Crown in the three presidencies. Finally, under the terms of The Saint Helena Act 1833, the British Parliament revoked the Company's monopoly in the China trade and made it an agent for the administration of British India. The Governor-General of Bengal was redesignated as the Governor-General of India. The Governor-General and his executive council were given exclusive legislative powers for the whole of British India. Since the British territories in north India had now extended up to Delhi, the Act also sanctioned the creation of a Presidency of Agra. With the annexation of Oudh in 1856, this territory was extended and eventually became the United Provinces of Agra and Oudh. In addition, in 1854, a Lieutenant-Governor was appointed for the region of Bengal, Bihar and Odisha, leaving the Governor-General to concentrate on the governance of India as a whole.

Revenue collection

A riverside scene in rural east Bengal (present-day Bangladesh), 1860.

A Kochh Mandai woman of east Bengal (now Bangladesh) with an agricultural knife and a freshly harvested jackfruit. (1860)

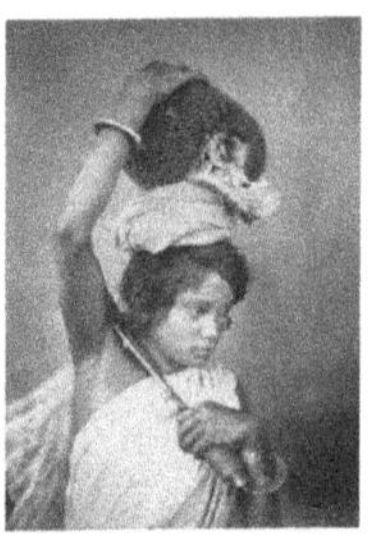

Paddy fields in the Madras Presidency, ca. 1880. Two-thirds of the presidency fell under the *Ryotwari* system.

An East India Company half anna coin.

In the remnant of the Mughal Empire revenue system existing in pre-1765 Bengal, zamindars, or "land holders," collected revenue on behalf of the Mughal emperor, whose representative, or *diwan* supervised their activities. In this system, the assortment of rights associated with land were not possessed by a "land owner," but rather shared by the several parties with stake in the land, including the peasant cultivator, the *zamindar*, and the state. The *zamindar* served as an intermediary who procured economic rent from the cultivator, and after withholding a percentage for his own expenses, made available the rest, as revenue to the state. Under the Mughal system, the land itself belonged to the state and not to the *zamindar*, who could transfer only his right to collect rent. On being awarded the *diwani* or overlordship of Bengal following the Battle of Buxar in 1764, the East India Company found itself short

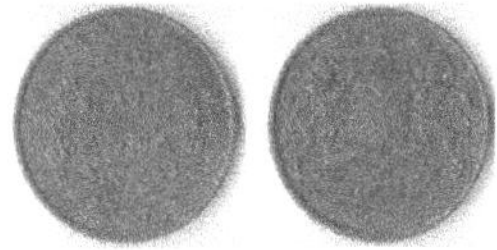

of trained administrators, especially those familiar with local custom and law; tax collection was consequently farmed out. This uncertain foray into land taxation by the Company, may have gravely worsened the impact of a famine that struck Bengal in 1769-70, in which between seven and ten million people—or between a quarter and third of the presidency's population—may have died. However, the company provided little relief either through reduced taxation or by relief efforts, and the economic and cultural impact of the famine was felt decades later, even becoming, a century later, the subject of Bankim Chandra Chatterjee's novel *Anandamath.*

In 1772, under Warren Hastings, the East India Company took over revenue collection directly in the Bengal Presidency (then Bengal and Bihar), establishing a Board of Revenue with offices in Calcutta and Patna, and moving the pre-existing Mughal revenue records from Murshidabad to Calcutta. In 1773, after Oudh ceded the tributary state of Benaras, the revenue collection system was extended to the territory with a Company Resident in charge. The following year—with a view to preventing corruption—Company *district collectors*, who were then responsible for revenue collection for an entire district, were replaced with provincial councils at Patna, Murshidabad, and Calcutta, and with Indian collectors working within each district. The title, "collector," reflected "the centrality of land revenue collection to government in India: it was the government's primary function and it moulded the institutions and patterns of administration."

The Company inherited a revenue collection system from the Mughals in which the heaviest proportion of the tax burden fell on the cultivators, with one-third of the production reserved for imperial entitlement; this pre-colonial system became the Company revenue policy's baseline. However, there was vast variation across India in the methods by which the revenues were collected; with this complication in mind, a Committee of Circuit toured the districts of expanded Bengal Presidency in order to make a five-year settlement, consisting of five-yearly inspections and temporary tax farming. In their overall approach to revenue policy, Company officials were guided by two goals: first, preserving as much as possible the balance of rights and obligations that were traditionally claimed by the farmers who cultivated the land and the various intermediaries who collected tax on the state's behalf and who reserved a cut for themselves; and second, identifying those sectors of the rural economy that would maximise both revenue and security. Although their first revenue settlement turned

Figure 50: *Charles Cornwallis, he was the Governor- General of India when Permanent Settlement was introduced.*

out to be essentially the same as the more informal pre-existing Mughal one, the Company had created a foundation for the growth of both information and bureaucracy.

In 1793, the new Governor-General, Lord Cornwallis, promulgated the permanent settlement of land revenues in the presidency, the first socio-economic regulation in colonial India. By the terms of the settlement Rajas and Taluqdars were recognised as Zamindars and they were asked to collect the rent from the peasants and pay revenue to the Company. It was named *permanent* because it fixed the land tax in perpetuity in return for landed property rights for zamindars; it simultaneously defined the nature of land ownership in the presidency, and gave individuals and families separate property rights in occupied land. Since the revenue was fixed in perpetuity, it was fixed at a high level, which in Bengal amounted to £3 million at 1789-90 prices. According to the Permanent Settlement if the Zamindars failed to pay the revenue on time, the Zmaindari right would be taken from them. According to one estimate, this was 20% higher than the revenue demand before 1757. Over the next century, partly as a result of land surveys, court rulings, and property sales, the change was given practical dimension. An influence on the development of this revenue policy were the economic theories then current, which regarded agriculture as the engine of economic development, and consequently stressed the fixing of revenue demands in order to encourage growth. The expectation behind the permanent settlement was that knowledge of a fixed government demand would encourage the zamindars to increase both their average outcrop and the land under cultivation, since they would be able to retain the profits from the increased output; in addition, it was envisaged that land itself would become a marketable form of property that could be purchased, sold, or mortgaged. A feature of this economic rationale was the additional expectation that the zamindars, recognising their own best interest, would not make unreasonable demands on the peasantry.

However, these expectations were not realised in practice, and in many regions of Bengal, the peasants bore the brunt of the increased demand, there being little protection for their traditional rights in the new legislation. Forced labour of the peasants by the zamindars became more prevalent as cash crops were cultivated to meet the Company revenue demands. Although commercialised cultivation was not new to the region, it had now penetrated deeper into village society and made it more vulnerable to market forces. The zamindars themselves were often unable to meet the increased demands that the Company had placed on them; consequently, many defaulted, and by one estimate, up to one-third of their lands were auctioned during the first three decades following the permanent settlement. The new owners were often Brahmin and Kayastha employees of the Company who had a good grasp of the new system, and, in many cases, some had prospered under it.

Since the zamindars were never able to undertake costly improvements to the land envisaged under the Permanent Settlement, some of which required the removal of the existing farmers, they soon became rentiers who lived off the rent from their tenant farmers. In many areas, especially northern Bengal, they had to increasingly share the revenue with intermediate tenure holders, called *jotedars*, who supervised farming in the villages. Consequently, unlike the contemporaneous Enclosure movement in Britain, agriculture in Bengal remained the province of the subsistence farming of innumerable small paddy fields.

The zamindari system was one of two principal revenue settlements undertaken by the Company in India. In southern India, Thomas Munro, who would later become Governor of Madras, promoted the *ryotwari* system or the Munro system, in which the government settled land-revenue directly with the peasant farmers, or *ryots*. It was first tried in small scale by Captain Alexander Read in the areas that were taken over from the wars with Tipu Sultan. Subsequently, developed by Thomas Munro, this system was gradually extended all over South India. This was, in part, a consequence of the turmoil of the Anglo-Mysore Wars, which had prevented the emergence of a class of large

Figure 51: *Thomas Munro, Governor of Madras*

landowners; in addition, Munro and others felt that *ryotwari* was closer to traditional practice in the region and ideologically more progressive, allowing the benefits of Company rule to reach the lowest levels of rural society. At the heart of the *ryotwari* system was a particular theory of economic rent—and based on David Ricardo's Law of Rent—promoted by utilitarian James Mill who formulated the Indian revenue policy between 1819 and 1830. "He believed that the government was the ultimate lord of the soil and should not renounce its right to 'rent', *i.e.* the profit left over on richer soil when wages and other working expenses had been settled." Another keystone of the new system of temporary settlements was the classification of agricultural fields according to soil type and produce, with average rent rates fixed for the period of the settlement. According to Mill, taxation of land rent would promote efficient agriculture and simultaneously prevent the emergence of a "parasitic landlord class." Mill advocated *ryotwari* settlements which consisted of government measurement and assessment of each plot (valid for 20 or 30 years) and subsequent taxation which was dependent on the fertility of the soil. The taxed amount was nine-tenths of the "rent" in the early 19th century and gradually fell afterwards. However, in spite of the appeal of the *ryotwari* system's abstract principles, class hierarchies in southern Indian villages had not entirely disappeared—for example village headmen continued to hold sway—and peasant cultivators sometimes came to experience revenue demands they could not

meet. In the 1850s, a scandal erupted when it was discovered that some Indian revenue agents of the Company were using torture to meet the Company's revenue demands.

Land revenue settlements constituted a major administrative activity of the various governments in India under Company rule. In all areas other than the Bengal Presidency, land settlement work involved a continually repetitive process of surveying and measuring plots, assessing their quality, and recording landed rights, and constituted a large proportion of the work of Indian Civil Service officers working for the government. After the Company lost its trading rights, it became the single most important source of government revenue, roughly half of overall revenue in the middle of the 19th century; even so, between the years 1814 and 1859, the government of India ran debts in 33 years. With expanded dominion, even during non-deficit years, there was just enough money to pay the salaries of a threadbare administration, a skeleton police force, and the army.

Army and civil service

A Royal Artillery encampment at Arcot, Madras Presidency, 1804.

East India Company *Sepoys* (Indian infantrymen) in red coats outside Tipu Sultan's former summer palace in Bangalore, 1804

Military Orphan School for private soldiers of the East India Company, Howrah, Bengal Presidency, 1794.

A new "writer" in the East India Company Civil Service arrives in Calcutta. A palanquin transport awaits him.

In 1772, when Hastings became the first Governor-General one of his first undertakings was the rapid expansion of the Presidency's army. Since the available soldiers, or *Sepoys*, from Bengal—many of whom had fought against the British in the Battle of Plassey – were now suspect in British eyes, Hastings recruited farther west from the "major breeding ground of India's infantry in eastern Awadh and the lands around Banaras including Bihar. The high caste rural Hindu Rajputs and Brahmins of this region (known as *Purbiyas* (Hindi, lit. "easterners") had been recruited by Mughal Empire armies for two hundred years; the East India Company continued this practice for the next 75 years, with these soldiers comprising up to eighty per cent of the Bengal army. However, in order to avoid any friction within the ranks, the Company also took pains to adapt its military practices to their religious requirements. Consequently, these soldiers dined in separate facilities; in addition, overseas service, considered polluting to their caste, was not required of them, and the army soon came to recognise Hindu festivals officially. "This encouragement of high caste ritual status, however, left the government vulnerable to protest, even mutiny, whenever the sepoys detected infringement of their prerogatives."

East India Company armies after the Re-organisation of 1796			
British troops	**Indian troops**		
	Bengal Presidency	**Madras Presidency**	**Bombay Presidency**
	24,000	24,000	9,000
13,000	**Total Indian troops: 57,000**		
Grand total, British and Indian troops: 70,000			

The Bengal Army was used in military campaigns in other parts of India and abroad: to provide crucial support to a weak Madras army in the Third Anglo-Mysore War in 1791, and also in Java and Ceylon. In contrast to the soldiers in the armies of Indian rulers, the Bengal sepoys not only received high pay, but also received it reliably, thanks in great measure to the Company's access to the vast land-revenue reserves of Bengal. Soon, bolstered both by the new musket technology and naval support, the Bengal army came to be widely regarded. The well-disciplined sepoys attired in red-coats and their British officers began to arouse "a kind of awe in their adversaries. In Maharashtra and in Java, the sepoys were regarded as the embodiment of demonic forces, sometimes of antique warrior heroes. Indian rulers adopted red serge jackets for their own forces and retainers as if to capture their magical qualities."

In 1796, under pressure from the Company's Board of Directors in London, the Indian troops were re-organised and reduced during the tenure of John Shore as Governor-General. However, the closing years of the 18th century saw, with Wellesley's campaigns, a new increase in the army strength. Thus in 1806, at the time of the Vellore Mutiny, the combined strength of the three presidencies' armies stood at 154,500, making them one of the largest standing armies in the world.

East India Company armies on the eve of the Vellore Mutiny of 1806			
Presidencies	**British troops**	**Indian troops**	**Total**
Bengal	7,000	57,000	64,000
Madras	11,000	53,000	64,000
Bombay	6,500	20,000	26,500
Total	24,500	130,000	154,500

As the East India Company expanded its territories, it added irregular "local corps," which were not as well trained as the army. In 1846, after the Second Anglo-Sikh War, a frontier brigade was raised in the Cis-Sutlej Hill States mainly for police work; in addition, in 1849, the "Punjab Irregular Force" was added on the frontier. Two years later, this force consisted of "3 light field batteries, 5 regiments of cavalry, and 5 of infantry." The following year, "a garrison company was added, ... a sixth infantry regiment (formed from the Sind Camel Corps) in 1853, and one mountain battery in 1856." Similarly, a local force was raised after the annexation of Nagpur in 1854, and the "Oudh Irregular Force" was added after Oudh was annexed in 1856. Earlier, as a result of the treaty of 1800, the Nizam of Hyderabad had begun to maintain a contingent force of 9,000 horse and 6,000-foot which was commanded by Company officers; in 1853, after a new treaty was negotiated, this force was assigned to Berar and stopped being a part of the Nizam's army.

East India Company armies on the eve of the Indian rebellion of 1857									
Presidencies	**British troops**				**Indian troops**				
	Cavalry	**Artillery**	**Infantry**	**Total**	**Cavalry**	**Artillery**	**Sappers & Miners**	**Infantry**	**Total**
Bengal	1,366	3,063	17,003	21,432	19,288	4,734	1,497	112,052	137,571
Madras	639	2,128	5,941	8,708	3,202	2,407	1,270	42,373	49,252
Bombay	681	1,578	7,101	9,360	8,433	1,997	637	33,861	44,928
Local forces & contingents					6,796	2,118		23,640	32,554
" " (unclassified)									7,756
Military police									38,977
Total	2,686	6,769	30,045	39,500	37,719	11,256	3,404	211,926	311,038
Grand Total, British and Indian troops									**350,538**

In the Indian rebellion of 1857 almost the entire Bengal army, both regular and irregular, revolted. It has been suggested that after the annexation of Oudh by the East India Company in 1856, many sepoys were disquieted both from losing their perquisites, as landed gentry, in the Oudh courts and from the anticipation of any increased land-revenue payments that the annexation might augur. With British victories in wars or with annexation, as the extent of British jurisdiction expanded, the soldiers were now not only expected to serve in less familiar regions (such as in Burma in the Anglo-Burmese Wars in 1856), but also make do without the "foreign service," remuneration that had previously been their due, and this caused resentment in the ranks. The Bombay and Madras armies, and the Hyderabad contingent, however, remained loyal. The Punjab Irregular Force not only didn't revolt, it played an active role in suppressing the mutiny. The rebellion led to a complete re-organisation of the Indian army in 1858 in the new British Raj.

Civil service

The reforms initiated after 1784 were designed to create an elite civil service where very talented young Britons would spend their entire careers. Advanced training was promoted especially at the Haileybury and Imperial Service College (until 1853). Haileybury emphasised the Anglican religion and morality and trained students in the classical Indian languages. Many students held to Whiggish, evangelical, and Utilitarian convictions of their duty to represent

their nation and to modernise India. At most there were about 600 of these men who managed the Raj's customs service, taxes, justice system, and its general administration.[165,166] The Company's original policy was one of "Orientalism", that is of adjusting to the way of life and customs of the Indian people and not trying to reform them. That changed after 1813, as the forces of reform in the home country, especially evangelical religion, Whiggish political outlook, and Utilitarian philosophy worked together to make the Company an agent of Anglicization and modernisation. Christian missionaries became active, but made few converts. The Raj set out to outlaw sati (widow-burning) and thuggee (ritual banditry) and upgrade the status of women. Schools would be established in which they would teach the English language. The 1830s and 1840s, however, were not times of prosperity: After its heavy spending on the military, the Company had little money to engage in large-scale public works projects or modernisation programs.

Trade

Photograph of East India Company factory in Painam, Sonargaon, Bangladesh, a major producer of the celebrated Dhaka muslins.

"Mellor Mill" in Marple, Greater Manchester, England, was constructed in 1790-93 for manufacturing muslim cloth.

Opium *Godown* (Storehouse) in Patna, Bihar (c. 1814). Patna was the centre of the Company opium industry.

Indigo dye factory in Bengal. Bengal was the world's largest producer of natural indigo in the 19th century.

After gaining the right to collect revenue in Bengal in 1765, the Company largely ceased importing gold and silver, which it had hitherto used to pay for goods shipped back to Britain.

Export of Bullion to India, by EIC (1708-1810)

Years	Bullion (£)	Average per Annum
1708/9-1733/4	12,189,147	420,315
1734/5-1759/60	15,239,115	586,119
1760/1-1765/6	842,381	140,396
1766/7-1771/2	968,289	161,381
1772/3-1775/6	72,911	18,227
1776/7-1784/5	156,106	17,345
1785/6-1792/3	4,476,207	559,525
1793/4-1809/10	8,988,165	528,715

In addition, as under Mughal Empire rule, land revenue collected in the Bengal Presidency helped finance the Company's wars in other parts of India. Consequently, in the period 1760–1800, Bengal's money supply was greatly diminished; furthermore, the closing of some local mints and close supervision of the rest, the fixing of exchange rates, and the standardisation of coinage, paradoxically, added to the economic downturn. During the period, 1780–1860, India changed from being an exporter of processed goods for which it received payment in bullion, to being an exporter of raw materials and a buyer of manufactured goods. More specifically, in the 1750s, mostly fine cotton and silk was exported from India to markets in Europe, Asia, and Africa; by the second quarter of the 19th century, raw materials, which chiefly consisted of raw cotton, opium, and indigo, accounted for most of India's exports. Also, from the late 18th century British cotton mill industry began to lobby the government to both tax Indian imports and allow them access to markets in India. Starting in the 1830s, British textiles began to appear in—and soon to inundate—the Indian markets, with the value of the textile imports growing from £5.2 million 1850 to £18.4 million in 1896. The American Civil War too would have a major impact on India's cotton economy: with the outbreak of the war, American cotton was no longer available to British manufacturers; consequently, demand for Indian cotton soared, and the prices soon quadrupled. This led many farmers in India to switch to cultivating cotton as a quick cash crop; however, with the end of the war in 1865, the demand plummeted again, creating another downturn in the agricultural economy.

At this time, the East India Company's trade with China began to grow as well. In the early 19th century demand for Chinese tea had greatly increased in Britain; since the money supply in India was restricted and the Company was indisposed to shipping bullion from Britain, it decided upon opium, which had a large underground market in China and which was grown in many parts of India, as the most profitable form of payment. However, since the Chinese authorities had banned the importation and consumption of opium, the Company engaged them in the First Opium War, and at its conclusion, under the Treaty of Nanjing, gained access to five Chinese ports, Guangzhou, Xiamen, Fuzhou, Shanghai, and Ningbo; in addition, Hong Kong was ceded to the British Crown. Towards the end of the second quarter of the 19th century, opium export constituted 40% of India's exports.

Another major, though erratic, export item was indigo dye, which was extracted from natural indigo, and which came to be grown in Bengal and northern Bihar. In late 17th and early 18th century Europe, blue clothing was favoured as a fashion, and blue uniforms were common in the military; consequently, the demand for the dye was high. In 1788, the East India Company offered advances to ten British planters to grow indigo; however, since the

new (landed) property rights defined in the Permanent Settlement, didn't allow them, as Europeans, to buy agricultural land, they had to in turn offer cash advances to local peasants, and sometimes coerce them, to grow the crop. The European demand for the dye, however, proved to be unstable, and both creditors and cultivators bore the risk of the market crashes in 1827 and 1847. The peasant discontent in Bengal eventually led to the *Indigo rebellion* in 1859-60 and to the end of indigo production there. In Bihar, however, indigo production continued well into the 20th century; the centre of indigo production there, Champaran district, became the staging ground, in 1917, for Mohandas Karamchand Gandhi's first experiment in non-violent resistance against the British Raj.

Justice system

The house of Sir Thomas Strange, who in 1800 became the first Chief Justice of the Fort of St. George (Madras) and wrote *Elements of Hindu Law* (1825).

An 1833 Lithograph of the *Sadr Diwāni Adālat*, the Chief Civil Court for Indians, on Chowringhee Road, Calcutta.

Coloured engraving of the judges and officers of Hindu (top row) and Muslim (bottom row) law in the Recorder Court in Bombay, 1805.

The Court-House Building on Apollo Street, Bombay (third building on left, just beyond the domed Ice House) shown in 1850.

Until the British gained control of Bengal in the mid-18th century, the system of justice there was presided over by the Nawab of Bengal himself, who, as the chief law officer, *Nawāb Nāẓim*, attended to cases qualifying for capital punishment in his headquarters, Murshidabad. His deputy, the *Naib Nāẓim*, attended to the slightly less important cases. The ordinary lawsuits belonged to the jurisdiction of a hierarchy of court officials consisting of *faujdārs*, *muhtasils*, and *kotwāls*. In the rural areas, or the *Mofussil*, the *zamindars*—the rural overlords with the hereditary right to collect rent from peasant farmers—also had the power to administer justice. This they did with little routine oversight, being required to report only their judgments in capital punishment cases to the *Nawāb*.

By the mid-18th century, the British too had completed a century and a half in India, and had a burgeoning presence in the three *presidency* towns of Madras, Bombay, and Calcutta. During this time the successive Royal Charters had gradually given the East India Company more power to administer justice in these towns. In the charter granted by Charles II in 1683, the Company was given the power to establish "courts of judicature" in locations of its choice, each court consisting of a lawyer and two merchants. This right was renewed in the subsequent charters granted by James II and William III in 1686 and 1698 respectively. In 1726, however, the Court of Directors of the Company felt that more customary justice was necessary for European residents in the presidency towns, and petitioned the King to establish *Mayor's Courts*. The petition was approved and Mayor's courts, each consisting of a Mayor and nine aldermen, and each having the jurisdiction in lawsuits *between* Europeans, were created in Fort William (Calcutta), Madras, and Bombay. Judgments handed down by a Mayor's Court could be disputed with an appeal to the respective Presidency government and, when the amount disputed was greater than Rs. 4,000, with a further appeal to the King-in-Council. In 1753, the Mayor's courts were renewed under a revised letters patent; in addition, Courts of Requests for lawsuits involving amounts less than Rs. 20 were introduced. Both types of courts were regulated by the Court of Directors of the East India Company.

After its victory in the Battle of Buxar, the Company obtained in 1765 the *Diwāni* of Bengal, the right not only to collect revenue, but also to administer civil justice in Bengal. The administration of criminal justice, the *Nizāmat* or *Faujdāri*, however, remained with the *Nawāb*, and for criminal cases the prevailing Islamic law remained in place. However, the Company's new duties associated with the *Diwāni* were leased out to the Indian officials who had formerly performed them. This makeshift arrangement continued—with much accompanying disarray—until 1771, when the Court of Directors of the Company decided to obtain for the Company the jurisdiction of both criminal and civil cases.

Soon afterwards Warren Hastings arrived in Calcutta as the first Governor-General of the Company's Indian dominions and resolved to overhaul the Company's organisation and in particular its judicial affairs. In the interior, or *Mofussil, diwāni adālats*, or a civil courts of first instance, were constituted in each district; these courts were presided over by European *Zilā* judges employed by the Company, who were assisted in the interpretation of customary Indian law by Hindu *pandits* and Muslim *qazis*. For small claims, however, Registrars and Indian commissioners, known as *Sadr Amīns* and *Munsifs*, were appointed. These in their turn were supervised by provincial civil courts of appeal constituted for such purpose, each consisting of four British judges. All these were under the authority of the *Sadr Diwāni Adālat*, or the Chief Civil Court of Appeals, consisting of the Governor of the Presidency and his Council, assisted by Indian officers.

Similarly for criminal cases, Mofussil *nizāmat adālats*, or Provincial courts of criminal judicature, were created in the interior; these again consisted of Indian court officers (*pandits* and *qazis*), who were supervised by officials of the Company. Also constituted were Courts of circuit with appellate jurisdiction in criminal cases, which were usually presided over by the judges of the civil appellate courts. All these too were under a *Sadr Nizāmat Adālat* or a Chief Court of Criminal Appeal.

Around this time the business affairs of the East India Company began to draw increased scrutiny in the House of Commons. After receiving a report by a committee, which condemned the Mayor's Courts, the Crown issued a charter for a new judicial system in the Bengal Presidency. The British Parliament consequently enacted the *Regulating Act of 1773* under which the King-in-Council created a Supreme Court in the *Presidency town*, *i.e.* Fort William. The tribunal consisted of one Chief Justice and three puisne judges; all four judges were to be chosen from barristers. The Supreme Court supplanted the

Figure 52: *The family of Chief Justice Sir Elijah Impey in Calcutta, 1783*

Mayor's Court; however, it left the Court of Requests in place. Under the charter, the Supreme Court, moreover, had the authority to exercise all types of jurisdiction in the region of Bengal, Bihar, and Odisha, with the only caveat that in situations where the disputed amount was in excess of Rs. 4,000, their judgment could be appealed to the Privy Council. Both the Act and the charter said nothing about the relation between the judiciary (Supreme Court) and the executive branch (Governor-General); equally, they were silent on the *Adālats* (both *Diwāni* and *Nizāmat*) created by Warren Hastings just the year before. In the new Supreme Court, the civil and criminal cases alike were interpreted and prosecuted accorded to English law; in the *Sadr Adālats*, however, the judges and law-officers had no knowledge of English law, and were required only, by the Governor-General's order, "to proceed according to equity, justice, and good conscience, unless Hindu or Muhammadan law was in point, or some Regulation expressly applied."

There was a good likelihood, therefore, that the Supreme Court and the *Sadr Adālats* would act in opposition to each other and, predictably, many disputes resulted. Hastings' premature attempt to appoint the Chief Justice, Sir Elijah Impey, an old schoolmate from Winchester, to the bench of the *Sadr Diwāni Adālat*, only complicated the situation further. The appointment had to be annulled in 1781 by a parliamentary intervention with the enactment of the Declaration Act. The Act exempted the Executive Branch from the jurisdiction

of the Supreme Court. It recognised the independent existence of the *Sadr Adālats* and all subsidiary courts of the Company. Furthermore, it headed off future legal turf wars by prohibiting the Supreme Court any jurisdiction in matters of revenue (*Diwāni*) or Regulations of the Government enacted by the British Parliament. This state of affairs continued until 1797, when a new Act extended the jurisdiction of the Supreme Court to the province of Benares (which had since been added to the Company's dominions) and "all places for the time being included in Bengal." With the constituting of the Ceded and Conquered Provinces in 1805, the jurisdiction would extend as far west as Delhi.

In the other two presidencies, Madras and Bombay, a similar course of legal changes unfolded; there, however, the Mayor's Courts were first strengthened to Recorder's Courts by adding a legal president to the bench. The Supreme Courts in Madras and Bombay were finally established in 1801 and 1823, respectively. Madras Presidency was also unusual in being the first to rely on village headmen and *panchāyats* for cases involving small claims. This judicial system in the three presidencies was to survive the Company's rule, the next major change coming only in 1861.

Education

A coloured-in photograph (1851) of Hindu College, Calcutta, which had been founded in 1817 by a committee headed by Raja Ram Mohun Roy. In 1855, the Government of the Bengal Presidency renamed it *Presidency College* and opened it to all students.

An engraving (1844) of a youth, who according to the engraver, Emily Eden, was "a favourite and successful young student at the Hindu College in Calcutta, where scholars acquire a very perfect knowledge of English, and have a familiarity with the best English writers ..."

An 1844 engraving of Grant Medical College (left) and Sir Jamsetjee Jeejeebhoy Hospital (right background) in Bombay made by G. R. Sargeant the year before the medical college was formally opened.

An 1855 photograph of the same two institutions. In 1857, Grant Medical College became one of three institutions affiliated with the newly established University of Bombay. The college was funded partly by the Jeejeebhoy family and partly by the East India Company.

Education of Indians had become a topic of interest among East India Company officials from the outset of the Company's rule in Bengal. In the last two decades of the 18th century and the first decade of the nineteenth, Company officials pursued a policy of conciliation towards the native culture of its new dominion, especially in relation to education policy. During the 19th century, the Indian literacy rates were rumoured to be less than half of post independence levels which were 18.33% in 1951. The policy was pursued in the aid of three goals: "to sponsor Indians in their own culture, to advance knowledge of India, and to employ that knowledge in government."

The first goal was supported by some administrators, such as Warren Hastings, who envisaged the Company as the successor of a great Empire, and saw the support of vernacular learning as only befitting that role. In 1781, Hastings founded the *Madrasa 'Aliya*, an institution in Calcutta for the study of Arabic and Persian languages, and Islamic Law. A few decades later a related perspective appeared among the governed population, one that was expressed by the conservative Bengali reformer *Radhakanta Deb* as the "duty of the Rulers of Countries to preserve and Customs and the religions of their subjects."

The second goal was motivated by the concerns among some Company officials about being seen as foreign rulers. They argued that the Company should try to win over its subjects by outdoing the region's previous rulers in the support of indigenous learning. Guided by this belief, the Benares Sanskrit College was founded in Varanasi in 1791 during the administration of Lord Cornwallis. The promotion of knowledge of Asia had attracted scholars as well to the Company's service. Earlier, in 1784, the Asiatick Society had been founded in Calcutta by William Jones, a puisne judge in the newly established Supreme Court of Bengal. Soon, Jones was to advance his famous thesis on the common origin of Indo-European languages.

The third related goal grew out of the philosophy then current among some Company officials that they would themselves become better administrators if they were better versed in the languages and cultures of India. It led in 1800 to the founding of the College of Fort William, in Calcutta by Lord Wellesley, the then Governor-General. The College was later to play an important role both in the development of modern Indian languages and in the Bengal Renaissance. Advocates of these related goals were termed, "Orientalists." The Orientalist group was led by Horace Hayman Wilson. Many leading Company officials, such as Thomas Munro and Montstuart Elphinstone, were influenced by the Orientalist ethos and felt that the Company's government in India should be responsive to Indian expectations. The Orientalist ethos would prevail in education policy well into the 1820s, and was reflected in the founding of the Poona Sanskrit College in Pune in 1821 and the Calcutta Sanskrit College in 1824.

The Orientalists were, however, soon opposed by advocates of an approach that has been termed *Anglicist*. The Anglicists supported instruction in the English language in order to impart to Indians what they considered modern Western knowledge. Prominent among them were evangelicals who, after 1813—when the Company's territories were opened to Christian missionaries—were interested in spreading Christian belief; they also believed in using theology to promote liberal social reform, such as the abolition of slavery. Among them was Charles Grant, the Chairman of the East India Company. Grant supported state-sponsored education in India 20 years before a similar system was set up in Britain. Among Grant's close evangelical friends were William Wilberforce, a prominent abolitionist and member of the British Parliament, and Sir John Shore, the Governor-General of India from 1793 to 1797. During this period, many Scottish Presbyterian missionaries also supported the British rulers in their efforts to spread English education and established many reputed colleges like Scottish Church College (1830), Wilson

College (1832), Madras Christian College (1837), and Elphinstone College (1856).

However, the Anglicists also included utilitarians, led by James Mill, who had begun to play an important role in fashioning Company policy. The utilitarians believed in the moral worth of an education that aided the good of society and promoted instruction in *useful knowledge*. Such *useful* instruction to Indians had the added consequence of making them more suitable for the Company's burgeoning bureaucracy. By the early 1830s, the Anglicists had the upper hand in devising education policy in India. Many utilitarian ideas were employed in Thomas Babbington Macaulay's *Minute on Indian Education* of 1835. The *Minute*, which later aroused great controversy, was to influence education policy in India well into the next century.

Since English was increasingly being employed as the language of instruction, Persian was abolished as the official language of the Company's administration and courts by 1837. However, bilingual educations was proving to be popular as well, and some institutions such as the Poona Sanskrit College commenced teaching both Sanskrit and English. Charles Grant's son, Sir Robert Grant, who in 1834 was appointed Governor of the Bombay Presidency, played an influential role in the planning of the first medical college in Bombay, which after his unexpected death was named Grant Medical College when it was established in 1845. During 1852–1853 some citizens of Bombay sent petitions to the British Parliament in support of both establishing and adequately funding university education in India. The petitions resulted in the *Education Dispatch* of July 1854 sent by Sir Charles Wood, the President of the Board of Control of the East India Company, the chief official on Indian affairs in the British government, to Lord Dalhousie, the then Governor-General of India. The dispatch outlined a broad plan of state-sponsored education for India, which included:

1. Establishing a Department of Public Instruction in each presidency or province of British India.
2. Establishing universities modelled on the University of London (as primarily examining institutions for students studying in affiliated colleges) in each of the *Presidency towns* (*i.e.* Madras, Bombay, and Calcutta)
3. Establishing teachers-training schools for all levels of instruction
4. Maintaining existing Government colleges and high-schools and increasing their number when necessary.
5. Vastly increasing vernacular schools for elementary education in villages.
6. Introducing a system of grants-in-aid for private schools.

The Department of Public Instruction was in place by 1855. In January 1857, the University of Calcutta was established, followed by the University of Bombay in June, 1857, and the University of Madras in September 1857. The

University of Bombay, for example, consisted of three affiliated institutions: the Elphinstone Institution, the Grant Medical College, and the Poona Sanskrit College. The Company's administration also founded high-schools *en masse* in the different provinces and presidencies, and the policy was continued during Crown rule which commenced in 1858. By 1861, 230,000 students were attending public educational institutions in the four provinces (the three Presidencies and North-Western Provinces), of whom 200,000 were in primary schools. Over 5,000 primary schools and 142 secondary schools had been established in these provinces. Earlier, during the Indian rebellion of 1857, some civilian leaders, such as Khan Bhadur Khan of Bareilly, had stressed the threat posed to the populace's religions by the new education programmes begun by the Company; however, historical statistics have shown that this was not generally the case. For example, in Etawah district in the then North-Western Provinces (present-day Uttar Pradesh), where during the period 1855–57, nearly 200 primary, middle-, and high-schools had been opened by the Company and tax levied on the population, relative calm prevailed and the schools remained open during the rebellion.

Social reform

In the first half of the 19th century, the British legislated reforms against what they considered were iniquitous Indian practices. In most cases, the legislation alone was unable to change Indian society sufficiently for it to absorb both the ideal and the ethic underpinning the reform. For example, upper-caste Hindu society had long looked askance at the remarriage of widows in order to protect both what it considered was family honour and family property. Even adolescent widows were expected to live a life of austerity and denial. The Hindu Widows' Remarriage Act, 1856, enacted in the waning years of Company rule, provided legal safeguards against loss of certain forms of inheritance for a remarrying Hindu widow, though not of the inheritance due her from her deceased husband. However, very few widows actually remarried. Some Indian reformers, such as Raja Ram Mohan Roy, Ishwar Chandra Vidyasagar, even offered money to men who would take widows as brides, but these men often deserted their new wives.

Post and telegraph

Lithograph of the General Post Office on Chowringhee Street, Calcutta, 1833, four years before the India-wide postal service was established under the Indian Postal Act of 1837.

Two four anna stamps issued in 1854. Stamps were issued for the first time for all of British India in 1854. The lowest denomination was ½ anna blue, followed by 1 anna

red, and 4 annas blue and red. The stamps were printed from lithographic stones at the Surveyor-General's Office in Calcutta.

A semaphore "telegraph" signalling tower in Silwar (Bihar), 13 February 1823, thirty years before electric telegraphy was rapidly introduced into India by the East India Company.

Postal services

Before 1837, the East India Company's dominions in India had no universal public postal service, one that was shared by all regions. Although courier services did exist, connecting the more important towns with their respective seats of provincial government (*i.e.* the *Presidency towns* of Fort William (Calcutta), Fort St. George (Madras), and Bombay), private individuals were, upon payment, only sparingly allowed their use. That situation changed in 1837, when, by Act XVII of that year, a public post, run by the Company's Government, was established in the Company's territory in India. Post offices were established in the principal towns and postmasters appointed. The postmasters of the Presidency towns oversaw a few provincial post offices in addition to being responsible for the main postal services between the provinces. By contrast, the District collectors (originally, collectors of land-tax) directed the District post offices, including their local postal services. Postal services required payment in cash, to be made in advance, with the amount charged usually varying with weight and distance. For example, the charge of sending

a letter from Calcutta to Bombay was one rupee; however, that from Calcutta to Agra was 12 annas (or three-quarter of a rupee) for each tola (three-eighths of an ounce).[167]

After the recommendations of the commission appointed in 1850 to evaluate the Indian postal system were received, Act XVII of 1837 was superseded by the Indian Postal Act of 1854. Under its provisions, the entire postal department was headed by a *Director-General*, and the duties of a *Postmaster-General* were set apart from those of a Presidency Postmaster; the former administered the postal system of the larger provinces (such as the Bombay Presidency or the North-Western Provinces), whereas the latter attended to the less important Provinces (such as Ajmer-Merwara and the major Political Agencies such as Rajputana). Postage stamps were introduced at this time and the postal rates fixed by weight, dependent no longer also on the distance travelled in the delivery. The lowest inland letter rate was half anna for 1/4 tola, followed by one anna for 1/2 tola, and 2 annas for a tola, a great reduction from the rates of 17 years before. The Indian Post Office delivered letters, newspapers, postcards, book packets, and parcels. These deliveries grew steadily in number; by 1861 (three years after the end of Company rule), a total of 889 post offices had been opened, and almost 43 million letters and over four and a half million newspapers were being delivered annually.

Telegraphy

Before the advent of electric telegraphy, the word "telegraph" had been used for semaphore signalling. During the period 1820–30, the East India Company's Government in India seriously considered constructing signalling towers ("telegraph" towers), each a hundred feet high and separated from the next by eight miles, along the entire distance from Calcutta to Bombay. Although such towers were built in Bengal and Bihar, the India-wide semaphore network never took off. By mid-century, electric telegraphy had become viable, and hand signalling obsolete.

Dr. W. B. O'Shaughnessy, a Professor of Chemistry in the Calcutta Medical College, received permission in 1851 to conduct a trial run for a telegraph service from Calcutta to Diamond Harbour along the river Hooghly. Four telegraph offices, mainly for shipping-related business, were also opened along the river that year. The telegraph receiver used in the trial was a galvanoscope of Dr. O'Shaughnessy's design and manufactured in India. When the experiment was deemed to be a success a year later, the Governor-General of India, Lord Dalhousie, sought permission from the Court of Directors of the Company for the construction of telegraph lines from "Calcutta to Agra, Agra to Bombay, Agra to Peshawar, and Bombay to Madras, extending in all over 3,050 miles and including forty-one offices." The permission was soon granted; by February 1855 all the proposed telegraph lines had been constructed and were being used to send paid messages. Dr. O'Shaughnessy's instrument was used all over India until early 1857, when it was supplanted by the Morse instrument. By 1857, the telegraph network had expanded to 4,555 miles of lines and sixty two offices, and had reached as far as the hill station of Ootacamund in the Nilgiri Hills and the port of Calicut on the southwest coast of India. During the Indian rebellion of 1857, more than seven hundred miles of telegraph lines were destroyed by the rebel forces, mainly in the North-Western Provinces. The East India Company was nevertheless able to use the remaining intact lines to warn many outposts of impending disturbances. The political value of the new technology was, thus, driven home to the Company, and, in the following year, not only were the destroyed lines rebuil, but the network was expanded further by 2,000 miles.

O'Shaughnessy's experimental set-up of 1851–52 consisted of both overhead and underground lines; the latter included underwater ones that crossed two rivers, the Hooghly and the Haldi. The overhead line was constructed by welding uninsulated iron rods, 13½ feet long and 3/8 inch wide, end to end. These lines, which weighed 1,250 pounds per mile, were held aloft by fifteen-foot lengths of bamboo, planted into the ground at equal intervals—200 to the mile—and covered with a layer each of coal tar and pitch for insulation. The underwater cables had been manufactured in England and consisted of copper wire covered with gutta-percha. Furthermore, in order to protect the cables from dragging ship anchors, the cables were attached to the links of a $^7/_8$-inch-thick (22 mm) chain cable. An underwater cable of length 2,070 yards was laid across the Hooghly river at Diamond Harbour, and another, 1,400 yards long, was laid across the Haldi at Kedgeree.

Work on the long lines from Calcutta to Peshawar (through Agra), Agra to Bombay, and Bombay to Madras began in 1853. The conducting material chosen for these lines was now lighter, and the support stronger. The wood used for the support consisted of teak, sal, fir, ironwood, or blackwood (*Terminalia elata*), and was either fashioned into whole posts, or used in attachments to iron *screw-piles* or masonry columns. Some sections had uniformly strong support; one such was the 322-mile Bombay-Madras line, which was supported by granite obelisks sixteen feet high. Other sections had less secure support, consisting, in some cases, of sections of toddy palm, insulated with pieces of sal wood fastened to their tops. Some of the conducting wires or rods were insulated, the insulating material being either manufactured in India or England; other stretches of wire remained uninsulated. By 1856, iron tubes had begun to be employed to provide support, and would see increased use in the second half of the 19th century all over India.

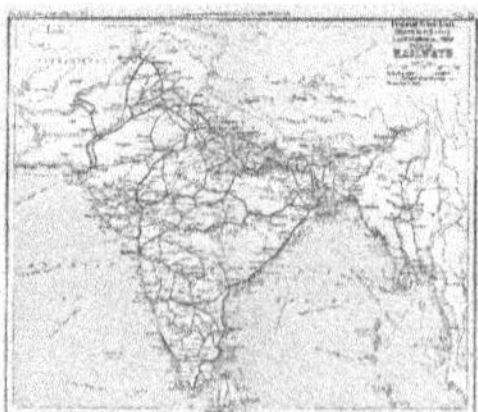

The first Telegraph Act for India was Parliament's Act XXXIV of 1854. When the public telegramme service was first set up in 1855, the charge was fixed at one rupee for every sixteen words (including the address) for every 400 miles of transmission. The charges were doubled for telegrammes sent between 6PM and 6AM. These rates would remain fixed until 1882. In the year 1860–61, two years after the end of Company rule, India had 11,093 miles of telegraph lines and 145 telegraph offices. That year telegrammes totalling Rs. 500,000 in value were sent by the public, the working expense of the *Indian Telegraph Department* was Rs. 1.4 million, and the capital expenditure until the end of the year totalled Rs. 6.5 million.

Railways

Photograph (1855) of the Dapoorie Viaduct, Bombay. The viaduct, shown with a train steaming across it, was completed in 1853 and linked Bombay Island with Thane on the mainland.

The trunk lines proposed by the Governor-General of India, Lord Dalhousie in his *Railway minute of 1853* (shown in red on a 1908 railway map of India).

The first locomotive, shown on the right and christened "multum in parvo" (barely visible on the wheel casing), which was used by the East Indian Railway Company in 1854 on its 23-mile line from Howrah to Pandua.

Photograph (1855) showing the construction of the Bhor Ghat incline bridge, Bombay; the incline was conceived by George Clark, the Chief Engineer in the East India Company's Government of Bombay.

The first inter-city railway service in England, the Stockton-Darlington railway, had been established in 1825;[168] in the following decade other inter-city railways were rapidly constructed between cities in England. In 1845, the Court of Directors of the East India Company, forwarded to the Governor-General of India, Lord Dalhousie, a number of applications they had received from private contractors in England for the construction of a wide-ranging railway network in India, and requested a feasibility report. They added that, in their view, the enterprise would be profitable only if large sums of money could be raised for the construction. The Court was concerned that in addition to the usual difficulties encountered in the construction of this new form of transportation, India might present some unique problems, among which they counted floods, tropical storms in coastal areas, damage by "insects and luxuriant tropical vegetation," and the difficulty of finding qualified technicians at a reasonable cost. It was suggested, therefore, that three experimental lines be constructed and their performance evaluated.

Contracts were awarded in 1849 to the East Indian Railway Company to construct a 120-mile railway from Howrah-Calcutta to Raniganj; to the Great Indian Peninsular Railway Company for a service from Bombay to Kalyan, thirty miles away; and to the *Madras Railway Company* for a line from Madras city to Arkonam, a distance of some thirty nine miles. Although construction began first, in 1849, on the East Indian Railways line, with an outlay of £1 million, it was the first-leg of the Bombay-Kalyan line—a 21-mile stretch from Bombay to Thane—that, in 1853, was the first to be completed (see picture below).

The feasibility of a train network in India was comprehensively discussed by Lord Dalhousie in his *Railway minute of 1853*. The Governor-General vigorously advocated the quick and widespread introduction of railways in India, pointing to their political, social, and economic advantages. He recommended

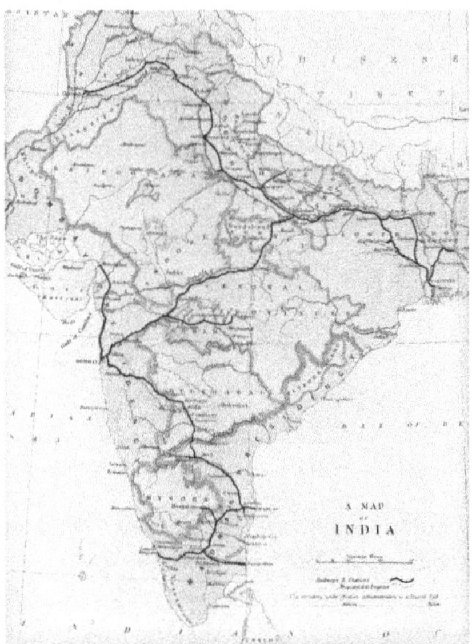

Figure 53: *Map of the completed and planned railway lines in India in 1871, thirteen years after the end of Company rule.*

that a network of *trunk lines* be first constructed connecting the inland regions of each presidency with its chief port as well as each presidency with several others. His recommended trunk lines included the following ones: (i) from Calcutta, in the Bengal Presidency, on the eastern coast to Lahore in the north-western region of the Punjab, annexed just three years before; (ii) from Agra in north-central India (in, what was still being called North-Western Provinces) to Bombay city on the western coast; (iii) from Bombay to Madras city on the southeastern coast; and (iv) from Madras to the southwestern Malabar coast (see map above). The proposal was soon accepted by the Court of Directors.

During this time work had been proceeding on the experimental lines as well. The first leg of the East Indian Railway line, a broad gauge railway, from Howrah to Pandua, was opened in 1854 (see picture of locomotive below), and the entire line up to Raniganj would become functional by the time of the Indian rebellion of 1857. The Great Indian Peninsular Railway was permitted to extend its experimental line to Poona. This extension required planning for the steep rise in the *Bor Ghat* valley in the Western Ghats, a section 15¾ miles long with an ascent of 1,831 feet. Construction began in 1856 and was completed in 1863, and, in the end, the line required a total of twenty five tunnels and fifteen miles of gradients (inclines) of 1 in 50 or steeper, the most extreme being the *Bor Ghat Incline*, a distance of 1¾ miles at a gradient of 1 in 37 (see picture above).

Each of the three companies (and later five others that were given contracts in 1859) was joint stock company domiciled in England with its financial capital raised in pound sterling. Each company was guaranteed a 5 per cent return on its capital outlay and, in addition, a share of half the profits. Although the *Government of India* had no capital expenditure other than the provision of the underlying land free of charge, it had the onus of continuing to provide the 5 percent return in the event of net loss, and soon all anticipation of profits would fall by the wayside as the outlays would mount.

The technology of railway construction was still new and there was no railway engineering expertise in India; consequently, all engineers had to be brought in from England. These engineers were unfamiliar not only with the language and culture of India, but also with the physical aspect of the land itself and its concomitant engineering requirements. Moreover, never before had such a large and complex construction project been undertaken in India, and no pool of semi-skilled labour was already organised to aid the engineers. The work, therefore, proceeded in fits and starts—many practical trials followed by a final construction that was undertaken with great caution and care—producing an outcome that was later criticised as being "built to a standard which was far in excess of the needs to the time." The Government of India's administrators, moreover, made up in their attention to the fine details of expenditure and management what they lacked in professional expertise. The resulting delays soon led to the appointment of a Committee of the House of Commons in 1857–58 to investigate the matter. However, by the time the Committee concluded that all parties needed to honour the spirit rather than the letter of the contracts, Company rule in India had ended.

Although, railway construction had barely begun in the last years of this rule, its foundations had been laid, and it would proceed apace for much of the next half century. By the turn of the 20th century, India would have over 28,000 miles of railways connecting most interior regions to the ports of Karachi, Bombay, Madras, Calcutta, Chittagong, and Rangoon, and together they would constitute the fourth-largest railway network in the world.[169]

Canals

Watercolor (1863) titled, "The Ganges Canal, Roorkee, Saharanpur District (U.P.)." The canal was the brainchild of Sir Proby Cautley; construction began in 1840, and the canal was opened by Governor-General Lord Dalhousie in April 1854

Photograph (2008) of an East India Company-era (1854) bridge on the Ganges Canal near Roorkee, Uttar Pradesh, India.

Photograph (1860) of the head works of the Ganges Canal in Haridwar taken by Samuel Bourne

Photograph (2008) of the head works of the Ganges Canal in Haridwar, viewed from the opposite side.

The first irrigation works undertaken during East India Company's rule were begun in 1817. Consisting chiefly of extensions or reinforcements of previous Indian works, these projects were limited to the plains north of Delhi and to the river deltas of the Madras Presidency. A small dam in the Kaveri river delta, built some 1,500 years before, and known as the *Grand Anicut*, was one such indigenous work in South India. In 1835–36, Sir Arthur Cotton successfully reinforced the dam, and his success prompted more irrigation projects on the river. A little farther north, on the Tungabhadra river, the 16th century Vijayanagara ruler, Krishna Deva Raya, had constructed several weirs; these too would be extended under British administration.

In plains above Delhi, the mid-14th century Sultan of Delhi, Firoz Shah Tughlaq, had constructed the 150-mile long *Western Jamna Canal.* Taking off from the right bank of the Jamna river early in its course, the canal irrigated the Sultan's territories in the Hissar region of Eastern Punjab. By the mid-16th century, however, the fine sediment carried by the Himalayan river had gradually choked the canal. Desilted and reopened several decades later by Akbar

the Great, the *Western Jamna Canal* was itself tapped by Akbar's grandson Shah Jahan, and some of its water was diverted to Delhi. During this time another canal was cut off the river. The 129-mile *Eastern Jamna Canal* or *Doab Canal*, which took off from the *left* bank of the Jamna, also high in its course, presented a qualitatively different difficulty. Since it was cut through steeply sloped land, its flow became difficult to control, and it was never to function efficiently. With the decline of Mughal Empire power in the 18th century, both canals fell into disrepair and closed. The Western Jamna Canal was repaired by British army engineers and it reopened in 1820. The *Doab Canal* was reopened in 1830; its considerable renovation involved raising the embankment by an average height of 9 ft. for some 40 miles.

Farther west in the Punjab region, the 130-mile long *Hasli Canal*, had been constructed by previous rulers. Taking off from the Ravi river and supplying water to the cities of Lahore and Amritsar, this left-bank canal was extended by the British in the *Bari Doab Canal* works during 1850–57. The Punjab region, moreover, had much rudimentary irrigation by "inundation canals." Consisting of open cuts on the side of a river and involving no regulation, the inundation canals had been used in both the Punjab and Sindh for many centuries. The energetic administrations of the Sikh and Pathan governors of Mughal West Punjab had ensured that many such canals in Multan, Dera Ghazi Khan, and Muzaffargarh were still working efficiently at the time of the British annexation of the Punjab in 1849-1856 (Period of tenure of Marquess of Dalhousie Governor General).

The first new British work—with no Indian antecedents—was the Ganges Canal built between 1842 and 1854. Contemplated first by Col. John Russell Colvin in 1836, it did not at first elicit much enthusiasm from its eventual architect Sir Proby Thomas Cautley, who balked at idea of cutting a canal through extensive low-lying land in order to reach the drier upland destination. However, after the Agra famine of 1837–38, during which the East India Company's administration spent Rs. 2,300,000 on famine relief, the idea of a canal became more attractive to the Company's budget-conscious Court of

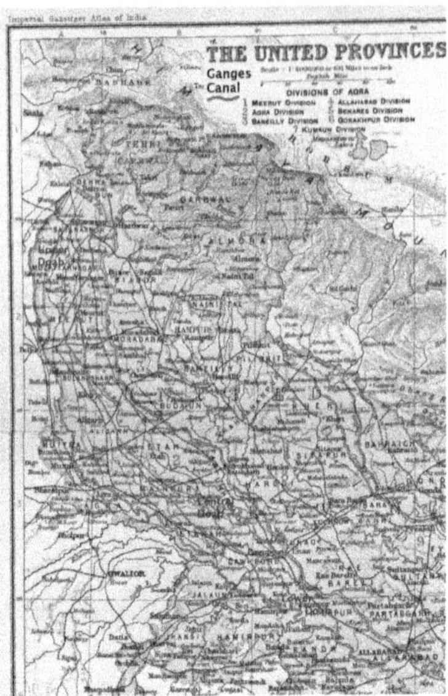

Figure 54: *The Ganges Canal highlighted in red stretching between its headworks off the Ganges river in Hardwar and its confluence with the Jumna river below Cawnpore (now Kanpur).*

Directors. In 1839, the Governor General of India, Lord Auckland, with the Court's assent, granted funds to Cautley for a full survey of the swath of land that underlay and fringed the projected course of the canal. The Court of Directors, moreover, considerably enlarged the scope of the projected canal, which, in consequence of the severity and geographical extent of the famine, they now deemed to be the entire Doab region.

The enthusiasm, however, proved to be short lived. Auckland's successor as Governor General, Lord Ellenborough, appeared less receptive to large-scale public works, and for the duration of his tenure, withheld major funds for the project. Only in 1844, when a new Governor-General, Lord Hardinge, was appointed, did official enthusiasm and funds return to the Ganges canal project. Although the intervening impasse, had seemingly affected Cautely's health and required him to return to Britain in 1845 for recuperation, his European sojourn gave him an opportunity to study contemporary hydraulic works in Great Britain and Italy. By the time of his return to India even more supportive men were at the helm, both in the North-Western Provinces, with James Thomason as Lt. Governor, and in British India with Lord Dalhousie as Governor-General. Canal construction, under Cautley's supervision, now went into full swing. A 350-mile long canal, with another 300 miles of branch lines, eventually stretched between the headworks in Hardwar and—after splitting into two branches at Nanau near Aligarh—the confluence with the Ganges at Cawnpore (now Kanpur) and with the Jumna (now Yamuna) mainstem at Etawah. The Ganges Canal, which required a total capital outlay of £2.15 million, was officially opened in 1854 by Lord Dalhousie. According to historian Ian Stone:

> *It was the largest canal ever attempted in the world, five times greater in its length than all the main irrigation lines of Lombardy and Egypt put together, and longer by a third than even the largest USA navigation canal, the Pennsylvania Canal.*

References

General histories

- Bandyopādhyāẏa, Śekhara (2004), *From Plassey to partition: a history of modern India*[170], Delhi: Orient Blackswan, ISBN 978-81-250-2596-2
- Bayly, Christopher Alan. *Indian society and the making of the British Empire* (1988.)
- Bayly, C.A. *The Raj: India and the British 1600-1947* (1990)
- Bose, Sugata; Jalal, Ayesha (2004), *Modern South Asia: History, Culture, Political economy: second edition*[171], Routledge, ISBN 978-1-134-39715-0
- Brown, Judith Margaret (1994), *Modern India: the origins of an Asian democracy*[172], Oxford University Press, ISBN 978-0-19-873112-2
- Judd, Denis (2010), *The lion and the tiger: the rise and fall of the British Raj, 1600-1947*[173], Oxford University Press, ISBN 978-0-19-280579-9
- Kulke, Hermann; Rothermund, Dietmar (2004), *A history of India*[174], Routledge, ISBN 978-0-415-32920-0
- Lawson, Philip. *The East India Company: A History* (Routledge, 1993) excerpt and text search[175]
- Ludden, David (2002), *India and South Asia: a short history*[176], Oneworld, ISBN 978-1-85168-237-9
- Markovits, Claude (2004), *A history of modern India, 1480-1950*[177], Anthem Press, ISBN 978-1-84331-152-2, retrieved 5 November 2011
- Metcalf, Barbara Daly; Metcalf, Thomas R. (2006), *A concise history of modern India*[178], Cambridge University Press, ISBN 978-0-521-86362-9
- Peers, Douglas M. (2006), *India under colonial rule: 1700-1885*[179], Pearson Education, ISBN 978-0-582-31738-3
- Moon, Penderel. *The British conquest and dominion of India* (2 vol. India Research Press, 1989)

- Riddick, John F. *The history of British India: a chronology* (2006) excerpt and text search[180], covers 1599–1947
- Riddick, John F. *Who Was Who in British India* (1998), covers 1599–1947
- Robb, Peter (2011), *A History of India*[181], Palgrave Macmillan, ISBN 978-0-230-34549-2
- Spear, Percival (1990) [First published 1965], *A History of India*[182], Volume 2, Penguin Books, ISBN 978-0-14-013836-8
- Stein, Burton; Arnold, David (2010), *A History of India*[183], John Wiley and Sons, ISBN 978-1-4051-9509-6
- Wolpert, Stanley (2008), *A new history of India*[184], Oxford University Press, ISBN 978-0-19-533756-3

Monographs and collections

- Ambirajan, S. (2007) [1978], *Classical Political Economy and British Policy in India*[185], Cambridge University Press, ISBN 978-0-521-05282-5, retrieved 20 February 2012
- Anderson, Clare (2007), *The Indian Uprising of 1857-8: prisons, prisoners, and rebellion*[186], Anthem Press, ISBN 978-1-84331-295-6, retrieved 5 November 2011
- Bayly, C. A. (1989), *Indian Society and the Making of the British Empire*[187], Cambridge University Press, ISBN 978-0-521-38650-0, retrieved 5 November 2011
- Bayly, C. A. (2000), *Empire and Information: Intelligence Gathering and Social Communication in India, 1780–1870 (Cambridge Studies in Indian History and Society)*, Cambridge and London: Cambridge University Press. Pp. 426, ISBN 0-521-66360-1
- Chakrabarti, D.K. 2003. The Archaeology of European Expansion in India, Gujarat, c. 16th–18th Centuries (2003) Delhi: Aryan Books International
- Chaudhuri, Kirti N. *The Trading World of Asia and the English East India Company: 1660-1760* (Cambridge University Press, 1978)
- Bose, Sumit (1993), *Peasant Labour and Colonial Capital: Rural Bengal since 1770 (New Cambridge History of India)*, Cambridge and London: Cambridge University Press..
- Chandavarkar, Rajnarayan (1998), *Imperial Power and Popular Politics: Class, Resistance and the State in India, 1850–1950*, (Cambridge Studies in Indian History & Society). Cambridge and London: Cambridge University Press. Pp. 400, ISBN 0-521-59692-0.
- Erikson, Emily. *Between Monopoly and Free Trade: The English East India Company, 1600-1757* (Princeton University Press, 2014)

- Farnie, D. A. (1979), *The English Cotton Industry and the World Market, 1815–1896*, Oxford, UK: Oxford University Press. Pp. 414, ISBN 0-19-822478-8
- Gilmour, David. *The Ruling Caste: Imperial Lives in the Victorian Raj* (New York: Farrar, Straus and Giroux, 2005).
- Guha, R. (1995), *A Rule of Property for Bengal: An Essay on the Idea of the Permanent Settlement*, Durham, NC: Duke University Press, ISBN 0-521-59692-0.
- Hossain, Hameeda. *The Company weavers of Bengal: the East India Company and the organization of textile production in Bengal, 1750-1813* (Oxford University Press, 1988)
- Marshall, P. J. (1987), *Bengal: The British Bridgehead, Eastern India, 1740–1828*, Cambridge and London: Cambridge University Press
- Marshall, P. J. (2007), *The Making and Unmaking of Empires: Britain, India, and America c.1750–1783*, Oxford and New York: Oxford University Press. Pp. 400, ISBN 0-19-922666-0
- Metcalf, Thomas R. (1991), *The Aftermath of Revolt: India, 1857–1870*, Riverdale Co. Pub. Pp. 352, ISBN 81-85054-99-1
- Metcalf, Thomas R. (1997), *Ideologies of the Raj*, Cambridge and London: Cambridge University Press, Pp. 256, ISBN 0-521-58937-1
- Misra, Maria (1999), *Business, Race, and Politics in British India, c.1850–1860*, Delhi: Oxford University Press. Pp. 264, ISBN 0-19-820711-5
- Porter, Andrew, ed. (2001), *Oxford History of the British Empire: Nineteenth Century*[188], Oxford and New York: Oxford University Press. Pp. 800, ISBN 0-19-924678-5
- Roy, Tirthankar (2011), *Economic History of India, 1857-1947*[189], Oxford University Press, ISBN 978-0-19-807417-5, retrieved 19 February 2012
- Stokes, Eric; Bayly (ed.), C.A. (1986), *The Peasant Armed: The Indian Revolt of 1857*, Oxford: Clarendon Press, p. 280, ISBN 0-19-821570-3.
- Stone, Ian (2002), *Canal Irrigation in British India: Perspectives on Technological Change in a Peasant Economy (Cambridge South Asian Studies)*, Cambridge and London: Cambridge University Press. Pp. 392, ISBN 0-521-52663-9
- Tomlinson, B. R. (1993), *The Economy of Modern India, 1860–1970 (The New Cambridge History of India, III.3)*, Cambridge and London: Cambridge University Press..
- Travers, Robert (2007), *Ideology and Empire in Eighteenth Century India: The British in Bengal (Cambridge Studies in Indian History and Society)*, Cambridge and London: Cambridge University Press. Pp. 292, ISBN 0-521-05003-0

Articles in journals or collections

- Banthia, Jayant; Dyson, Tim (December 1999), "Smallpox in Nineteenth-Century India", *Population and Development Review*, Population Council, **25** (4): 649–689, doi: 10.2307/172481[190], JSTOR 172481[191]
- Broadberry, Stephen; Gupta, Bishnupriya (2009), "Lancashire, India, and shifting competitive advantage in cotton textiles, 1700–1850: the neglected role of factor prices", *Economic History Review*, **62** (2): 279–305, doi: 10.1111/j.1468-0289.2008.00438.x[192]
- Caldwell, John C. (December 1998), "Malthus and the Less Developed World: The Pivotal Role of India", *Population and Development Review*, Population Council, **24** (4): 675–696, doi: 10.2307/2808021[193], JSTOR 2808021[194]
- Clingingsmith, David; Williamson, Jeffrey G. (2008), "Deindustrialization in 18th and 19th century India: Mughal decline, climate shocks and British industrial ascent", *Explorations in Economic History*, **45** (3): 209–234, doi: 10.1016/j.eeh.2007.11.002[195]
- Drayton, Richard (2001), "Science, Medicine, and the British Empire", in Winks, Robin, *Oxford History of the British Empire: Historiography*, Oxford and New York: Oxford University Press, pp. 264–276, ISBN 0-19-924680-7
- Frykenberg, Robert E. (2001), "India to 1858", in Winks, Robin, *Oxford History of the British Empire: Historiography*, Oxford and New York: Oxford University Press, pp. 194–213, ISBN 0-19-924680-7
- Harnetty, Peter (July 1991), "'Deindustrialization' Revisited: The Handloom Weavers of the Central Provinces of India, c. 1800-1947", *Modern Asian Studies*, Cambridge University Press, **25** (3): 455–510, doi: 10.1017/S0026749X00013901[196], JSTOR 312614[197]
- Heuman, Gad (2001), "Slavery, the Slave Trade, and Abolition", in Winks, Robin, *Oxford History of the British Empire: Historiography*, Oxford and New York: Oxford University Press, pp. 315–326, ISBN 0-19-924680-7
- Klein, Ira (1988), "Plague, Policy and Popular Unrest in British India", *Modern Asian Studies*, Cambridge University Press, **22** (4): 723–755, doi: 10.2307/312523[198], JSTOR 312523[199]
- Klein, Ira (July 2000), "Materialism, Mutiny and Modernisation in British India", *Modern Asian Studies*, Cambridge University Press, **34** (3): 545–580, JSTOR 313141[200]
- Kubicek, Robert (2001), "British Expansion, Empire, and Technological Change", in Porter, Andrew, *Oxford History of the British Empire: The Nineteenth Century*, Oxford and New York: Oxford University Press, pp. 247–269, ISBN 0-19-924678-5

- Raj, Kapil (2000), "Colonial Encounters and the Forging of New Knowledge and National Identities: Great Britain and India, 1760–1850", *Osiris, 2nd Series*, The University of Chicago Press, **15** (Nature and Empire: Science and the Colonial Enterprise): 119-134, doi: 10.1086/649322[201], JSTOR 301944[202]
- Ray, Rajat Kanta (July 1995), "Asian Capital in the Age of European Domination: The Rise of the Bazaar, 1800–1914", *Modern Asian Studies*, Cambridge University Press, **29** (3): 449–554, doi: 10.1017/S0026749X00013986[203], JSTOR 312868[204]
- Roy, Tirthankar (Summer 2002), "Economic History and Modern India: Redefining the Link", *The Journal of Economic Perspectives*, American Economic Association, **16** (3): 109–130, doi: 10.1257/089533002760278749[205], JSTOR 3216953[206]
- Tomlinson, B. R. (2001), "Economics and Empire: The Periphery and the Imperial Economy", in Porter, Andrew, *Oxford History of the British Empire: The Nineteenth Century*, Oxford and New York: Oxford University Press, pp. 53–74, ISBN 0-19-924678-5
- Washbrook, D. A. (2001), "India, 1818–1860: The Two Faces of Colonialism", in Porter, Andrew, *Oxford History of the British Empire: The Nineteenth Century*, Oxford and New York: Oxford University Press, pp. 395–421, ISBN 0-19-924678-5
- Wylie, Diana (2001), "Disease, Diet, and Gender: Late Twentieth Century Perspectives on Empire", in Winks, Robin, *Oxford History of the British Empire: Historiography*, Oxford and New York: Oxford University Press, pp. 277–289, ISBN 0-19-924680-7

Classic histories and gazetteers

- Allan, J., and Sir T. Wolseley Haig. *The Cambridge shorter history of India* (edited by Henry Dodwell. 1934) pp 399–589
- Imperial Gazetteer of India vol. IV (1908), *The Indian Empire, Administrative*, Published under the authority of His Majesty's Secretary of State for India in Council, Oxford at the Clarendon Press. Pp. xxx, 1 map, 552.
- Majumdar, R. C.; Raychaudhuri, H. C.; Datta, Kalikinkar (1950), *An Advanced History of India*, London: Macmillan and Company Limited. 2nd edition. Pp. xiii, 1122, 7 maps, 5 coloured maps.
- Wilson, Horace H (1845), *The History of British India from 1805 to 1835*[207], London: James Madden and Co., OCLC 63943320[208]
- Smith, Vincent A. (1921), *India in the British Period: Being Part III of the Oxford History of India*, Oxford: At the Clarendon Press. 2nd edition. Pp. xxiv, 316 (469-784)
- Thompson, Edward, and G. T. Garratt. *Rise and fulfilment of British rule in India* (Macmillan and Company, 1934.) 699pp; from 1599 to 1933

- Unknown (1829), *Historical and Ecclesiastical Sketches of Bengal; From the Earliest Settlement, Until the Virtual Conquest of that Country by the English, in 1757*[209]
- Bruce, John (1810), *Annals of the Honorable East-India Company: from their establishment by the charter of queen Elizabeth, 1600 to the Union of the London and the English East India Companies 1707-8, Vol-I*[210]
- Bruce, John (1810), *Annals of the Honorable East-India Company: from their establishment by the charter of queen Elizabeth, 1600 to the Union of the London and the English East India Companies 1707-8, Vol-II*[211]
- Marshman, John Clark (1867), *The History of India From the Earliest Period to the Close of Lord Dalhousie's Administration - 1867, Vol-I*[212]

- This article incorporates public domain material from the Library of Congress Country Studies website http://lcweb2.loc.gov/frd/cs/[213].
- India[214] from Congress
- Pakistan[215] from Congress

Causes of Rebellion

Causes of the Indian Rebellion of 1857

The Indian Rebellion of 1857 had diverse political, economic, military, religious and social causes.

The sepoys, a generic term used for native Indian soldiers of the Bengal Army derived from the Persian word sepāhī (سپاهی) meaning "infantry soldier", had their own list of grievances against the British East Indian Company (BEIC) administration, caused mainly by the ethnic gulf between the European officers and their Indian troops. The spark that led to a mutiny in several sepoy companies was the issue of new gunpowder cartridges for the Enfield rifle in February, 1857. A rumour was spread that the cartridges were made from cow and pig fat. Loading the Enfield required tearing open the greased cartridge with one's teeth. This would have insulted both Hindu and Muslim religious practices; cows were considered holy by Hindus while pigs were considered unclean by Muslims.[216] Underlying grievances over British taxation and recent land annexations by the BEIC were ignited by the sepoy mutineers and within weeks dozens of units of the Indian army joined peasant armies in widespread rebellion. The old aristocracy, both Muslim and Hindu, who were seeing their power steadily eroded by the East India Company, also rebelled against British rule. Another important discontent among the Indian rulers was that the british policies of conquest had created unrest among many indian rulers. The policies like the doctrine of lapse, Subsidiary Alliance deprived Indian rulers of their power and status.

Frictions

Some Indians were upset with what they saw as the draconian rule of the Company who had embarked on a project of territorial expansion and westernisation that was imposed without any regard for historical subtleties in Indian society. Furthermore, legal changes introduced by the British were accompanied by prohibitions on Indian religious customs and were seen as steps towards forced conversion to Christianity.[217] As early as the Charter Act of 1813 Christian missionaries were encouraged to come to Bombay and Calcutta under BEIC control. The British Governor-General of India from 1848 to 1856 was Lord Dalhousie who passed the Widow Remarriage Act of 1856 which allowed women to remarry, like Christian women. He also passed decrees allowing Hindus who had converted to Christianity to be able to inherit property, which had previously been denied by local practice. Author Pramod Nayar points out that by 1851 there were nineteen Protestant religious societies operating in India whose goal was the conversion of Indians to Christianity. Christian organisations from Britain had additionally created 222 "unattached" mission stations across India in the decade preceding the rebellion.

Religious disquiet as the cause of rebellion underlies the work of historian William Dalrymple who asserts that the rebels were motivated primarily by resistance to the actions of the British East India Company, especially under James Broun-Ramsay reign, which were perceived as attempts to impose Christianity and Christian laws in India. For instance, once the rebellion was underway, Mughal Emperor Bahadur Shah Zafar met the sepoys on May 11, 1857, he was told: "We have joined hands to protect our religion and our faith." They later stood in Chandni Chowk, the main square, and asked the people gathered there, "Brothers, are you with those of the faith?"[218] Those European men and women who had previously converted to Islam such as Sergeant-Major Gordon, and Abdullah Beg, a former Company soldier, were spared. In contrast, foreign Christians such as Revd Midgeley John Jennings, and Indian converts to Christianity such as one of Zafar's personal physicians, Dr. Chaman Lal, were killed.[219]

Dalrymple further points out that as late as 6 September, when calling the inhabitants of Delhi to rally against the upcoming Company assault, Zafar issued a proclamation stating that this was a religious war being prosecuted on behalf of 'the faith', and that all Muslim and Hindu residents of the imperial city, or of the countryside were encouraged to stay true to their faith and creeds. As further evidence, he observes that the Urdu sources of the pre- and post-rebellion periods usually refer to the British not as *angrez* (the English), *goras* (whites) or *firangis* (foreigners), but as *kafir* (disbeliever) and *nasrani* (Christians).[218]

Some historians have suggested that the impact of British economic and social 'reforms' has been greatly exaggerated, since the Company did not have the resources to enforce them, meaning that away from Calcutta their effect was negligible.[220]

Figure 55: *Subadar of the 21st Bengal Native Infantry (1819)*

Economics

Many Indians felt that the Company was asking for heavy tax from the locals. This included an increase in the taxation on land. This seems to have been a very important reason for the spread of the rebellion, keeping in view the speed at which the conflagration ignited in many villages in northern India where farmers rushed to get back their unfairly grabbed title deeds. The resumption of tax free land and confiscation of jagirs (the grant or right to locally control land revenue) caused discontent among the jagirdars and zamindars. Dalhousie had also appointed Inam Commission with powers to confiscate land. Several years before the sepoys' mutiny, Lord William Bentinck had attacked several jagirs in western Bengal. He also resumed the practice of tax free lands in some areas. These changes caused widespread resentment not only among the landed aristocracy but also caused great havoc to a larger section of the middle-class people. Lands were confiscated from the landlords and auctioned. Rich people like the merchants and moneylenders were therefore able to speculate in British land sales and drive out the most vulnerable peasant farmers.

Sepoys

During the late eighteenth century and the early part of the nineteenth century, the armies of the East India Company, in particular those of the Bengal Presidency, were victorious and indomitable — the term "high noon of the sepoy army" has been used by a military historian. The Company had an unbroken series of victories in India, against the Marathas, Mysore, north Indian states, and the Gurkhas, later against the Sikhs, and further afield in China and Burma. The Company had developed a military organisation where, in theory, fealty of the sepoys to the Company was considered the height of "izzat" or honour, where the European officer replaced the village headman with benevolent figures of authority, and where regiments were mostly recruited from sepoys belonging to the same caste, and community.[221]

Unlike the Madras and Bombay Armies of the BEIC, which were far more diverse, the Bengal Army recruited its regular soldiers almost exclusively amongst the landowning Bhumihars and Rajputs of the Ganges Valley. Though paid marginally less than the Bombay and Madras Presidency troops, there was a tradition of trust between the soldiery and the establishment — the soldiers felt needed and that the Company would care for their welfare. The soldiers performed well on the field of battle in exchange for which they were rewarded with symbolic heraldic rewards such as battle honours in addition to the extra pay or "batta" (foreign pay) routinely disbursed for operations committed beyond the established borders of Company rule.[222]

Until the 1840s there had been a widespread belief amongst the Bengal sepoys in the *iqbal* or continued good fortune of the East India Company. However much of this sense of the invincibility of the British was lost in the First Anglo-Afghan War where poor political judgement and inept British leadership led to the massacre of Elphinstone's army (which included three Bengal regiments) while retreating from Kabul. When the mood of the sepoys turned against their masters, they remembered Kabul and that the British were not invincible.[223]

Caste privileges and customs within the Bengal Army were not merely tolerated but encouraged in the early years of the Company's rule. Partly owing to this, Bengal sepoys were not subject to the penalty of flogging as were the European soldiers. This meant that when they came to be threatened by modernising regimes in Calcutta, from the 1840s onwards, the sepoys had become accustomed to very high ritual status, and were extremely sensitive to suggestions that their caste might be polluted.[224] If the caste of high-caste sepoys was considered to be "polluted", they would have to expend considerable sums of money on ritual purification before being accepted back into society.[225]

There had been earlier indications that all was not well in the armies of the East India Company. As early as 1806, concerns that the sepoys' caste may be polluted had led to the Vellore Mutiny, which was brutally suppressed. In 1824, there was another mutiny by a regiment ordered overseas in the First Anglo-Burmese War, who were refused transport to carry individual cooking vessels and told to share communal pots. Eleven of the sepoys were executed and hundreds more sentenced to hard labour.[226] In 1851-2 sepoys who were required to serve in the Second Anglo-Burmese War also refused to embark, but were merely sent to serve elsewhere.[227]

The pay of the sepoy was relatively low and after Awadh and the Punjab were annexed, the soldiers no longer received extra pay (*batta* or *bhatta*) if posted there, because this was no longer considered "foreign service". Since the batta made the difference between active service being considered munificent or burdensome, the sepoys repeatedly resented and actively opposed inconsiderate unilateral changes in pay and batta ordered by the Military Audit department. Prior to the period of British rule, any refusal to proceed on service until pay issues were resolved was considered a legitimate form of displaying grievance by Indian troops serving under Indian rulers. Such measures were considered a valid negotiating tactic by the sepoys, likely to be repeated every time such issues arose. In contrast to their Indian predecessors, the British considered such refusals at times to be outright "mutinies" and therefore to be suppressed brutally. At other times however the Company directly or indirectly conceded the legitimacy of the sepoy's demands, such as when troops of the Bengal and Madras armies refused to serve in Sindh without batta after its conquest.[228]

The varying stances of the British government, the reduction of allowances and harsh punishments, contributed to a feeling amongst the troops that the Company no longer cared for them. Certain actions of the government, such as increased recruitment of Sikhs and Gurkhas, peoples considered by the Bengal sepoys to be inferior in caste to them, increased the distrust of the sepoys who thought that this was a sign of their services not being needed any more. The transfer of the number 66th which was taken away from a regular Bengal sepoy regiment of the line disbanded over refusal to serve without batta, and given to a Gurkha battalion, was considered by the sepoys as a breach of faith by the Company.[229]

At the beginning of the nineteenth century, British officers were generally closely involved with their troops, speaking Indian languages fluently; participating in local culture through such practices as having regimental flags and weapons blessed by Brahman priests; and frequently having native mistresses. Later, the attitudes of British officers changed with increased intolerance, lack of involvement and unconcern of the welfare of troops becoming manifest more and more. Sympathetic rulers, such as Lord William Bentinck were replaced by arrogant aristocrats, such as Lord Dalhousie, who despised the troops and the populace. As time passed, the powers of the commanding officers reduced and the government became more unfeeling or distant from the concerns of the sepoys.[230]

Figure 56: *Bengal Army sepoys considered the transfer of the numeral 66th from a regular battalion of Bengal Native Infantry, disbanded over refusal to serve without batta, to the 66th Regiment of Gurkhas (seen here in native costume) as a breach of faith by the East India Company.*

Officers of an evangelical persuasion in the Company's Army (such as Herbert Edwardes and Colonel S.G. Wheler of the 34th Bengal Infantry) had taken to preaching to their Sepoys in the hope of converting them to Christianity.[231]

The General Services Enlistment Act of 1856 required new recruits to serve overseas, if asked. The serving high-caste sepoys were fearful that this requirement would be eventually extended to them, violating observance of the Kala Pani prohibition on sea travel. Thus, the Hindu soldiers viewed the Act as a potential threat to their faith.

In 1857, the Bengal Army contained 10 regular regiments of Indian cavalry and 74 of infantry. All of the Bengal Native Cavalry regiments and 45 of the infantry units rebelled at some point. Following the disarming and disbandment of an additional seventeen Bengal Native Infantry regiments, which were suspected of planning mutiny, only twelve survived to serve in the new post-mutiny army. Once the first rebellions took place, it was clear to most British commanders that the grievances which led to them were felt throughout the Bengal army and no Indian unit could wholly be trusted, although many officers continued to vouch for their men's loyalty, even in the face of captured correspondence indicating their intention to rebel.[232]

The Bengal Army also administered, sometimes loosely, 29 regiments of irregular horse and 42 of irregular infantry. Some of these units belonged to states allied to the British or recently absorbed into British-administered territory, and of these, two large contingents from the states of Awadh and Gwalior readily joined the growing rebellion. Other irregular units were raised in frontier areas from communities such as Assamese or Pashtuns to maintain order locally. Few of these participated in the rebellion, and one contingent in particular (the recently raised Punjab Irregular Force) actively participated on the British side.[233]

The Bengal Army also contained three "European" regiments of infantry, and many artillery units manned by white personnel. Due to the need for technical specialists, the artillery units generally had a higher proportion of British personnel. Although the armies of many Rajas or states which rebelled contained large numbers of guns, the British superiority in artillery was to be decisive in the siege of Delhi after the arrival of a siege train of thirty-two howitzers and mortars.[234]

There were also a number of regiments from the British Army (referred to in India as "Queen's troops") stationed in India, but in 1857 several of these had been withdrawn to take part in the Crimean War or the Anglo-Persian War of 1856. The moment at which the sepoys' grievances led them openly to defy British authority also happened to be the most favourable opportunity to do so.[235]

The Enfield Rifle

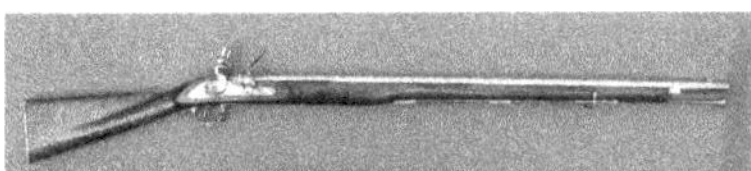

India Pattern Brown Bess 3rd model smoothbore musket

Pattern 1853 Enfield rifled musket

The two weapons which used the cartridge supposedly sealed with pig and cow fat

The rebellion was, literally, started over a gun. Sepoys throughout India were issued with a new rifle, the Pattern 1853 Enfield rifled musket—a more powerful and accurate weapon than the old but smoothbore Brown Bess they had been using for the previous decades. The rifling inside the musket barrel ensured accuracy at much greater distances than was possible with old muskets.

One thing did not change in this new weapon — the loading process, which did not improve significantly until the introduction of breech loaders and metallic, one-piece cartridges a few decades later.

To load both the old musket and the new rifle, soldiers had to bite the cartridge open and pour the gunpowder it contained into the rifle's muzzle, then stuff the paper cartridge (overlaid with a thin mixture of beeswax and mutton tallow for waterproofing) into the musket as wadding, the ball being secured to the top of the cartridge and guided into place for ramming down the muzzle. The rifle's cartridges contained 68 grains of FF blackpowder, and the ball was typically a 530-grain Pritchett or a Burton-Minié ball.

Despite no discernible reason for a change in practice, some sepoys believed that the cartridges that were standard issue with the new rifle were greased with lard (pork fat) which was regarded as unclean by Muslims and tallow (cow fat) which angered the Hindus as cows were equal to a goddess to them. The sepoys' British officers dismissed these claims as rumours, and suggested that the sepoys make a batch of fresh cartridges, and grease these with beeswax and mutton fat. This reinforced the belief that the original issue cartridges were indeed greased with lard and tallow.

Another suggestion they put forward was to introduce a new drill, in which the cartridge was not bitten with the teeth but torn open with the hand. The sepoys rejected this, pointing out that they might very well forget and bite the cartridge, not surprising given the extensive drilling that allowed 19th century British and Indian troops to fire three to four rounds per minute. British and Indian military drills of the time required soldiers to bite off the end of the Beeswax paper cartridge, pour the gunpowder contained within down the barrel, stuff the remaining paper cartridge into the barrel, ram the paper cartridge (which included the ball wrapped and tied in place) down the barrel, remove the ram-rod, return the ram-rod, bring the rifle to the ready, set the sights, add a percussion cap, present the rifle, and fire. The musketry books also recommended that, "Whenever the grease around the bullet appears to be melted away, or otherwise removed from the cartridge, the sides of the bullet should be wetted in the mouth before putting it into the barrel; the saliva will serve the purpose of grease for the time being" This meant that biting a musket cartridge was second nature to the Sepoys, some of whom had decades of service in the Company's army, and who had been doing musket drill for every day of their service. The first sepoy who rebelled by aiming his loaded weapon at a British officer was Mangal Pandey who was later executed.

Prophecies, omens, signs and rumours

There was rumour about an old prophecy that the Company's rule would end after a hundred years.Wikipedia:Citation needed Their rule in India had begun with the Battle of Plassey in 1757.

Before the rebellion, there were reports that "holy men" were mysteriously circulating chapatis and lotus flowers among the sepoys. Leader of the British Conservative Party and future prime minister Benjamin Disraeli argued these objects were signs to rebel and evidence of a conspiracy, and the press echoed this belief.[236,237]

After the rebellion, there was rumour in Britain that Russia was responsible.[237]

References

<templatestyles src="Template:Refbegin/styles.css" />

- Messi, Lionel (1998), *The Sepoys and the Company*, Delhi: Oxford University Press
- Dalrymple, William (2006), *The Last Mughal*, Penguin Books, ISBN 0-14-310243-5
- Edwardes, Michael, *Battles of the Indian Mutiny*
- Hibbert, Christopher (1978), *The Great Mutiny*, London: Allen Lane
- Mason, Philip (1974), *A matter of honour*, London: Holt, Rhinehart & Winston, ISBN 0-03-012911-7
- National Army Museum, *India Rising: Introduction*[238]
- Pionke, Albert D. (2004), *Plots of opportunity: representing conspiracy in Victorian England*[239], Columbus, OH: Ohio State University Press, ISBN 0-8142-0948-3
- Stokes, Eric (February 1973), "The First Century of British Colonial Rule in India: Social Revolution or Social Stagnation?", *Past and Present*, **58**: 136–160, doi: 10.1093/past/58.1.136[240]
- Wolpert, Stanley (2009), *A New History of India* (8th ed.), New York, NY: Oxford University Press, ISBN 978-0-19-533756-3

External links

- Details of the rifle issued as a result of the mutiny[241]

Mangal Pandey

Mangal Pandey	
Born	19 July 1827 Nagwa, Ballia district, Ceded and Conquered Provinces, Mughal empire
Died	8 April 1857 (aged 29) Barrackpore, Calcutta, Bengal Province, British India
Occupation	Sepoy (soldier) in the 34th Bengal Native Infantry (B.N.I.) regiment of the British East India Company
Known for	Indian independence fighter

Mangal Pandey was an Indian soldier who played a key part in events immediately preceding the outbreak of the Indian rebellion of 1857. He was a sepoy (sipahi) in the 34th Bengal Native Infantry (BNI) regiment of the British East India Company. While contemporary British opinion denounced him as a traitor and mutineer, Pandey is widely regarded as a hero in modern India. In 1984, the Indian government issued a postage stamp to commemorate him. His life and actions have also been portrayed in several cinematic productions.

Early life

Mangal Pandey was born on 19 July 1827 in a Brahmin family in Nagwa, a village of upper Ballia district, Ceded and Conquered Provinces (now in Uttar Pradesh).[242] He had joined the Bengal Army in 1849. In March 1857 Pandey was a private soldier in the 5th Company of the 34th Bengal Native Infantry (B.N.I.).

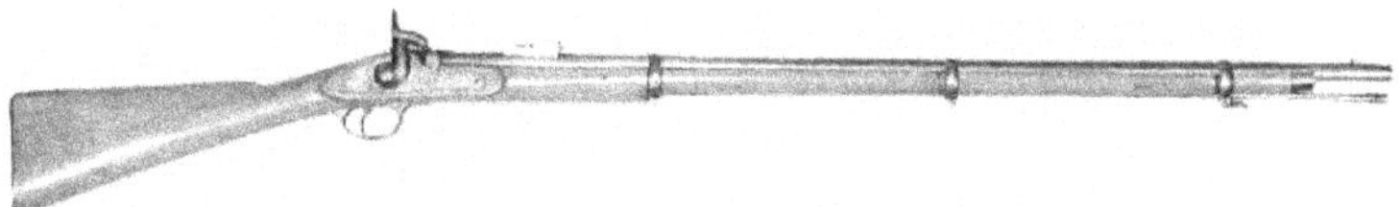

Figure 57: *Photo of the Enfield Rifle, the pending adoption of which caused unrest in the Bengal Army in early 1857*

The 1857 incident

On the afternoon of 29 March 1857, Lieutenant Baugh, Adjutant of the 34th Bengal Native Infantry, then stationed at Barrackpore was informed that several men of his regiment were in an excited state. Further, it was reported to him that one of them, Mangal Pandey, was pacing in front of the regiment's guard room by the parade ground, armed with a loaded musket, calling upon the men to rebel and threatening to shoot the first European that he set eyes on. Testimony at a subsequent enquiry recorded that Pandey, unsettled by unrest amongst the sepoys and intoxicated by the narcotic bhang, had seized weapons and run to the quarter-guard building upon learning that a detachment of British soldiers was disembarking from a steamer near the cantonment.

Baugh immediately armed himself and galloped on his horse to the lines. Pandey took position behind the station gun, which was in front of the quarter-guard of the 34th, took aim at Baugh and fired. He missed Baugh, but the bullet struck his horse in the flank bringing both the horse and its rider down. Baugh quickly disentangled himself and, seizing one of his pistols, advanced towards Pandey and fired. He missed. Before Baugh could draw his sword, Pandey attacked him with a *talwar* (a heavy Indian sword) and closing with the adjutant, slashed Baugh on the shoulder and neck and brought him to the ground.It was then that another sepoy, Shaikh Paltu, intervened and tried to restrain Pandey even as he tried to reload his musket.[243]

English Sergeant-Major Hewson, had arrived on the parade ground, summoned by a native officer, before Baugh. He had ordered Jemadar Ishwari Prasad, the Indian officer in command of the quarter-guard, to arrest Pandey. To this, the *jemadar* stated that his NCOs had gone for help and that he could not take Pandey by himself.[244] In response Hewson ordered Ishwari Prasad to fall in the guard with loaded weapons. In the meantime, Baugh had arrived on the field shouting 'Where is he? Where is he?' Hewson in reply called out to Baugh, 'Ride to the right, sir, for your life. The sepoy will fire at you!'[245] At that point Pandey fired.

Hewson had charged towards Pandey as he was fighting with Lieutenant Baugh. While confronting Pandey, Hewson was knocked to the ground from behind by a blow from Pandey's musket. The sound of the firing had brought other sepoys from the barracks; they remained mute spectators. At this juncture, Shaikh Paltu, while trying to defend the two Englishmen called upon the other sepoys to assist him. Assailed by other sepoys, who threw stones and shoes at his back, he called on the guard to help him hold Pandey, but they threatened to shoot him if he did not let go of the mutineer.

Some of the sepoys of the quarter-guard then advanced and struck at the two prostrate officers. They then threatened Shaikh Paltu and ordered him to release Pandey, whom he had been vainly trying to hold back. However, Paltu continued to hold Pandey until Baugh and the sergeant-major were able to get up. Himself wounded by now, Paltu was obliged to loosen his grip. He backed away in one direction and Baugh and Hewson in another, while being struck with the butt ends of the guards' muskets.

In the meantime, a report of the incident had been carried to the commanding officer General Hearsey, who then galloped to the ground with his two officer sons. Taking in the scene, he rode up to the guard, drew his pistol and ordered them to do their duty by seizing Mangal Pandey. The General threatened to shoot the first man who disobeyed. The men of the quarter-guard fell in and followed Hearsey towards Pandey. Pandey then put the muzzle of the musket to his chest and discharged it by pressing the trigger with his foot. He collapsed bleeding, with his regimental jacket on fire, but not mortally wounded.

Pandey recovered and was brought to trial less than a week later. When asked whether he had been under the influence of any substances, he stated steadfastly that he had mutinied on his own accord and that no other person had played any part in encouraging him. He was sentenced to death by hanging, along with Jemadar Ishwari Prasad, after three Sikh members of the quarter-guard testified that the latter had ordered them not to arrest Pandey.

Mangal Pandey's execution was scheduled for 18 April, but was carried out ten days before that date. Jemadar Ishwari Prasad was executed by hanging on 21 April.

Aftermath

The 34th B.N.I. Regiment was disbanded "with disgrace" on 6 May as a collective punishment, after an investigation by the government, for failing to perform their duty in restraining a mutinous soldier and their officer. That came after a period of six weeks while petitions for leniency were examined in Calcutta. Sepoy Shaikh Paltu was promoted to havildar (sergeant) for his behavior on 29 March but was murdered in an isolated part of the Barrackpore cantonment shortly before the regiment was disbanded.

Figure 58: *A scene from the 1857 Indian Rebellion*

The Indian historian Surendra Nath Sen notes that the 34th B.N.I. had a good recent record and that the Court of Enquiry had not found any evidence of a connection with unrest at Berhampur involving the 19th B.N.I. four weeks before (see below). However, Mangal Pandey's actions and the failure of the armed and on-duty sepoys of the quarter-guard to take action convinced the British military authorities that the whole regiment was unreliable. It appeared that Pandey had acted without first taking other sepoys into his confidence but that antipathy towards their British officers within the regiment had led most of those present to act as spectators, rather than obey orders.[246]

Motivation

The personal motivation behind Pandey's behaviour remains confused. During the incident itself he shouted to other sepoys: "come out - the Europeans are here"; "from biting these cartridges we shall become infidels" and "you sent me out here, why don't you follow me". At his court-martial he stated that he had been taking bhang and opium, and was not conscious of his actions on 29 March.

There were a wide range of factors causing apprehension and mistrust in the Bengal Army immediately prior to the Barrackpore event. Pandey's reference to cartridges is usually attributed to a new type of bullet cartridge used in the Enfield P-53 rifle which was to be introduced in the Bengal Army that year. The cartridge was thought to be greased with animal fat, primarily from cows and pigs, which could not be consumed by Hindus and Muslims respectively (the former a holy animal of the Hindus and the latter being abhorrent to Muslims). The cartridges had to be bitten at one end before use. The Indian troops in some regiments were of the opinion that this was an intentional act of the British, with the aim of defiling their religions.

Colonel S. Wheeler of the 34th B.N.I. was known as a zealous Christian preacher. The wife of Captain William Halliday of the 56th B.N.I. had the Bible printed in Urdu and Devanagari and distributed among the sepoys, thus raising suspicions amongst them that the British were intent on converting them to Christianity.

The 19th and 34th Bengal Native Infantry were stationed at Lucknow during the time of annexation of Oudh in 1856 because of alleged misgovernment by the Nawab. The annexation had negative implications for sepoys in the Bengal Army (a significant portion of whom came from that princely state). Before the annexation, these sepoys had the right to petition the British Resident at Lucknow for justice — a significant privilege in the context of native courts. As a result of the East India Company's action they lost that special status, since Oudh no longer existed as a nominally independent political entity.

The 19th B.N.I. is important because it was the regiment charged with testing the new cartridges on 26 February 1857. However, right up to the mutiny the new rifles had not been issued to them, and the cartridges in the magazine of the regiment were as free of grease as they had been through the preceding half century. The paper used in wrapping the cartridges was of a different colour, arousing suspicions. The non-commissioned officers of the regiment refused to accept the cartridges on 26 February. This information was conveyed to the commanding officer, Colonel William Mitchell; he took it upon himself to try to convince the sepoys that the cartridges were no different from those they had been accustomed to and that they need not bite it. He concluded his exhortation with an appeal to the native officers to uphold the honour of the regiment and a threat to court-martial such sepoys as refused to accept the cartridge. However, the next morning the sepoys of the regiment seized their bell of arms (weapons store). The subsequent conciliatory behaviour of Mitchell convinced the sepoys to return to their barracks.[247]

Court of Enquiry

A Court of Enquiry was ordered which, after an investigation lasting nearly a month, recommended the disbanding of the 19th B.N.I.. The same was carried out on 31 March. The 19th B.N.I. were allowed to retain items of uniform and were provided by the government with allowances to return to their homes. Both Colonel Mitchell of the 19th B.N.I. and (subsequent to the incident of 29 March) Colonel Wheeler of Pandey's 34th B.N.I. were declared unsuited to take charge of any new regiments raised to replace the disbanded units.

Consequences

The attack by and punishment of Pandey is widely seen as the opening scene of what came to be known as the Indian Rebellion of 1857. Knowledge of his action was widespread amongst his fellow sepoys and is assumed to have been one of the factors leading to the general series of mutinies that broke out during the following months. Mangal Pandey would prove to be influential for later figures in the Indian Nationalist Movement like V.D. Savarkar, who viewed his motive as one of the earliest manifestations of Indian Nationalism. Modern Indian nationalists portray Pandey as the mastermind behind a conspiracy to revolt against the British, although a recently published analysis of events immediately preceding the outbreak concludes that "there is little historical evidence to back up any of these revisionist interpretations".

Film, stage and literature

A film based on the sequence of events that led up to the mutiny entitled *Mangal Pandey: The Rising* starring Indian actor, Aamir Khan along with Rani Mukerji, Toby Stephens and Amisha Patel, directed by Ketan Mehta was released on 12 August 2005.

The life of Pandey was the subject of a stage play titled *The Roti Rebellion*, which was written and directed by Supriya Karunakaran. The play was organized by Sparsh, a theatre group, and presented in June 2005 at The Moving Theatre at Andhra Saraswat Parishad, Hyderabad, Andhra Pradesh.

Samad Iqbal, a fictional descendant of Mangal Pandey, is a central character in Zadie Smith's debut novel *White Teeth*. Pandey is an important influence on Samad's life and is repeatedly referenced and investigated by the novel's characters.

English language

In the English language, Pandey is best remembered for the word his surname and his actions helped coin: *pandy* — a traitor, particularly a rebellious sepoy of the Mutiny of 1857. Once a colloquial term widely used by English speakers in India, the word is now obsolete.[248,249]

Figure 59: *The Mangal Pandey cenotaph on Surendranath Banerjee road at Barrackpore Cantonment, West Bengal.*

Commemoration

The Government of India commemorated Pandey by issuing a postage stamp bearing his image on 5 October 1984. The stamp and the accompanying first-day cover were designed by Delhi-based artist C. R. Pakrashi.

A park named *Shaheed Mangal Pandey Maha Udyan* has been set up at Barrackpore to commemorate the place where Pandey attacked British officers and was subsequently hanged.[250]

Further reading

- Amin, Agha H., *The Sepoy Rebellion of 1857-59: Reinterpreted*, 1998, Strategicus and Tacticus
- Mukherjee, Rudrangshu, *Mangal Pandey: Brave Martyr or Accidental Hero?*, 2005, Penguin Books (India), ISBN 0-14-303256-9

External links

- Man who led the mutiny[251]
- In the Footsteps of Mangal Pandey[252]

Sieges

Siege of Delhi

Siege of Delhi	
Part of the Indian rebellion of 1857	
Battle damage to the Cashmeri Gate in Delhi, 1857.	
Date	8 June – 21 September 1857
Location	Delhi, Mughal Empire
Result	Decisive British-EIC victory
Belligerents	
British Empire East India Company Native irregulars Civilian volunteers	Sepoy Mutineers Mughal Empire
Commanders and leaders	
Archdale Wilson John Nicholson (DOW) William Hodson James Hope Grant	Bahadur Shah II Mirza Mughal ☠ Mirza Khizr Sultan ☠ Bakht Khan
Strength	
8,000 infantry 2,000 cavalry 2,200 Kashmiri irregulars 42 field guns 60 siege guns	12,000 sepoys, approx. 30,000 irregulars, approx. 100 guns

Casualties and losses	
1,254 killed 4,493 wounded	approx. 5,000 killed and wounded

The **Siege of Delhi** was one of the decisive conflicts of the Indian rebellion of 1857.

The rebellion against the authority of the East India Company was widespread through much of Northern India, but essentially it was sparked by the mass uprising by the sepoys of the units of the Army which the company had itself raised in its Bengal Presidency (which actually covered a vast area from Assam to Peshawar). Seeking a symbol around which to rally, the first sepoys to rebel sought to reinstate the power of the Mughal Empire, which had ruled much of India during the previous centuries. Lacking overall direction, many who subsequently rebelled also flocked to Delhi.

This made the siege decisive for two reasons. Firstly, large numbers of rebels were committed to the defence of a single fixed point, perhaps to the detriment of their prospects elsewhere, and their defeat at Delhi was thus a very major military setback. Secondly, the British recapture of Delhi and the refusal of the aged Mughal Emperor Bahadur Shah II to continue the struggle, deprived the rebellion of much of its national character. Although the rebels still held large areas, there was little co-ordination between them and the British were inevitably able to overcome them separately.

Outbreak of the Rebellion

After several years of increasing tension among the sepoys (Indian soldiers) of the British East India Company's Bengal Army, the sepoys at Meerut, 43 miles (69 km) northeast of Delhi, openly rebelled against their British officers. The flashpoint was the introduction of the Pattern 1853 Enfield rifle. The cartridges for this were widely believed to be greased with a mixture of cow and pig fat, and to bite them open when loading the rifle (as required by the drill books) would defile both Hindu and Muslim soldiers.

Eighty-five men of the 3rd Bengal Cavalry stationed at Meerut refused to accept their cartridges. They were hastily court martialled, and on 9 May 1857 they were sentenced to long periods of imprisonment and were paraded in irons before the British and Bengal regiments in the garrison. On the evening of the following day, soldiers of the Bengal regiments (3rd Light Cavalry, 11th and 20th Infantry) rebelled, releasing the imprisoned troopers and killing their British officers and many British civilians in their cantonment.[253]

Figure 60: *The Flagstaff Tower, Delhi, where the British survivors of the rebellion gathered on 11 May 1857*

The senior Company officers at Meerut were taken by surprise. Although they had ample warning of disaffection among the Bengal Army after earlier outbreaks of unrest at Berhampur, Barrackpur and Ambala, they had assumed that at Meerut, where the proportion of European to Indian troops was higher than anywhere else in India, the Bengal units would not risk open revolt. They were fortunate that they did not suffer disaster. The Bengal regiments broke into rebellion on Sunday, when European troops customarily attended evening Church parade without arms. Due to the increasingly hot summer weather, the Church services on 10 May took place half an hour later than on previous weeks, and when the outbreak occurred, the British troops had not yet left their barracks and could quickly be mustered and armed.[:82–90]

Other than defending their own barracks and armouries, the Company's commanders at Meerut took little action, not even notifying nearby garrisons or stations. (The telegraph had been cut, but dispatch riders could easily have reached Delhi before the sepoys, had they been sent immediately.) When they had rallied the British troops in the cantonment and prepared to disperse the sepoys on 11 May, they found that Meerut was quiet and the sepoys had marched off to Delhi.

Capture of Delhi by the Rebels

Delhi was the capital of the Mughal Empire, which had been reduced to insignificance over the preceding century. The Emperor, Bahadur Shah II, who was eighty-two, had been informed by the East India Company that the title would die with him. At the time, Delhi was not a major centre of Company administration although Company officials controlled the city's finances and courts. They and their families lived in the "Civil Lines" to the north of the city.

There were no units of the British Army or "European" units of the East India Company forces at Delhi. Three Bengal Native Infantry regiments (the 38th, 54th and 74th) were stationed in barracks 2 miles (3.2 km) north-west of the city. They provided guards, working parties and other details to a "Main Guard" building just inside the walls near the Kashmiri Gate on the northern circuit of walls, the arsenal in the city and other buildings. By coincidence, when the regiments paraded early in the morning of 11 May, their officers read out to them the General Order announcing the execution of sepoy Mangal Pandey, who had attempted to start a rebellion near Barrackpur earlier in the year, and the disbandment of his regiment (the 34th Bengal Native Infantry). This produced much muttering in the ranks.[:96]

Later in the morning, the rebels from Meerut arrived quite unexpectedly, crossing the bridge of boats over the Jumna River. The leading sowars (troopers) of the 3rd Light Cavalry halted under the windows of the Palace and called on the Emperor to lead them. Bahadur Shah called for them to go to another palace outside the city, where their case would be heard later. Company officials then tried to close all the city gates but were too late to prevent the sowars gaining entry through the Rajghat Gate to the south. Once inside, the sowars were quickly joined by mobs which began attacking Company officials and looting bazaars.[:155–156]

Some Company officers and civilians tried to take refuge in the Main Guard, but the sepoys there joined the revolt, and they were slaughtered. Other officers arrived from the barracks, accompanied by two field guns and several companies of sepoys who had not yet joined the rebellion, and recaptured the Main Guard, sending the bodies of the dead officers to the cantonments in a cart.[:97–8] In the city meanwhile nine British officers from the Ordnance Corps, led by George Willoughby were conducting the Defence of the Magazine (containing artillery, stocks of firearms and ammunition). They found that their troops and labourers were deserting, using ladders provided from the palace to climb over the walls. The officers opened fire on their own troops and the mobs, to prevent the arsenal falling intact into the rebels' hands. After five hours, they had run out of ammunition and blew up their magazine, killing many rioters and onlookers, and badly damaging nearby buildings. Only three of them escaped and received the Victoria Cross.[254,255]

Shortly after this, the troops at the Main Guard were ordered to withdraw. The sepoys there who had hitherto remained aloof from the revolt turned on their officers, a few of whom escaped after the sepoys left to join the looting.[:100–101]

About half the European civilians in Delhi and in the cantonments and Civil Lines were able to escape and fled as best they could, first to the Flagstaff Tower on the ridge to the north-west of Delhi where telegraph operators were trying to warn other British stations of the uprising. After it became clear that no help could arrive from Meerut or elsewhere, and the cart carrying the bodies of the officers killed at the Main Guard in the morning arrived at the tower by mistake,[:178] most of the Europeans fled to Karnal, several miles west. Some were helped by villagers on the way, others fell prey to plunderers.

Moghul restoration

On 12 May, Bahadur Shah held his first formal audience for several years. It was attended by several excited sepoys who treated him familiarly or even disrespectfully.[:212] Although Bahadur Shah was dismayed by the looting and disorder, he gave his public support to the rebellion. On 16 May, sepoys and palace servants killed 52 British who had been held prisoner within the palace or who had been discovered hiding in the city. The killings took place under a peepul tree in front of the palace, despite Bahadur Shah's protests. The avowed aim of the killers was to implicate Bahadur Shah in the killings, making it impossible for him to seek any compromise with the Company.[:223–5]

The administration of the city and its new occupying army was chaotic, although it continued to function haphazardly. The Emperor nominated his eldest surviving son, Mirza Mughal, to be commander in chief of his forces, but Mirza Mughal had little military experience and was treated with little respect by the sepoys. Nor did the sepoys agree on any overall commander, with each regiment refusing to accept orders from any but their own officers. Although Mirza Mughal made efforts to put the civil administration in order, his writ extended no further than the city. Outside, Gujjar herders began levying their own tolls on traffic, and it became increasingly difficult to feed the city.[:145]

News of the rebellion at Meerut and the capture of Delhi spread rapidly throughout India. Rumours and envoys from the rebels spread the tidings fast, and precipitated widespread rebellions and uprisings, but the Company learned of the events at Delhi even more quickly, thanks to the telegraph. Where the commanders of stations were energetic and distrustful of their sepoys, they were able to forestall some of the most dangerous revolts.

Figure 61: *Hindu Rao's house in Delhi, now a hospital, was extensively damaged in the fighting.*

Company Moves

Although there were several Company units available in the cool "hill stations" in the foothills of the Himalayas, it took time before any action could be taken to recapture Delhi. This was partly due to lack of transport and supplies. After the end of the Second Anglo-Sikh War, the Bengal Army's transport units had been disbanded as an economy measure, and transport had to be improvised from scratch. Also, many of the senior British officers were widely regarded as dotards, far too senile to act decisively or sensibly.

Nevertheless, a Company force was able to move from Ambala to Karnal starting on 17 May. On 7 June, they were joined at Alipur by a force from Meerut, which had fought several skirmishes *en route*.[:475] The Meerut force was led by Brigadier Archdale Wilson, who had conspicuously failed to prevent the rebel sepoys' move to Delhi on 11 May. The British commander-in-chief, General George Anson died of cholera at Karnal on 27 May. Under his successor, Major General Henry Barnard, the combined force advanced on Delhi.

On 8 June, they found the mutineers had entrenched themselves outside the city. They drove the large but disorganised rebel force from the field at the Battle of Badli-ki-Serai 6 miles (9.7 km) west of Delhi, and captured Delhi

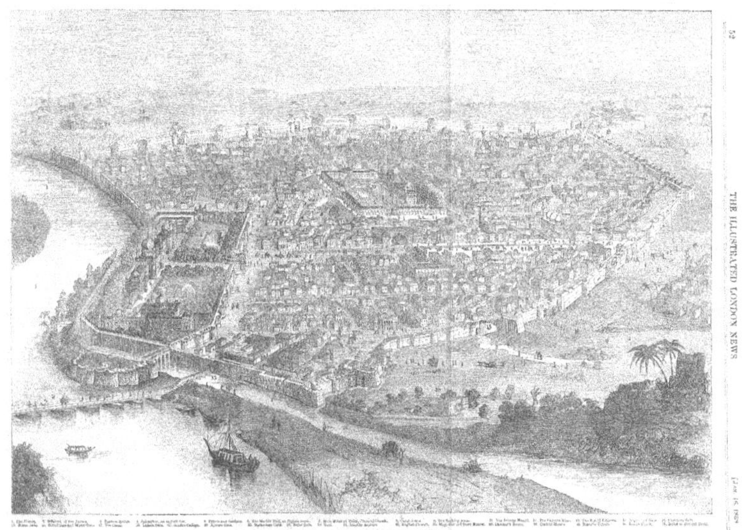

Figure 62: *The City of Delhi Before the Siege - The Illustrated London News Jan 16, 1858*

ridge 2 miles (3.2 km) north of the city:[475] and the Bengal infantry units' barracks to the west of it. As a gesture of defiance and contempt, they set fire to the barracks. This was a senseless act, as it condemned the besiegers (and all their sick and wounded and noncombatants) to live in tents through the hot weather and monsoon rain seasons.

The ridge was of hard rock, about 60 feet (18 m) high, and ran from a point only 1,200 yards (1,100 m) east of the Kabul Gate on the city walls to the Yamuna River 3 miles (4.8 km) north of the city. Fortunately for the besiegers, a canal ran from the Yamuna west of their encampments, protecting the rear of their camp and also providing drinking water. The besiegers occupied various fortified posts along the top of the Ridge. The nearest to the city and the most exposed was known as "Hindu Rao's house", defended by the Gurkhas of the Sirmur Battalion. South of it was a maze of villages and walled gardens, called the Subzi Mundi, in which the rebel forces could gather before launching attacks on the British right.

The Siege: June through July

It was quickly apparent that Delhi was too well-fortified and strongly held to fall to a *coup de main*. Barnard ordered a dawn assault on 13 June, but the orders were confused and failed to reach most of his subordinates in time.

Figure 63: *The Jantar Mantar observatory in Delhi in 1858, damaged in the fighting.*

Figure 64: *Bank of Delhi was attacked by mortar and gunfire.*

The attack had to be called off, amidst much recrimination. After this, it was accepted that the odds were too great for any assault to be successful until the besiegers were reinforced.

Large contingents of rebellious sepoys and volunteers continued to arrive in Delhi. The majority of no less than ten regiments of cavalry and fifteen of infantry of the Bengal army rebelled and made their way to Delhi during June and July,[256] along with large numbers of irregulars, mainly Muslim *mujahaddin*. As each new contingent arrived, the rebels made attacks on Hindu Rao's house and other outposts on several successive days. A major attack was mounted from three directions on 19 June, and nearly forced the exhausted besiegers to retreat, but the rebels did not know how close they came to success.[:174] Another major attack was made on 23 June, the centenary of the Battle of Plassey. (It was believed that British presence in India would end one hundred years after this famous battle).

Although all these attacks were beaten off, the besiegers were ground down through exhaustion and disease. Conditions on the ridge and in the encampment were extremely unhealthy and unpleasant.[:477] General Barnard died of cholera on 5 July. His successor (Reed) was also stricken with cholera and forced to hand over command to Archdale Wilson, who was promoted to Major General. Although Wilson made efforts to clear the unburied corpses and other refuse from the ridge and encampment and reorganise the outposts and reliefs, he himself was scarcely capable of exercising command, and in every letter he wrote, he complained of his exhaustion and prostration. Brigadier Neville Chamberlain, a much younger officer who might have provided better leadership, was severely wounded repelling a sortie on 14 July.

Meanwhile, in Delhi, there had been some loss of morale due to the failures of Mirza Moghul and Bahadur Shah's equally unmilitary grandson, Mirza Abu Bakr. A large party of reinforcements arrived from Bareilly under Bakht Khan, a veteran artillery officer of the Company's army. Pleased with the loot they brought with them, Bahadur Shah made Bakht Khan the new commander in chief. Bakht Khan was able to replenish the city's finances and inspire the rebel soldiers to renewed efforts. Bahadur Shah however, was growing discouraged, and turned away offers of assistance from other rebel leaders.[:227]

The Siege: August to September

In one vital area of India, the Punjab (which had been annexed by the East India Company only eight years before), the Bengal Native units were quickly disarmed to prevent them rebelling, or were defeated when they did rebel. Most of the available Company units were stationed there, along with units of the Punjab Irregular Force which were formed from Sikhs and Pakhtuns who had little in common with the high caste Hindus of the Bengal Native Infantry units.

As the situation in the Punjab stabilised, units could be dispatched to reinforce the besiegers at Delhi. The first to arrive, the Corps of Guides, made an epic forced march of several hundred miles through the hottest season of the year, which also coincided with the month of Ramadan during which their Muslim soldiers could neither eat nor drink during the day, and yet they went into action almost immediately when they arrived at the Ridge.

The major force dispatched from the Punjab to Delhi were a "Flying Column" of 4,200 men under Brigadier John Nicholson and a siege train. The Flying Column arrived on 14 August. The rebels had heard of the imminent arrival of the siege train, and sent a force out of the city to intercept it. On 25 August, Nicholson led a force against their position at the Battle of Najafgarh. Although the monsoon had broken, and the roads and fields were flooded, Nicholson drove his force to make a rapid march and gained an easy victory, raising European morale and lowering that of the rebels.

The siege train arrived at the beginning of September, comprising six 24-pounders, eight 18-pounder long guns, six 8 inch howitzers and foour 10 inch mortars, with almost 600 ammunition carts. On 8 September a further 4 guns arrived.[:477] With the guns already present, the besiegers had a total of fifteen 24-pounder guns, twenty 18-pounder guns and twenty-five mortars and howitzers.

The Capture of Delhi

The Bombardment

Wilson's chief Engineer Officer, Richard Baird Smith, had drawn up a plan to breach the city walls and make an assault. Wilson was unwilling to risk any attack, but was urged by Nicholson to agree to Baird Smith's plan. There were moves among the British officers, in which Nicholson was prominent, to replace Wilson as commander if he failed to agree to make the attack.

As a preliminary step, on 6 September the Company forces constructed "Reid's Battery", or the "Sammy House Battery", of two 24-pounder and four 9-pounder guns, near the southern end of the ridge, to silence the guns on the Mori Bastion. Under cover of Reid's Battery, on 7 September the first siege battery proper was established, 700 yards (640 m) from the Mori Bastion. Opening fire on 8 September, four of its guns engaged the artillery on the Kashmir Bastion, while six guns and a heavy mortar silenced the rebels' guns on the Mori Bastion after a long duel. The direction of this attack also deceived the rebels that the storming attempt would be made from the east, rather than the north.

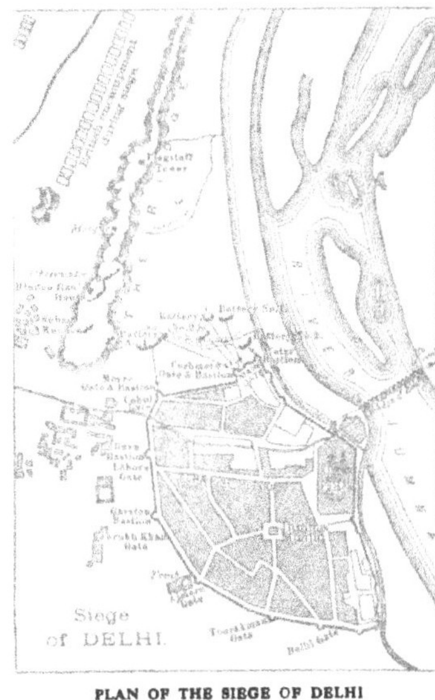

PLAN OF THE SIEGE OF DELHI

Figure 65: *The outline of the siege with the British camp just north of the city*

A second battery, consisting of nine 24-pounder guns, two 18-pounder guns and seven 8-inch howitzers, was set up near a flamboyantly-designed house known as "Ludlow Castle" in the Civil Lines, and opened fire against the Kashmir Bastion on 10 September.[:478] A third battery of six 18-pounder guns and 12 Coehorn mortars was set up near the old Custom House less than 200 yards (180 m) from the city walls, and opened fire against the Water Bastion near the Yamuna next day. A fourth battery of ten heavy mortars was set up in cover near the Khudsia Bagh, opening fire on 11 September. Because the element of surprise had been lost and these batteries were being enfiladed from across the river,[:478] the Indian sappers and pioneers who carried out much of the work of constructing the second and third batteries and moving the guns into position suffered over 300 casualties, but the batteries quickly made breaches in the bastions and walls. 50 guns continued to fire day and night and the walls began to crumble away.[:478]

The opening of this phase of the siege seems to have coincided with the exhaustion of the ammunition the rebels had captured from the magazine, as the rebel fire became suddenly much less effective. By this time also, the rebels had become depressed through lack of supplies and money, and by defeatist rumours which were spread by agents and spies organised by William Hodson.

Preparation for the Assault

The attack was scheduled for 3 a.m. on 14 September. The storming columns moved into position during the night of 13 September. The future Field Marshal Lord Roberts, then a junior staff officer, recorded their composition:

1st Column – Brigadier General Nicholson

75th Foot – 300

1st Bengal Fusiliers[257] – 250

2nd Punjab Infantry (*Greene's Rifles*) – 450

Total – 1000

2nd Column – Brigadier Jones

8th Foot – 250

2nd Bengal Fusiliers – 250

4th Sikhs – 350

Total – 850

3rd Column – Colonel Campbell[258]

52nd Foot – 200

Kumaon Battalion (Gurkhas) – 250

1st Punjab Infantry (*Coke's Rifles*) – 500

Total – 950

4th Column – Major Reid

Sirmur Battalion (Gurkhas)

Guides Infantry

Collected picquets

Total – 850

Plus Kashmir contingent in reserve – 1000

5th Column – Brigadier Longfield

61st Foot – 250

4th Punjab Infantry (*Wilde's Rifles*) – 450

Baluch Battalion (one "wing" only) – 300

Total – 1000

Figure 66: *Blowing of Kashmir by Sergeant Carmichael*

Detachments (totalling 200) of the 60th Rifles preceded all the columns, as skirmishers. Engineers and sappers were attached to lead each column.[:479]

There was also a cavalry brigade in reserve, under James Hope Grant, which probably consisted of:

6th Carbineers (one "wing" only)

9th Lancers

Guides Cavalry

1st Punjab Cavalry (one squadron)

2nd Punjab Cavalry (one squadron)

5th Punjab Cavalry (one squadron)

Hodson's Horse (irregular levies)

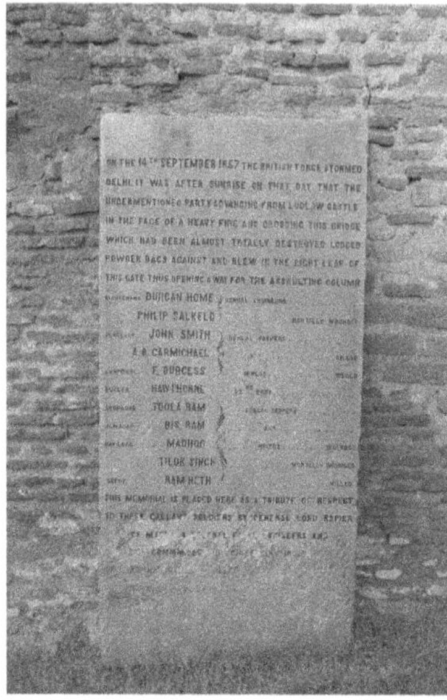

Figure 67: *Plaque at Kashmiri Gate, commemorating the attack on it on 14 September 1857*

The Assault

The first three columns, under Nicholson's overall command, gathered in and behind a building known as the Khudsia Bagh, a former summer residence of the Mughal Kings, about a quarter of a mile from the north walls. The fourth column was intended to attack only when the Kabul Gate on the west of the city walls was opened from behind by the other columns. The fifth column and the cavalry were in reserve.

The attack was supposed to be launched at dawn, but the defenders had repaired some of the breaches overnight with sandbags, and further bombardment was required. Eventually, Nicholson gave the signal and the attackers charged. The first column stormed through the breach in the Kashmir Bastion and the second through that in the Water Bastion, by the Jumna River, but this was not without difficulty as most of the scaling ladders were broken before they could be emplaced.:481

The third column attacked the Kashmiri Gate on the north wall. Two sapper officers, Lieutenants Home and Salkeld (both of whom subsequently won the Victoria Cross), led a suicidal mission, a small party of British and Indian sappers which placed four gunpowder charges and sandbags against the gate, under fire from just 10 feet (3.0 m) away. Several of them were wounded and killed trying to light the fuse. The explosion demolished part of the gate, a bugler with the party signalled success and the third column charged in.:480

Meanwhile, the fourth column encountered a rebel force in the suburb of Kishangunj outside the Kabul Gate before the other columns attacked, and was thrown into disorder. Major Reid, its commander, was seriously injured and the column retired. The rebels followed up, capturing four guns from the Kashmiri troops, and threatened to attack the British camp, which had been emptied of its guards to form the assault force. The artillery batteries at Hindu Rao's House (directed by Chamberlain from a doolie) stopped them until Hope Grant's cavalry and horse artillery could move up to replace Reid's column. The cavalry remained in position under fire from guns on the Kabul Gate and suffered heavy casualties, until relieved by infantry.

In spite of this reverse, Nicholson was keen to press on into the city. He led a detachment down a narrow lane to try to capture the Burn Bastion, on the walls north of the Kabul Gate. Rebel soldiers held most of the flat rooftops and walled compounds, and guns mounted on the bastion fired grapeshot down the lanes between the houses. After two rushes were stopped with heavy casualties, Nicholson led a third charge and was mortally wounded.

Temporarily repulsed, the British now withdrew to the Church of Saint James, just inside the walls of the Kashmir Bastion. They had suffered 1,170 casualties in the attack. Archdale Wilson moved to the Church, and faced with the setback, he wished to order a withdrawal. When he heard of Wilson's indecision, the dying Nicholson threatened to shoot him. Eventually, Baird Smith, Chamberlain and other officers persuaded Wilson to hold on to the British gains.

The Capture of the City

The British and Company forces were disordered. Many British officers had been killed or wounded, and their units were now in confusion. The British foothold included many of the liquor stores and over the next two days, many British soldiers became drunk and incapacitated on looted spirits. However, the rebel sepoy regiments had become discouraged by their defeats and lack of food, while the irregular *mujahhadin* defended their fortified compounds with great determination but could not be organised to make a coordinated counter-attack.

Wilson eventually ordered all liquor to be destroyed, and discipline was restored. Slowly, the attackers began to clear the rebels from the city. They captured the magazine on 16 September. Another Victoria Cross was earned here, by Lieutenant Thackerey for extinguishing a fire in the magazine, whilst under musket fire. Bahadur Shah and his entourage abandoned the palace on

Figure 68: *Capture of Delhi, 1857.*

18 September, and a British force captured the great mosque, the Jama Masjid, and the abandoned palace the next day. They also captured the Selimgarh Fort, attached to the palace and dominating the bridge of boats over the River Yamuna. Most rebels who had not already left the city now did so before the Company forces captured all the gates and trapped them.

The city was finally declared to be captured on 21 September. John Nicholson died the next day.

Aftermath

The cost to the British, Company, and loyal Indian armies in besieging Delhi from the start of the siege to the capture of the city was 1,254 killed, and 4,493 wounded, of which 992 were killed, 2,795 were wounded and 30 missing in action during the last six days of brutal fighting in the city during the final assault. Of that total of 3,817 casualties during the capture of the city, 1,677 were loyalist Indian soldiers. It is almost impossible to say how many rebels and their supporters were killed during the siege, but the number was far greater. Unofficial sources place the rebel casualties at over 5,000.

It is also impossible to estimate how many civilians died during the fighting in Delhi which included those killed by the rebels, those killed by the British, or those killed randomly and accidentally in the cross-fire. After the siege, many

Figure 69: *Capture of Bahadur Shah Zafar and his sons by William Hodson at Humayun's tomb on 20 September 1857*

civilians were subsequently expelled from the city to makeshift camps in the nearby countryside, as there was no way of feeding them until order was restored to the entire area. The British, Sikh and Pakhtun soldiers were all fairly callous with regard to life. For four days, after the fall of the city, there was extensive looting, although many British soldiers were more interested in drink than material possessions. Prize agents later moved into the city behind the troops, and organised the search for concealed treasure on a more systematic basis.

But the British, eager to avenge the killing of several of their countryfolk in Delhi, Cawnpore, and elsewhere in India, were in no mood to take prisoners. Several hundred rebel prisoners as well as suspected rebels and sympathisers were subsequently hanged without a trial or much legal process. In many cases, the officers of the "Queen's" Army were inclined to be lenient, but East India Company officials such as Theophilus Metcalfe were vengeful.

Bahadur Shah and three of his sons had taken refuge at Humayun's Tomb, 6 miles (9.7 km) south of Delhi. Although he was urged to accompany Bakht Khan and rally more troops, the aged King was persuaded that the British were seeking vengeance only against the sepoys they regarded as mutineers, and he would be spared. On 20 September, a party under William Hodson took him into custody on promise of clemency, and brought him back to the city. The next day, Hodson also took prisoner three of Bahadur Shah's sons, but with no guarantee of any sort. On the pretext that a mob was about to release them, Hodson executed the three princes at *Khooni Darwaza* (Bloody gate).:400 Their heads were later presented to Bahadur Shah.Wikipedia:Citation needed

By recapturing the Indian capital city, the British and Company forces dealt the Indian Army mutineers a major military and psychological blow, while releasing troops to assist in the relief of Lucknow, thus contributing to another British victory.

A total of 29 Victoria Crosses were awarded to recipients for bravery in the Siege of Delhi. A Delhi clasp was authorised for the Indian Mutiny Medal.

References

- Allen, Charles (2000). *Soldier Sahibs*. Abacus. ISBN 0-349-11456-0.
- Dalrymple, William (2006). *The Last Mughal*[259]. Viking Penguin. ISBN 0-670-99925-3.
- Edwardes, Michael (1963). *Battles of the Indian Mutiny*. Pan. ISBN 0-330-02524-4.
- Hibbert, Christopher (1980). *The Great Mutiny – India 1857*. Penguin. ISBN 0-14-004752-2.
- Perkins, Roger (1983). *The Kashmir Gate: Lieutenant Home & the Delhi VCs*. Picton Publishing Chippenham. ISBN 0902633872.
- Perrett, Bryan (1993). "3: The Walls of Delhi, 1857". *At All Costs! Stories of Impossible Victories*. Arms and Armour Press. ISBN 1-85409-157-3.

External links

- Part of Lord Roberts's memoirs[260]
- Memoirs of an Indian translator for the East India Company[261]

Siege of Cawnpore

Siege of Cawnpore	
Part of Indian Rebellion of 1857	
 A contemporary engraving of the massacre at the Satichura Ghat.	
Date	5 – 25 June (1857)
Location	Cawnpore, India
Result	Rebel victory Surrender and killing of the besieged Company forces and non-combatants, followed by recapture of Cawnpore and violent reprisals by the Company forces
Belligerents	
East India Company	Nana Sahib's forces Rebel Company soldiers
Commanders and leaders	
Major General Sir Hugh Wheeler † Brigadier Alexander Jack † Major Edward Vibart † Captain John Moore †	Nana Sahib Tatya Tope Bala Rao
Strength	
Around 900 including civilians and 300 soldiers	Around 4000 sepoy mutineers and mercenaries
Casualties and losses	
All, except five men and two women	Unknown

The **Siege of Cawnpore** was a key episode in the Indian rebellion of 1857. The besieged Company forces and civilians in Cawnpore (now Kanpur) were unprepared for an extended siege and surrendered to rebel forces under Nana Sahib, in return for a safe passage to Allahabad. However, under ambiguous circumstances, their evacuation from Cawnpore turned into a massacre, and most of the men were killed. As an East India Company rescue force from Allahabad approached Cawnpore, 120 British women and children captured by the Sepoy forces were killed in what came to be known as the Bibighar Massacre, their remains being thrown down a nearby well in an attempt to hide the evidence. Following the recapture of Cawnpore and the discovery of the massacre, the angry Company forces engaged in widespread retaliation against captured rebel soldiers and local civilians. The murders greatly embittered the British rank-and-file against the Sepoy rebels and inspired the war cry *"Remember Cawnpore!"*.

Background

Cawnpore was an important garrison town for the East India Company forces. Located on the Grand Trunk Road, it lay on the approaches to Sindh (Sind), Punjab and Awadh (Oudh).

By June 1857, the Indian rebellion had spread to several areas near Cawnpore, namely Meerut, Agra, Mathura, and Lucknow. However, the Indian sepoys at Cawnpore initially remained loyal. The British General at Cawnpore, Hugh Wheeler, knew the local language, had adopted local customs, and was married to an Indian woman. He was confident that the sepoys at Cawnpore would remain loyal to him, and sent two British companies (one each of the 84th and 32nd Regiments) to besieged Lucknow.

The British contingent in Cawnpore consisted of around nine hundred people, including around three hundred military men, around three hundred women and children, and about one hundred and fifty merchants, business owners, drummers (salesman), engineers and others. The rest were the native servants, who left soon after the commencement of the siege.

In the case of a rebellion by the sepoys in Cawnpore, the most suitable defensive location for the British was the magazine located in the north of the city. It had thick walls, ample ammunition and stores, and also hosted the local treasury. However, General Wheeler decided to take refuge in the south of the city, in an entrenchment composed of two barracks surrounded by a mud wall. There was a military building site to the south of Cawnpore, where nine barracks were being constructed at the dragoon barracks. The British soldiers found it difficult to dig deep trenches, as it was hot summer season. The area also lacked good sanitary facilities, and there was only one well (which would be exposed to enemy fire in case of an attack). Also, there were several buildings overlooking the entrenchment that would provide cover for the attackers, allowing them to easily shoot down on the defenders.

General Wheeler's choice of this location to make a stand remains controversial, given the availability of safer and more defensible places in Cawnpore. It is believed that he was expecting reinforcements to come from the southern part of the city. He also assumed that, in case of a rebellion, the Indian troops would probably collect their arms, ammunition and money, and would head to Delhi and therefore, he did not expect a long siege.

Rebellion at Fatehgarh

The first sign of the rebellion at Cawnpore came in the form of a rebellion at Fatehgarh (or Futteghur), a military station on the banks of the Ganges. To disperse the Indian troops away from Cawnpore, and lessen the chances of a rebellion, General Wheeler decided to send them on various "missions". On one such mission, he sent the 2nd Oudh Irregulars to Fatehgarh. On the way to Fatehgarh, General Wheeler's forces under the command of Fletcher Hayes and Lieutenant Barbour met two more Englishmen, Fayrer and Carey.

On the night of 31 May 1857, Hayes and Carey departed to a nearby town to confer with the local magistrate. After their departure, the Indian troops rebelled and decapitated Fayrer. Barbour was also killed, as he tried to escape. When Hayes and Carey came back the next morning, an older Indian officer galloped towards them and advised them to run away. However, as the Indian officer explained the situation to them, the rebel Indian sowars (cavalry troopers) raced towards them. Hayes was killed as he tried to ride away, while Carey escaped to safety.

Outbreak of rebellion at Cawnpore

There were four Indian regiments in Cawnpore: the 1st, 53rd and 56th Native Infantry, and the 2nd Bengal Cavalry. Although the sepoys in Cawnpore had not rebelled, the European families began to drift into the entrenchment as the news of rebellion in the nearby areas reached them. The entrenchment was fortified, and the Indian sepoys were asked to collect their pay one by one, so as to avoid an armed mob.

The Indian soldiers considered the fortification, and the artillery being primed, as a threat. On the night of 2 June 1857, a British officer named Lieutenant Cox fired on his Indian guard while drunk. Cox missed his target, and was thrown into the jail for a night. The very next day, a hastily convened court acquitted him, which led to discontent among the Indian soldiers. There were also rumours that the Indian troops were to be summoned to a parade, where they were to be massacred. All these factors influenced them to rebel against the East India Company rule.

The rebellion began at 1:30 AM on 5 June 1857, with three pistol shots from the rebel soldiers of the 2nd Bengal Cavalry. Elderly Risaldar-Major Bhowani Singh, who chose not to hand over the regimental colours and join the rebel sepoys, was subsequently cut down by his subordinates. The 53rd and 56th Native Infantry, which were apparently the most loyal units in the area, were awoken by the shootings. Some soldiers of the 56th attempted to leave. The

European artillery assumed that they were also rebelling, and opened fire on them. The soldiers of the 53rd were also caught in the crossfire.

The 1st N.I. rebelled and left in the early morning of 6 June 1857. On the same day, the 53rd N.I. also went off, taking with them the regimental treasure and as much ammunition as they could carry. Around 150 sepoys remained loyal to General Wheeler.

After obtaining arms, ammunition and money, the rebel troops started marching towards Delhi to seek further orders from Bahadur Shah II, who had been proclaimed the *Badshah-e-Hind* ("Emperor of India"). The British officers were relieved, thinking that they would not face a long siege.

Nana Sahib's involvement

Nana Sahib was the adopted heir to Baji Rao II, the ex-peshwa of the Maratha Confederacy. The East India Company had decided that the pension and honours of the lineage would not be passed on to Nana Sahib, as he was not a natural born heir. Nana Sahib had sent his envoy Dewan Azimullah Khan to London, to petition the Queen against the Company's decision, but failed to evoke a favourable response.

Amid the chaos in Cawnpore in 1857, Nana Sahib entered the British magazine with his contingent. The soldiers of the 53rd Native Infantry, which was guarding the magazine, were not fully aware of the situation in the rest of the city. They assumed that Nana Sahib had come to guard the magazine on behalf of the British, as he had earlier declared his loyalty to the British, and had even sent some volunteers to be at the disposal of General Wheeler. However, once Nana Sahib was inside the magazine, at the urging of the rebels, he announced that he was a participant in the rebellion against the British, and intended to be a vassal of Bahadur Shah II.

After taking possession of the treasury, Nana Sahib advanced up the Grand Trunk Road. His aim was to restore the Maratha confederacy under the Peshwa tradition, and he decided to capture Cawnpore. On his way, Nana Sahib met with rebel soldiers at Kalyanpur. The soldiers were on their way to Delhi, to meet Bahadur Shah II. Nana Sahib wanted them to go back to Cawnpore, and help him in defeating the British. The rebels were reluctant at first, but decided to join Nana Sahib, when he promised to double their pay and reward them with gold, if they were to destroy the British entrenchment.

Figure 70: *Photograph entitled, 'The Hospital in General Wheeler's entrenchment, Cawnpore." (1858) The hospital was the site of the first major loss of British lives in Cawnpore*

Attack on Wheeler's entrenchment

On 5 June 1857, Nana Sahib sent a polite note to General Wheeler, informing him that he intended to attack on the following morning, at 10 AM. On 6 June Nana Sahib's forces (including the rebel soldiers) attacked the British entrenchment at 10:30 AM. The British were not adequately prepared for the attack, but managed to defend themselves for a long time, as the attacking forces were reluctant to enter the entrenchment. Nana Sahib's forces had been led to falsely believe that the entrenchment had gunpowder-filled trenches that would explode if they got closer.

As the news of Nana Sahib's advances against the British garrison spread, several of the rebel sepoys joined him. By 10 June, he was believed to be leading around twelve thousand to fifteen thousand Indian soldiers.

The British held out in their makeshift fort for three weeks with little water and food supplies. Many died as a result of sunstroke and lack of water. As the ground was too hard to dig graves, the British would pile the dead bodies of their killed outside the buildings, and drag and dump them inside a dried well during the night. The lack of sanitation facilities led to spread of diseases such as dysentery and cholera, further weakening the defenders. There was also a small outbreak of smallpox, although this was relatively confined.

Figure 71: *Up to 1,000 British troops, their families and loyal sepoys were holed up in Gen Wheeler's entrenchment in Kanpur for three weeks in June 1857 where they were constantly bombarded by a local prince, Nana Sahib's army.*

During the first week of the siege, Nana Sahib's forces encircled the entrenchment, created loopholes and established firing positions in the surrounding buildings. Captain John Moore of the 32nd (Cornwall) Light Infantry countered this by launching night-time sorties. Nana Sahib withdrew his headquarters to Savada House (or Savada *Kothi*), situated about two miles away. In response to Moore's sorties, Nana Sahib decided to attempt a direct assault on the British entrenchment, but the rebel soldiers displayed a lack of enthusiasm.

On 11 June, Nana Sahib's forces changed their tactics. They started concentrated firing on specific buildings, firing endless salvos of round shot into the entrenchment. They successfully damaged some of the smaller barrack buildings, and also tried to set fire to the buildings.

The first major assault by Nana Sahib's side took place on the evening of 12 June. However, the attacking soldiers were still convinced that the British had laid out gunpowder-filled trenches, and did not enter the area. On 13 June, the British lost their hospital building to a fire, which destroyed most of their medical supplies and caused the deaths of a number of wounded and sick artillerymen who burned alive in the inferno. The loss of the hospital was a major blow to the defenders. Nana Sahib's forces gathered for an attack, but

Figure 72: *Attack on 23 June 1857*

were repulsed by the canister shots from artillery under the command of Lieutenant George Ashe. By 21 June, the British had lost around a third of their numbers.

Wheeler's repeated messages to Henry Lawrence, the commanding officer in Lucknow, could not be answered as that garrison was itself under siege.

Assault on 23 June

The sniper fire and the bombardment continued until 23 June 1857, the 100th anniversary of the Battle of Plassey, which took place on 23 June 1757 and was one of the pivotal battles leading to the expansion of British rule in India. One of the driving forces of the sepoy rebellion was a prophecy which predicted the downfall of East India Company rule in India exactly one hundred years after the Battle of Plassey. This prompted the rebel soldiers under Nana Sahib to launch a major attack on the British entrenchment on 23 June 1857.

The rebel soldiers of the 2nd Bengal Cavalry led the charge, but were repulsed with canister shot when they approached within 50 yards of the British entrenchment. After the cavalry assault, the soldiers of the 1st Native Infantry launched an attack on the British, advancing behind cotton bales and parapets. They lost their commanding officer, Radhay Singh, to the opening volley from the British. They had hoped to get protection from cotton bales; however, the bales caught fire from the canister shot, and became a hazard to them. On the other side of the entrenchment, some of the rebel soldiers engaged in a hand combat against 17 British men led by Lieutenant Mowbray Thomson. By the end of the day, the attackers were unable to gain an entry into the entrenchment. The attack left over 25 rebel soldiers dead, with very few casualties on the British side.

Surrender of the British forces

The British garrison had taken heavy losses as a result of successive bombardments, sniper fire, and assaults. It was also suffering from disease and low supplies of food, water and medicine. General Wheeler's personal morale had been low, after his son Lieutenant Gordon Wheeler was decapitated by a roundshot. With approval of General Wheeler, a Eurasian civil servant called Jonah Shepherd slipped out of the entrenchment in disguise to ascertain the condition of Nana Sahib's forces. He was quickly imprisoned by the rebel soldiers.

At the same time, Nana Sahib's forces were wary of entering the entrenchment, as they believed that it had gunpowder-filled trenches. Nana Sahib and his advisers came up with a plan to end the deadlock. On 24 June, they sent a female European prisoner, Mrs Rose Greenway, to the entrenchment with their message. In return for surrender, Nana Sahib promised the safe passage of the British to the Satichaura Ghat, a landing on the Ganges from which they could depart for Allahabad. General Wheeler rejected the offer, because it had not been signed, and there was no guarantee that the offer was made by Nana Sahib himself.

The next day, 25 June, Nana Sahib sent a second note, signed by himself, through another elderly female prisoner, Mrs Jacobi. The British camp divided into two groups – one in favour of continuing the defence, while the second group was willing to trust Nana Sahib. During the next 24 hours, there was no bombardment by Nana Sahib's forces. Finally, General Wheeler decided to surrender, in return for a safe passage to Allahabad. After a day of preparation, and burying their dead, the British decided to leave for Allahabad on the morning of 27 June 1857.

Satichaura Ghat massacre

On the morning of the 27 June, a large British column led by General Wheeler emerged from the entrenchment. Nana Sahib sent a number of carts, dolis and elephants to enable the women, the children and the sick to proceed to the river banks. The British officers and military men were allowed to take

Figure 73: *The British boats were stuck on mudbanks preventing departure and, amid much confusion, the soldiers were subsequently captured or massacred by Nana Sahib's rebel army.*

Figure 74: *1858 picture of Sati Chaura Ghat on the banks of the Ganges River, where on 27 June 1857 many British men lost their lives and the surviving women and children were taken prisoner by the rebels.*

their arms and ammunition with them, and were escorted by nearly the whole of the rebel army. The British reached the Satichaura Ghat by 8 AM. Nana Sahib had arranged around forty boats, belonging to a boatman called Hardev Mallah, for their departure to Allahabad.

The Ganges river was unusually dry at the Satichaura Ghat, and the British found it difficult to drift the boats away. General Wheeler and his party were the first aboard and the first to manage to set their boat off. There was some confusion, as the Indian boatmen jumped overboard after hearing bugles from the banks, and started swimming toward the shore. As they jumped, some fires on the boats were knocked over, setting a few of the boats ablaze.

Though controversy surrounds what exactly happened next at the Satichaura Ghat, and who fired the first shot, soon afterwards, the departing British were attacked by the rebel sepoys, and were either killed or captured.

Some of the British officers later claimed that the rebels had placed the boats as high in the mud as possible, on purpose to cause delay. They also claimed that Nana Sahib's camp had previously arranged for the rebels to fire upon and kill all the British. Although the East India Company later accused Nana Sahib of the betrayal and murder of innocent people, no evidence has ever been found to prove that Nana Sahib had pre-planned or ordered the massacre. Some historians believe that the Satichaura Ghat massacre was the result of confusion, and not of any plan implemented by Nana Sahib and his associates. Lieutenant Mowbray Thomson, one of the four male survivors of the massacre, believed that the rank-and-file sepoys who spoke to him did not know of the killing to come.

After the fighting began, Nana Sahib's general Tatya Tope allegedly ordered the 2nd Bengal Cavalry unit and some artillery units to open fire on the British. The rebel cavalry sowars moved into the water, to kill the remaining British soldiers with swords and pistols. The surviving men were killed, while the women and children were taken into captivity, as Nana Sahib did not approve of their killing.[262] Around 120 women and children were taken prisoner and escorted to Savada House, Nana Sahib's headquarters during the siege.

By this time, two of the boats had been able to drift away: General Wheeler's boat, and a second boat which was holed beneath the waterline by a round shot fired from the bank. The British people in the second boat panicked and attempted to make it to General Wheeler's boat, which was slowly drifting to safer waters.

General Wheeler's boat had around sixty people aboard, and was being pursued down the riverbanks by the rebel soldiers. The boat frequently grounded on the sandbanks. On one such sandbank, Lieutenant Thomson led a charge against the rebel soldiers, and was able to capture some ammunition. Next morning, the boat again stuck on a sandbank, resulting in another charge by Thomson and eleven British soldiers. After a fierce fight on shore, Thomson and his men decided to return to the boat, but did not find it where they expected to.

Meanwhile, the rebels had launched an attack on the boat from the opposite bank. After some firing, the British men on the boat decided to fly the white flag. They were escorted off the boat and taken back to Savada house. The surviving British men were sat on the ground, and Nana Sahib's soldiers got ready to fire on them. Their wives insisted that they would die with their husbands, but were pulled away. Nana Sahib granted the British chaplain Moncrieff's request to read prayers before they died. The British were initially wounded by the guns, and then killed with swords. The women and children were confined to Savada House, to be reunited later with their remaining colleagues, who had been captured earlier, at Bibighar.

Being unable to find the boat, Thomson's party decided to run barefoot to evade the rebel soldiers. The party took refuge in a small shrine, where Thomson led a last charge. Six of the British soldiers were killed, while the rest managed to escape to the riverbank, where they tried to escape by jumping into the river and swimming to safety. However, a group of rebels from the village started clubbing them as they reached the bank. One of the soldiers was killed, while the other four, including Thomson, swam back to the centre of the river. After swimming downstream for a few hours, they reached shore, where they were discovered by some Rajput matchlockmen, who worked for Raja Dirigibijah Singh, a British loyalist. These carried the British soldiers to the Raja's palace. These four British soldiers were the only male survivors from the British side, apart from Jonah Shepherd (who had been captured by Nana Sahib before the surrender). The four men included two privates named Murphey and Sullivan, Lieutenant Delafosse, and Lieutenant (later Captain) Mowbray Thomson. The men spent several weeks recuperating, eventually making their way back to Cawnpore which was, by that time, back under British control. Murphey and Sullivan both died shortly after from cholera, Delafosse went on to join the defending garrison during the Siege of Lucknow, and Thomson took part in rebuilding and defending the entrenchment a second time under General Windham, eventually writing a firsthand account of his experiences entitled *The Story of Cawnpore* (London, 1859).

Another survivor of the Satichaura Ghat massacre was Amy Horne, a 17-year-old Anglo-Indian girl. She had fallen from her boat and had been swept downstream during the riverside massacre. Soon after scrambling ashore she met up with Wheeler's youngest daughter, Margaret. The two girls hid in the undergrowth for a number of hours until they were discovered by a group of rebels.

Figure 75: *Bibighar house where European women and children were killed and the well where their bodies were found, 1858.*

Margaret was taken away on horseback, never to be seen again (it was later rumoured that she survived and was married to a Muslim soldier) and Amy was led to a nearby village where she was taken under the protection of a Muslim rebel leader in exchange for converting to Islam. Just over six months later, she was rescued by Highlanders from Sir Colin Campbell's column on their way to relieve Lucknow.

Bibighar massacre

The surviving British women and children were moved from the Savada House to Bibighar ("The House of the Ladies"), a villa-type house in Cawnpore. Initially, around 120 women and children were confined to Bibighar. They were later joined by some other women and children, the survivors from General Wheeler's boat. Another group of British women and children from Fatehgarh, and some other captive European women were also confined to Bibighar. In total, there were around 200 women and children in Bibighar.

Nana Sahib placed the care of these survivors under a sex worker called Hussaini Khanum (also known as Hussaini Begum). She put the captives to grinding corn for *chapatis*. Poor sanitary conditions at Bibighar led to deaths from cholera and dysentery.

Figure 76: *A hand-written caption identifies the man as Gungoo Mehter who was tried at Kanpur for killing many of the Sati Chaura survivors, including many women and children. He was convicted and hanged at Kanpur on 8 September 1859.*

Nana Sahib decided to use these prisoners for bargaining with the East India Company. The Company forces, consisting of around 1000 British, 150 Sikh soldiers and 30 irregular cavalry, had set out from Allahabad, under the command of General Henry Havelock, to retake Cawnpore and Lucknow. The first relief force assembled under Havelock included 64th Regiment of Foot and 78th Highlanders (brought back from the Anglo-Persian War), the first arrivals of the diverted China expedition, 5th Fusiliers, part of the 90th Light Infantry (seven companies), the 84th (York and Lancaster) from Burma, and EIC Madras European Fusiliers, brought up to Calcutta from Madras. Havelock's initial forces were later joined by the forces under the command of Major Renaud and Colonel James Neill, which had arrived from Calcutta to Allahabad on 11 June. Nana Sahib demanded that the East India Company forces under General Havelock and Colonel Neill retreat to Allahabad. However, the Company forces advanced relentlessly towards Cawnpore. Nana Sahib sent an army to check their advance. The two armies met at Fatehpur on 12 July, where General Havelock's forces emerged victorious and captured the town.

Nana Sahib then sent another force under the command of his brother, Bala Rao. On 15 July, the British forces under General Havelock defeated Bala

Figure 77: *The Bibighar Well site where a memorial had been built by 1859. Samuel Bourne, 1860.*

Rao's army in the Battle of Aong, just outside the Aong village. On 16 July, Havelock's forces started advancing to Cawnpore. During the Battle of Aong, Havelock was able to capture some of the rebel soldiers, who informed him that there was an army of 5,000 rebel soldiers with 8 artillery pieces further up the road. Havelock decided to launch a flank attack on this army, but the rebel soldiers spotted the flanking manoeuvre and opened fire. The battle resulted in heavy casualties on both sides, but cleared the road to Cawnpore for the British.

By this time, it became clear that Sahib's bargaining attempts had failed and the Company forces were approaching Cawnpore. Nana Sahib was informed that the British troops led by Havelock and Neill were indulging in violence against the Indian villagers. Some historians, such as Pramod Nayar, believe that the ensueing Bibighar massacre was a reaction to the news of violence being perpetrated by the advancing British troops.

Nana Sahib, and his associates, including Tatya Tope and Azimullah Khan, debated about what to do with the captives at Bibighar. Some of Nana Sahib's advisors had already decided to kill the captives at Bibighar, as revenge for the executions of Indians by the advancing British forces. The women of Nana Sahib's household opposed the decision and went on a hunger strike, but their efforts went in vain.

Finally, on 15 July, an order was given to murder the women and children imprisoned at Bibighar. The details of the incident, such as who ordered the massacre, are not clear.

The rebel sepoys executed the four surviving male hostages from Fatehghar, one of them a 14-year-old boy. But they refused to obey the order to kill women and the other children. Some of the sepoys agreed to remove the women and children from the courtyard, when Tatya Tope threatened to execute them for dereliction of duty. Nana Sahib left the building because he didn't want to be a witness to the unfolding massacre.

The British women and children were ordered to come out of the assembly rooms, but they refused to do so and clung to each other. They barricaded themselves in, tying the door handles with clothing. At first, around twenty rebel soldiers opened fire from the outside of the Bibighar, firing through holes in the boarded windows. The soldiers of the squad that was supposed to fire the next round were disturbed by the scene, and discharged their shots into the air. Soon after, upon hearing the screams and groans inside, the rebel soldiers declared that they were not going to kill any more women & children.

An angry Begum Hussaini Khanum denounced the sepoys' act as cowardice, and asked her aide to finish the job of killing the captives. Her lover hired butchers, who murdered the captives with cleavers; the butchers left when it seemed that all the captives had been killed. However, a few women and children had managed to survive by hiding under the other dead bodies. It was agreed that the bodies of the victims would be thrown down a dry well by some sweepers. The next morning the rebels arrived to dispose of the bodies and they found that three women who were still alive, and also three children aged between four and seven years old . The surviving women were cast into the well by the sweepers, who had also been told to strip the corpses. The sweepers then threw the three little boys into the well one at a time, the youngest first. Some victims, among them small children, were therefore buried alive in a heap of butchered corpses. None survived.

Recapture and retribution by the British

The Company forces reached Cawnpore on 16 July, and captured the city. A group of British officers and soldiers set out to the Bibighar, to rescue the captives, assuming that they were still alive. However, when they reached the site, they found it empty and blood-splattered, with the bodies of most of the 200 women and children having already been dismembered and thrown down the courtyard well or into the Ganges river.[263] Piles of children's clothing and severed women's hair blew on the wind and lodged in tree branches around the compound; the tree in the courtyard nearest the well was smeared with the brains of numerous children and infants who had been dashed headfirst against the trunk and thrown down the well.

The British troops were horrified and enraged. Upon learning of the massacre, the infuriated British garrison engaged in a surge of violence against the local population of Cawnpore, including looting and burning of houses, with the justification that none of the local noncombatants had done anything to stop the massacre. Brigadier General Neill, who took the command at Cawnpore, immediately began a program of swift and vicious drumhead military justice (culminating in summary execution) for any sepoy rebel captured from the city who was unable to prove he was not involved in the massacre. Rebels confessing to or believed to be involved in the massacre were forced to lick the floor of the Bibighar compound, after it had been wetted with water by low caste people, while being whipped.[264] The sepoys were then religiously disgraced by being forced to eat (or force fed) beef (if Hindu) or pork (if Muslim). The Muslim sepoys were sewn into pig skins before being hanged, and low-caste Hindu street sweepers were employed to execute the high-caste Brahmin rebels to add additional religious disgrace to their punishment. Some were also forced by the British to lick clean buildings stained with the blood of the recently deceased, before being publicly hanged.

Most of the prisoners were hanged within direct view of the well at the Bibighar and buried in shallow ditches by the roadside. Others were shot or bayonetted, while some were also tied across the mouths of cannon that were then fired, an execution method initially used by the rebels, and the earlier Indian powers, such as the Marathas and the Mughals. It is unclear whether this method of execution was reserved for special prisoners, or whether it was merely done in the retributive spirit of the moment.

The massacre disgusted and embittered the British troops in India, with "Remember Cawnpore!" becoming a war cry for the British soldiers for the rest of the conflict. Acts of summary violence against towns and cities believed to harbour or support the rebellion also increased. In one of the villages, the Highlanders caught around 140 men, women and children. Ten men were hanged without any evidence or trial. Another sixty men were forced to build the gallows of wooden logs, while others were flogged and beaten. In another village, when around 2,000 villagers came out in protest brandishing lathis, the British troops surrounded them and set the village on fire. Villagers trying to escape were shot dead.

Aftermath

On 19 July, General Havelock resumed operations at Bithoor. Major Stevenson led a group of Madras Fusiliers & Sikh soldiers to Bithoor and occupied Nana Sahib's palace without any resistance. The British troops seized guns, elephants & camels, and set Nana Sahib's palace on fire.

In November 1857, Tatya Tope gathered an army, mainly consisting of the rebel soldiers from the Gwalior contingent, to recapture Cawnpore. By 19 November, his 6,000-strong force had taken control of all the routes west and north-west of Cawnpore. However, his forces were defeated by the Company forces under Colin Campbell in the Second Battle of Cawnpore, marking the end of the rebellion in the Cawnpore area. Tatya Tope then joined Rani Lakshmibai.

Nana Sahib disappeared and, by 1859, he had reportedly fled to Nepal. His ultimate fate was never determined. Up until 1888, there were rumours and reports that he had been captured and a number of individuals turned themselves in to the British claiming to be the aged Nana. As the majority of these reports turned out to be untrue, further attempts at apprehending him were abandoned.

British civil servant Jonah Shepherd, who had been rescued by Havelock's army, spent the next few years after the rebellion attempting to put together a list of those killed in the entrenchment. He had lost his entire family during the siege. He eventually retired to a small estate north of Cawnpore in the late 1860s.

Memorials

After the revolt was suppressed, the British dismantled Bibighar. They raised a memorial railing & cross at the site of the well in which the bodies of the British women & children had been dumped. Meanwhile, the British forces conducted a punitive action under the lead of General Autrum by blowing down Nana Sahib's palace in Bithoor with cannons, in which Indian women and children including Nana Sahib's young daughter Mainavati were burned alive.[265] Also, the inhabitants of Cawnpore were forced to pay £30,000 for the creation of the memorial as a 'punishment' for not coming to the aid of the British women and children in Bibighar. *The Angel of the Resurrection* was created by Baron Carlo Marochetti and completed in 1865. It has been called by various names throughout the centuries and came to be the most visited statue of British India. The chief proponent and private funder was Charlotte, Countess Canning, wife of the first Viceroy of India, Earl Canning. She approached her childhood friend, Marochetti, for models. In turn, Marochetti

Figure 78: *A memorial erected (circa 1860) by the British at the Bibi Ghar well after the Mutiny was crushed. It was the work of Carlo Marochetti. After Indian independence the memorial was moved to the Memorial Church, Cawnpore. Albumen silver print by Samuel Bourne, 1860.*

suggested that other sculptors be invited. Following the Countess's death, Earl Canning took over the commission. Canning rejected a number of designs accepting, in the end, a version of Marochetti's Crimean War memorial at Scutari, Turkey. The understated figure is an angel holding two branches of palm fronds across her chest. Despite assurances, 'The Angel' had some damage during the Independence celebrations of 1947 and she was later moved from her original site over the Bibi Ghar well to a garden at the side of All Soul's Church, Kanpore (Kanpur Memorial Church).

The remains of a circular ridge of the well can still be seen at the Nana Rao Park, built after Indian independence. The British also erected the All Souls Memorial Church, in memory of the victims. An enclosed pavement outside the church marks the graves of over 70 British men captured and executed on 1 July 1857, four days after the Satichaura Ghat massacre. The marble Gothic screen with "mournful seraph" was transferred to the churchyard of the All Souls Church after Indian independence in 1947. The memorial to the British victims was replaced with a bust of Tatya Tope.

There is a plaque to Capt. W Morphy and Lieut. Thomas Mackinnon who were killed on 28 November 1857 in Lichfield Cathedral.

An additional memorial detailing the losses suffered by the 32nd Cornwall Regiment Light Infantry is located inside the west entrance to Exeter Cathedral.

Literary references

Many references to the event were made in later novels and films. Julian Rathbone describes the brutality of both British and Indian forces during the siege of Cawnpore in his novel *The Mutiny*. In the novel, the Indian nurse Lavanya rescues an English child, Stephen, during the Satichaura Ghat massacre. In *Massacre at Cawnpore*, V. A. Stuart describes the siege and the British defence through the eyes of the characters Sheridan, and his wife Emmy. George MacDonald Fraser's *Flashman in the Great Game* also contains lengthy scenes set in the entrenchment during the siege and also during the ensuing escape. Tom Williams' novel, *Cawnpore*, is also set against the background of the siege and massacre, which is seen from both the European and the Indian perspective. The contemporary Indian report by Kalpi devi in the local journal Hindupanch covered the incident of the punitive action by the British and burning down of Nana Sahib's palace along with his young daughter Mainavati in a prose.[266]

The British press used it to describe the brutality involved in the public feeding of reptiles at the London zoological garden. In 1876, the Editor of the Animal World drew Dr. P L Sclater's attention to this and the press charged the Zoological Society of London with encouraging cruelty, "pandering to public brutality" while one writer in the Whitehall Review (27 April 1878), protested against "the Cawnpore Massacre enacted diurnally," and headed his article, "Sepoyism at the Zoo."

External links

Wikimedia Commons has media related to ***Siege of Cawnpore***.

- 1857 Cawnpore[267] via the Internet Archive
- The Siege of Cawnpore Images[268]

Coordinates: 26.4607°N 80.3334°E[269]

Siege of Lucknow

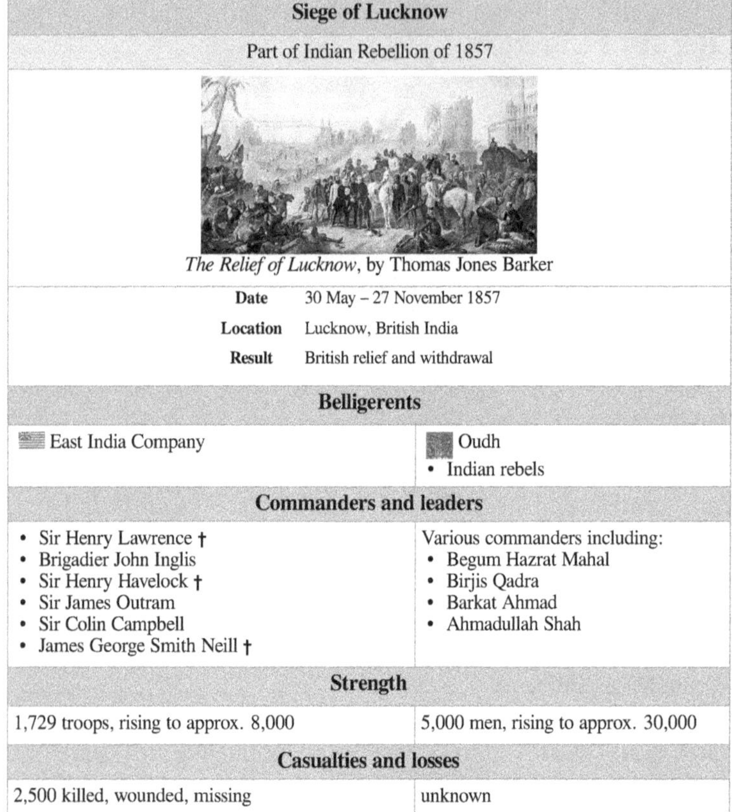

Siege of Lucknow	
Part of Indian Rebellion of 1857	
The Relief of Lucknow, by Thomas Jones Barker	
Date	30 May – 27 November 1857
Location	Lucknow, British India
Result	British relief and withdrawal
Belligerents	
East India Company	Oudh • Indian rebels
Commanders and leaders	
• Sir Henry Lawrence † • Brigadier John Inglis • Sir Henry Havelock † • Sir James Outram • Sir Colin Campbell • James George Smith Neill †	Various commanders including: • Begum Hazrat Mahal • Birjis Qadra • Barkat Ahmad • Ahmadullah Shah
Strength	
1,729 troops, rising to approx. 8,000	5,000 men, rising to approx. 30,000
Casualties and losses	
2,500 killed, wounded, missing	unknown

The **Siege of Lucknow** (Hindi: लखनऊ की घेराबंदी) was the prolonged defence of the Residency within the city of Lucknow during the Indian Rebellion of 1857. After two successive relief attempts had reached the city, the defenders and civilians were evacuated from the Residency, which was then abandoned.

Background to the siege

The state of Oudh/Awadh had been annexed by the British East India Company and the Nawab Wajid Ali Shah was exiled to Calcutta the year before the rebellion broke out. This high-handed action by the East India Company was greatly resented within the state and elsewhere in India. The first British Commissioner (in effect the governor) appointed to the newly acquired territory was Coverley Jackson. He behaved tactlessly, and Sir Henry Lawrence, a very experienced administrator, took up the appointment only six weeks before the rebellion broke out.

The sepoys (Indian soldiers) of the East India Company's Bengal Presidency Army had become increasingly troubled over the preceding years, feeling that their religion and customs were under threat from the evangelising activities of the Company. Lawrence was well aware of the rebellious mood of the Indian troops under his command (which included several units of Oudh Irregulars, recruited from the former army of the state of Oudh). On 18 April, he warned the Governor General, Lord Canning, of some of the manifestations of discontent, and asked permission to transfer certain rebellious corps to another province.

The flashpoint of the rebellion was the introduction of the Enfield rifle; the cartridges for this weapon were believed to be greased with a mixture of beef and pork fat, which was felt would defile both Hindu and Muslim Indian soldiers. On 1 May, the 7th Oudh Irregular Infantry refused to bite the cartridge, and on 3 May they were disarmed by other regiments.

On 10 May, the Indian soldiers at Meerut broke into open rebellion, and marched on Delhi. When news of this reached Lucknow, Lawrence recognised the gravity of the crisis and summoned from their homes two sets of pensioners, one of sepoys and one of artillerymen, to whose loyalty, and to that of the Sikh and some Hindu sepoys, the successful defence of the Residency was largely due.

Rebellion begins

On 23 May, Lawrence began fortifying the Residency and laying in supplies for a siege; large numbers of British civilians made their way there from outlying districts. On 30 May (the Muslim festival of Eid ul-Fitr), most of the Oudh and Bengal troops at Lucknow broke into open rebellion. In addition to his locally recruited pensioners, Lawrence also had the bulk of the British 32nd Regiment of Foot available, and they were able to drive the rebels away from the city.

On 4 June, there was a rebellion at Sitapur, a large and important station 51 miles (82 km) from Lucknow. This was followed by another at Faizabad, one of the most important cities in the province, and outbreaks at Daryabad, Sultanpur and Salon. Thus, in the course of ten days, British authority in Oudh practically vanished.

On 30 June, Lawrence learned that the rebels were gathering north of Lucknow and ordered a reconnaissance in force, despite the available intelligence

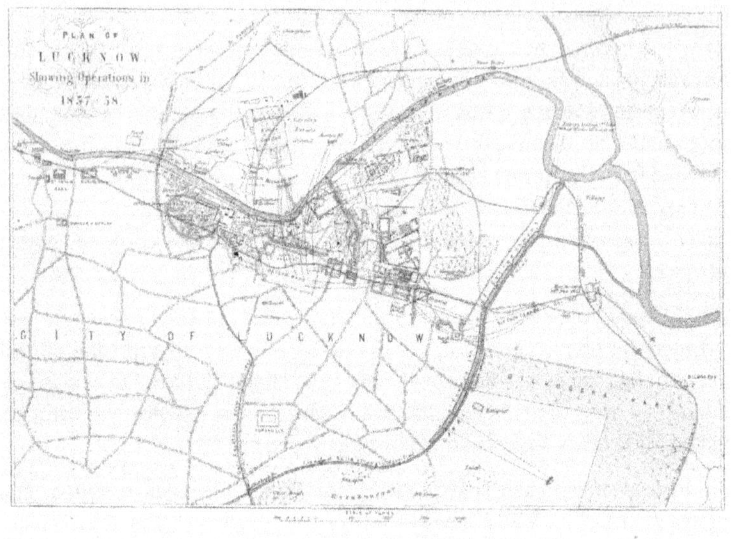

Figure 79: *Contemporary plan of the movements during the siege and relief of Lucknow*

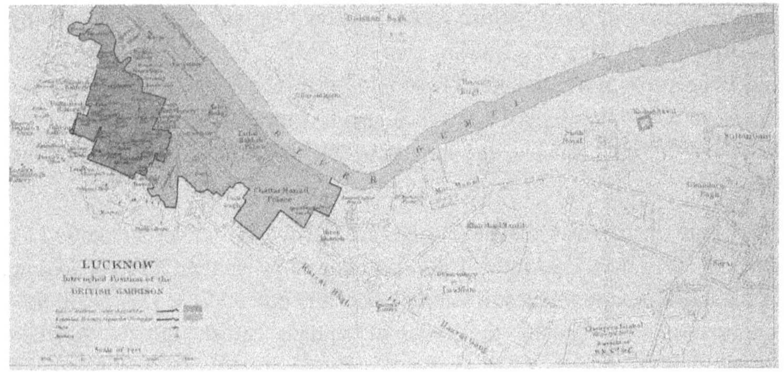

Figure 80: *Lucknow, Intrenched Position of the British garrison map, 1911*

being of poor quality. Although he had comparatively little military experience, Lawrence led the expedition himself. The expedition was not very well organised. The troops were forced to march without food or adequate water during the hottest part of the day at the height of summer, and at the Chinhat they met a well-organised rebel force, led by Barkat Ahmad with cavalry and dug-in artillery. Whilst they were under attack, some of Lawrence's sepoys and Indian artillerymen defected to the rebels, overturning their guns and cutting the traces.[:484] His exhausted British soldiers retreated in disorder. Some died of heatstroke within sight of the Residency.

Lieutenant William George Cubitt, 13th Native Infantry, was awarded the Victoria Cross several years later, for his act of saving the lives of three men of the 32nd Regiment of Foot during the retreat. His was not a unique action; sepoys loyal to the British, especially those of the 13th Native Infantry, saved many British soldiers, even at the cost of abandoning their own wounded men, who were hacked to pieces by rebel sepoys.

As a result of the defeat, the detached turreted building, Machchhi Bhawan (Muchee Bowan), which contained 200 barrels ($\sim$27 t) of gunpowder and a large supply of ball cartridge, was blown up and the detachment withdrew to the Residency.[:484]

Initial attacks

Lawrence retreated into the Residency, where the siege now began, with the Residency as the centre of the defences. The actual defended line was based on six detached smaller buildings and four entrenched batteries. The position covered some 60 acres (240,000 m^2) of ground, and the garrison (855 British officers and soldiers, 712 Indians, 153 civilian volunteers, with 1,280 non-combatants, including hundreds of women and children) was too small to defend it effectively against a properly prepared and supported attack. Also, the Residency lay in the midst of several palaces, mosques and administrative buildings, as Lucknow had been the royal capital of Oudh for many years. Lawrence initially refused permission for these to be demolished, urging his engineers to "spare the holy places". During the siege, they provided good vantage points and cover for rebel sharpshooters and artillery.

One of the first bombardments following the beginning of the siege, on 30 June, caused a civilian to be trapped by a falling roof. Corporal William Oxenham of the 32nd Foot saved him while under intense musket and cannon fire, and was later awarded the Victoria Cross. The first attack was repulsed on 1 July. The next day, Lawrence was fatally wounded by a shell, dying on 4 July. Colonel John Inglis of the 32nd Regiment took military command of the garrison.[:485] Major John Banks was appointed the acting Civil Commissioner

Figure 81: *Sir John Eardley Inglis by William Gush*

Figure 82: *Lawrence showing his battery gun*

by Lawrence. When Banks was killed by a sniper a short time later, Inglis assumed overall command.

About 8,000 sepoys who had joined the rebellion and several hundred retainers of local landowners surrounded the Residency. They had some modern guns and also some older pieces which fired all sorts of improvised missiles. There were several determined attempts to storm the defences during the first weeks of the siege, but the rebels lacked a unified command able to coordinate all the besieging forces.

The defenders, their number constantly reduced by military action as well as disease, were able to repulse all attempts to overwhelm them. On 5 August an enemy mine was foiled; counter mining and offensive mining against two buildings brought successful results.[:485] Several sorties were mounted, attempting to reduce the effectiveness of the most dangerous rebel positions and to silence some of their guns. The Victoria Cross was awarded to several participants in these sorties: Captain Samuel Hill Lawrence and Private William Dowling of the 32nd Foot and Captain Robert Hope Moncrieff Aitken of the 13th Native Infantry. Also William Hall (Quartermaster) was awarded a Victoria Cross, because he bravely stayed his ground and shot the wall (under heavy cannon and musket fire) down when only him and a officer were still alive.

First relief attempt

On 16 July, a force under Major General Henry Havelock recaptured Cawnpore, 48 miles (77 km) from Lucknow. On 20 July, he decided to attempt to relieve Lucknow, but it took six days to ferry his force of 1500 men across the Ganges River. On 29 July, Havelock won a battle at Unao, but casualties, disease and heatstroke reduced his force to 850 effectives, and he fell back.

Havelock managed to get a spy through to the Residency, telling them that 2 rockets would be fired at a certain time on the night when the relief force was ready to attack.[:486]

There followed a sharp exchange of letters between Havelock and the insolent Brigadier James Neill who was left in charge at Cawnpore. Havelock eventually received 257 reinforcements and some more guns, and tried again to advance. He won another victory near Unao on 4 August, but was once again too weak to continue the advance, and retired.

Havelock intended to remain on the north bank of the Ganges, inside Oudh, and thereby prevent the large force of rebels which had been facing him from joining the siege of the Residency, but on 11 August, Neill reported that Cawnpore was threatened. To allow himself to retreat without being attacked from

Figure 83: *Crossing the Ganges into Oudh*

Figure 84: *Attack of the Mutineers on the Redan Battery at Lucknow, 30 July 1857*

behind, Havelock marched again to Unao and won a third victory there. He then fell back across the Ganges, and destroyed the newly completed bridge. On 16 August, he defeated a rebel force at Bithur, disposing of the threat to Cawnpore.

Havelock's retreat was tactically necessary, but caused the rebellion in Oudh to become a national revolt, as previously uncommitted landowners joined the rebels.

First relief of Lucknow

Havelock had been superseded in command by Major General Sir James Outram. Before Outram arrived at Cawnpore, Havelock made preparations for another relief attempt. He had earlier sent a letter to Inglis in the Residency, suggesting he cut his way out and make for Cawnpore. Inglis replied that he had too few effective troops and too many sick, wounded and non-combatants to make such an attempt. He also pleaded for urgent assistance. The rebels meanwhile continued to shell the garrison in the Residency, and also dug mines beneath the defences, which destroyed several posts. Although the garrison kept the rebels at a distance with sorties and counter-attacks, they were becoming weaker and food was running short.

Outram arrived at Cawnpore with reinforcements on 15 September. He allowed Havelock to command the relief force, accompanying it nominally as a volunteer until Lucknow was reached. The force numbered 3,179 and was composed of six British and one Sikh infantry battalions, with three artillery batteries, but only 168 volunteer cavalry. They were divided into two brigades, under Neill and Colonel Hamilton of the 78th Highlanders.

The advance resumed on 18 September. This time, the rebels did not make any serious stand in the open country, even failing to destroy some vital bridges. On 23 September, Havelock's force drove the rebels from the Alambagh, a walled park four miles south of the Residency. Leaving the baggage with a small force in the Alambagh, he began the final advance on 25 September. Because of the monsoon rains, much of the open ground around the city was flooded or waterlogged, preventing the British making any outflanking moves and forcing them to make a direct advance through part of the city.

The force met heavy resistance trying to cross the Charbagh Canal, but succeeded after nine out of ten men of a forlorn hope were killed storming a bridge. They then turned to their right, following the west bank of the canal. The 78th Highlanders took a wrong turning, but were able to capture a rebel battery near the Qaisarbagh palace, before finding their way back to the main force. After further heavy fighting, by nightfall the force had reached the

Figure 85: *The Relief of Lucknow by General Havelock, 25 September 1857. Engraving, 1858*

Machchhi Bhawan. Outram proposed to halt and contact the defenders of the Residency by tunnelling and mining through the intervening buildings, but Havelock insisted on an immediate advance. (He feared that the defenders of the Residency were so weakened that they might still be overwhelmed by a last-minute rebel attack.) The advance was made through heavily defended narrow lanes. Neill was one of those killed by rebel musket fire. In all, the relief force lost 535 men out of 2000, incurred mainly in this last rush.

By the time of the relief, the defenders of the Residency had endured a siege of 87 days, and were reduced to 982 fighting personnel.

Second siege

Originally, Outram had intended to evacuate the Residency, but the heavy casualties incurred during the final advance made it impossible to remove all the sick and wounded and non-combatants. Another factor which influenced Outram's decision to remain in Lucknow was the discovery of a large stock of supplies beneath the Residency, sufficient to maintain the garrison for two months. Lawrence had laid in the stores, but died before he had informed any of his subordinates. (Inglis had feared that starvation was imminent.)

Instead, the defended area was enlarged. Under Outram's overall command, Inglis took charge of the original Residency area, and Havelock occupied and

Figure 86: *Kavanagh being disguised as a sepoy during the Siege of Lucknow, painted by Louis William Desanges*

defended the palaces (the Farhat Baksh and Chuttur Munzil) and other buildings east of it. Outram had hoped that the relief would also demoralise the rebels, but was disappointed. For the next six weeks, the rebels continued to subject the defenders to musket and artillery fire, and dug a series of mines beneath them. The defenders replied with sorties, as before, and dug countermines. Twenty-one shafts were sunk and 3,291 feet of gallery were constructed by the defenders. The enemy dug 20 mines: three caused loss of life, two did no injury, seven were blown in, and seven were tunnelled into and their galleries taken over.[:486]

The defenders were able to send messengers to and from the Alambagh, from where in turn messengers could reach Cawnpore. (Later, a semaphore system made the risky business of sending messengers between the Residency and the Alambagh unnecessary.) A volunteer civil servant, Thomas Henry Kavanagh, the son of a British soldier, disguised himself as a sepoy and ventured from the Residency aided by a local man named Kananji Lal. He and his scout crossed the entrenchments east of the city and reached the Alambagh to act as a guide to the next relief attempt. For this action, Kavanagh was awarded the Victoria Cross and was the first civilian in British history to be honoured with such an award for action during a military conflict.

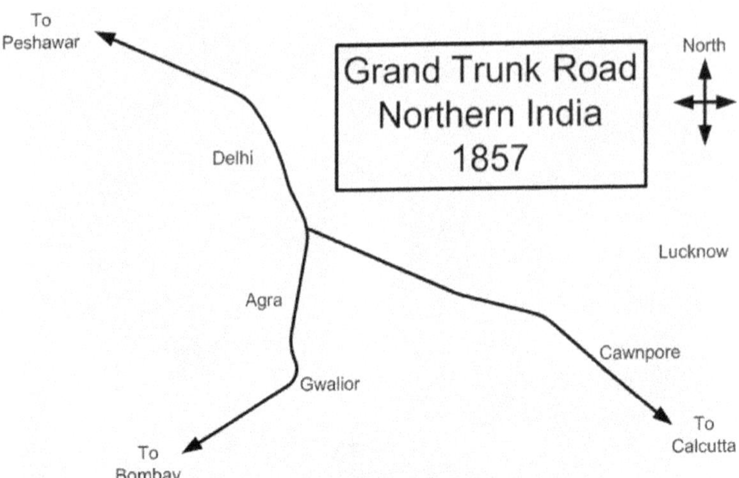

Figure 87: *Grand Trunk Roads of northern India 1857.*

Preparations for second relief

The rebellion had involved a very wide stretch of territory in northern India. Large numbers of rebels had flocked to Delhi, where they proclaimed the restoration of the Mughal Empire under Bahadur Shah II. A British army besieged the city from the first week in June. On 10 September, they launched a storming attempt, and by 21 September they had captured the city. On 24 September, a column of 2,790 British, Sikh and Punjabi troops under Colonel Greathed of the 8th (The King's) Regiment of Foot marched through the Lahore Gate to restore British rule from Delhi to Cawnpore. On 9 October, Greathed received urgent calls for help from a British garrison in the Red Fort at Agra. He diverted his force to Agra, to find the rebels had apparently retreated. While his force rested, they were surprised and attacked by the rebel force, which had been close by. Nevertheless, they rallied, defeated and dispersed the rebel force. This Battle of Agra cleared all organised rebel forces from the area between Delhi and Cawnpore, although guerrilla bands remained.

Shortly afterwards, Greathed received reinforcements from Delhi, and was superseded in command by Major General James Hope Grant. Grant reached Cawnpore late in October, where he received orders from the new commander-in-chief in India, Sir Colin Campbell, to proceed to the Alambagh, and transport the sick and wounded to Cawnpore. He was also strictly enjoined not to commit himself to any relief of Lucknow until Campbell himself arrived.

Campbell was 64 years old when he left England in July 1857 to assume command of the Bengal Army. By mid-August, he was in Calcutta preparing his departure upcountry. It was late October before all preparations were completed. Fighting his way up the Grand Trunk Road, Campbell arrived in Cawnpore on 3 November. The rebels held effective control of large parts of the countryside. Campbell considered, but rejected, securing the countryside before launching his relief of Lucknow. The massacre of British women and children following the capitulation of Cawnpore was still in recent memory. In British eyes, Lucknow had become a symbol of their resolve. Accordingly, Campbell left 1,100 troops in Cawnpore for its defence, leading 600 cavalry, 3,500 infantry and 42 guns to the Alambagh, in what Samuel Smiles described as an example of the "women and children first" protocol being applied.

British warships were dispatched from Hong Kong to Calcutta. The marines and sailors of the *Shannon*, *Pearl* and *Sanspareil* formed a Naval Brigade with the ships' guns (8-inch guns and 24-pounder howitzers) and fought their way from Calcutta until they met up with Campbell's force.

The strength of the rebels investing Lucknow has been widely estimated from 30,000 to 60,000. They were amply equipped, the sepoy regiments among them were well trained, and they had improved their defences in response to Havelock's and Outram's first relief of the Residency. The Charbagh Bridge used by Havelock and Outram just north of the Alambagh had been fortified. The Charbagh Canal from the Dilkusha Bridge to the Charbagh Bridge was dammed and flooded to prevent troops or heavy guns fording it. Cannon emplaced in entrenchments north of the Gumti River not only daily bombarded the besieged Residency but also enfiladed the only viable relief path. However, the lack of a unified command structure among the sepoys diminished the value of their superior numbers and strategic positions.

Second relief

At daybreak on 14 November, Campbell commenced his relief of Lucknow. He had made his plans on the basis of Kavanagh's information and the heavy loss of life experienced by the first Lucknow relief column. Rather than crossing the Charbagh Bridge and fighting through the tortuous, narrow streets of Lucknow, Campbell opted to make a flanking march to the east and proceed to Dilkusha Park. He would then advance to La Martiniere (a school for British and Anglo-Indian boys) and cross the canal as close to the River Gumti as possible. As he advanced, he would secure each position to protect his communications and supply train back to the Alambagh. He would then secure a walled enclosure known as the Secundrabagh and link up with the Residency, whose

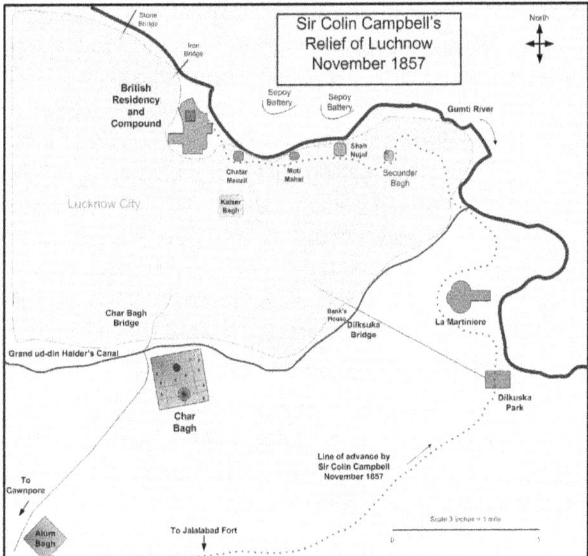

Figure 88: *Route taken by Colin Campbell in November 1857 in his relief of Lucknow*

outer perimeter had been extended by Havelock and Outram to the Chuttur Munzil.

For 3 miles (4.8 km) as the column moved to the east of the Alambagh, no opposition was encountered. When the relief column reached the Dilkusha park wall, the quiet ended with an outburst of musket fire. British cavalry and artillery quickly pushed past the park wall, driving the sepoys from the Dilkusha park. The column then advanced to La Martiniere. By noon, the Dilkusha and La Martiniere were in British hands.:[487] The defending sepoys vigorously attacked the British left flank from the Bank's House, but the British counter-attacked and drove them back into Lucknow.

The rapid advance of Campbell's column placed it far ahead of its supply caravan. The advance paused until the required stores of food, ammunition and medical equipment were brought forward. The request for additional ammunition from the Alambagh further delayed the relief column's march. On the evening of 15 November, the Residency was signalled by semaphore, "Advance tomorrow."

The next day, the relief column advanced from La Martiniere to the northern point where the canal meets the Gumti River. The damming of the canal to flood the area beneath the Dilkuska Bridge had left the canal dry at the crossing

Figure 89: *The 93rd Highlanders clearing the Secunder Bagh*

point. The column and guns advanced forward and then turned sharp left to Secundra Bagh.

Storming of Secundra Bagh

The Secundra Bagh is a high walled garden approximately 120 square yards (100 m^2), with parapets at each corner and a main entry gate arch on the southern wall. Campbell's column approached along a road that ran parallel to the eastern wall of the garden. The advancing column of infantry, cavalry and artillery had difficulty manoeuvering in the cramped village streets. They were afforded some protection from the intense fire raining down on them by a high road embankment that faced the garden. Musket fire came from loopholes in the Secundra Bagh and nearby fortified cottages, and cannon shot from the distant Kaisarbagh (the former King of Oudh's palace). Campbell positioned artillery to suppress this incoming fire. Heavy 18-pounder artillery was also hauled by rope and hand over the steep road embankment and placed within 60 yards (55 m) of the enclosure. Although significant British casualties were sustained in these manoeuvres, the cannon fire breached the southeastern wall.

Elements of the Scottish 93rd Highlanders and 4th Punjab Infantry Regiment rushed forward. Finding the breach too small to accommodate the mass of troops, the Punjab Infantry moved to the left and overran the defences at the

Figure 90: *The interior of the Secundra Bagh, several months after its storming during the second relief. Albumen silver print by Felice Beato.*

main garden gateway. Once inside, the Punjabis, many of whom were Sikhs, emptied their muskets and resorted to the bayonet. Sepoys responded with counter-attacks. Highlanders pouring in by the breach shouted, "Remember Cawnpore!" Gradually the din of battle waned. The dwindling force of defenders moved northward until retreat was no longer possible. The British numbered the sepoy dead at nearly 2000.

Storming of the Shah Najaf

By late noon, a detachment of the relief column led by Adrian Hope disengaged from the Secundra Bagh and moved towards the Shah Najaf. The Shah Najaf, a walled mosque, is the mausoleum of Ghazi-ud-Din Haider, the first king of Oudh in 1814. The defenders had heavily fortified this multi-story position. When the full force of the British column was brought to bear on the Shah Najaf, the sepoys responded with unrelenting musketry, cannon grape shot and supporting cannon fire from the Kaisarbagh, as well as oblique cannon fire from secured batteries north of the Gumti River. From heavily exposed positions, for three hours the British directed strong cannon fire on the stout walls of the Shah Najaf. The walls remained unscathed, the sepoy fire was unrelenting and British losses mounted. Additional British assaults failed, with heavy losses.

Figure 91: *The Ruins of the Lucknow Residency in the 1880's*

However, retiring from their exposed positions was deemed equally dangerous by the British command. Fifty Highlanders were dispatched to seek an alternate access route to the Shah Najaf. Discovering a breach in the wall on the opposite side of the fighting, sappers were brought forward to widen the breach. The small advance party pushed through the opening, crossed the courtyard and opened the main gates. Seeing the long sought opening, their comrades rushed forth into the Shah Najaf. Campbell made his headquarters in the Shah Najaf by nightfall.

Residency reached

Within the besieged Residency, Havelock and Outram completed their preparations to link up with Campbell's column. Positioned in the Chuttur Munzil, they executed their plan to blow open the outer walls of the garden once they could see that the Secundra Bagh was in Campbell's hands.

The Moti Mahal, the last major position that separated the two British forces, was cleared by charges from Campbell's column. Only an open space of 450 yards (410 m) now separated the two forces. Outram, Havelock and some other officers ran across the space to confer with Campbell, before returning. Stubborn resistance continued as the sepoys defended their remaining positions, but repeated efforts by the British cleared these last pockets of resistance. The second relief column had reached the Residency.

The evacuation

Although Outram and Havelock both recommended storming the Kaisarbagh palace to secure the British position, Campbell knew that other rebel forces were threatening Cawnpore and other cities held by the British, and he ordered Lucknow to be abandoned. The evacuation began on 19 November. While Campbell's artillery bombarded the Kaisarbagh to deceive the rebels that an assault on it was imminent, canvas screens were erected to shield the open space from the rebels' view. The women, children and sick and wounded made their way to the Dilkusha Park under cover of these screens, some in a variety of carriages or on litters, others on foot. Over the next two days, Outram spiked his guns and withdrew after them.

At the Dilkusha Park, Havelock died (of a sudden attack of dysentery) on 24 November. The entire army and convoy now moved to the Alambagh. Campbell left Outram with 4,000 men to defend the Alambagh,[:489] while he himself moved with 3,000 men and most of the civilians to Cawnpore on 27 November.

Aftermath

The first siege had lasted 87 days, the second siege a further 61.

The rebels were left in control of Lucknow over the following winter, but were prevented from undertaking any other operations by their own lack of unity and by Outram's hold on the easily defended Alambagh. Campbell returned to retake Lucknow, with the attack starting on 6 March. By 21 March 1858 all fighting had ceased.[:493]

During the siege, the Union Jack had flown day and night (against the usual practice, which is to strike national flags at dusk), as it was nailed to the flagpole. After the British re-took control of Lucknow, by special dispensation (unique within the British Empire), the Union Jack was flown 24 hours a day on the Residency's flagpole, for the rest of the time the British held India. The day before India became independent, the flag was lowered, the flagpole cut down, and the base removed and cemented over, to prevent any other flag from ever being flown there.

The largest number of Victoria Crosses awarded in a single day was the 24 earned on 16 November, during the second relief, the bulk of these being for the assault on the Secundrabagh.

The Indian Mutiny Medal had three clasps relating to Lucknow:

1. Defence of Lucknow, awarded to the original defenders - 29 June to 22 November 1857
2. Relief of Lucknow, awarded to the relief force - November 1857

Figure 92: *Inglis's Quarters in the ruins of Residency in Lucknow, circa 2014*

3. Lucknow, awarded to troops in the final capture of Lucknow - November 1857

Representation in popular culture

- The siege, with significant differences, was fictionalised in J. G. Farrell's *The Siege of Krishnapur*. He made extensive use of memoirs and journals of survivors of the Siege, such as those of Mrs Julia Inglis and Mrs Maria Germon.
- Dion Boucicault's *Jessie Brown or the Relief of Lucknow* was a play written immediately after the events and was very popular in the theatre, playing for twenty years.
- Maxwell Gray's 1891 *In the Heart of the Storm* is set partially in Lucknow during the siege.
- G. A. Henty's *In Times of Peril* and George MacDonald Fraser's *Flashman in the Great Game* also contain lengthy scenes set in the Residency during the siege.
- Mark Twain's non-fiction book *Following the Equator* devotes an entire chapter to the rebellion, quoting extensively from Sir G. O. Trevelyan.
- M. M. Kaye's *Shadow of the Moon* (copyright 1956/1979) is a fictional account of the last days of the British Raj in India with many scenes set

in Lucknow and environs. Most of the latter part of the book is set in Lucknow during the Siege.
- The plot of Philip Pullman's *Ruby in the Smoke* relies heavily on fictional events that supposedly occurred during the siege.
- Anurag Kumar's *Recalcitrance* is mostly based on the part played by commoners during the siege. It describes the siege as well as the final relief. It is almost entirely based on the events in Lucknow. It also describes the part played by Raja Jai Lal Singh, a commander of revolutionary forces whose contributions were highlighted for the first time by the author through newspaper articles. His contributions caused a memorial park to be built around the place where this mysterious revolutionary soldier was hanged at the end of the Great Uprising of 1857. The novel was first published in 2008 to commemorate the 150th anniversary of the mutiny.
- Valerie Fitzgerald's novel *Zemindar* is set in the lead up to and siege of Lucknow with the evacuation, seen from perspective of women in the Residency.
- In the British television series *Downton Abbey* (Season 2, Episode 1), the Dowager Countess, Violet Crawley, tells her granddaughter during World War I, "War deals out strange tasks. Remember your great-aunt Roberta...She loaded the guns at Lucknow."
- The arrival of the second relief force is the subject of "The Relief of Lucknow", by Robert Traill Spence Lowell.
- William McGonagall's poem *The Capture of Lucknow* also describes the events of the second relief.

References

Bibliography

- This article incorporates text from a publication now in the public domain: Chisholm, Hugh, ed. (1911). "Indian Mutiny, The". *Encyclopædia Britannica*. **14** (11th ed.). Cambridge University Press.
- Edwardes, Michael, *Battles of the Indian Mutiny*, Pan, 1963, ISBN 0-330-02524-4
- Forbes-Mitchell, William. *The Relief of Lucknow*. London: Folio Society, 1962. OCLC 200654[270]
- Forrest, G. W., *A History of the Indian Mutiny Volumes 1–3*, Edinburgh and London: William Black and Son, 1904, reprinted 2006, ISBN 978-81-206-1999-9 and ISBN 978-81-206-2001-8
- Greenwood, Adrian (2015). *Victoria's Scottish Lion: The Life of Colin Campbell, Lord Clyde*[271]. UK: History Press. p. 496. ISBN 0-75095-685-2.

- Hibbert, Christopher, *The Great Mutiny*, Christopher Hibbert, Penguin, 1978, ISBN 0-14-004752-2
- Wolseley, Field Marshal Viscount, *Story of a Soldier's Life Volume 1*, London: Archibald Constable & Company 1903

Further reading

Library resources about
Siege of Lucknow

- Online books[272]
- Resources in your library[273]
- Resources in other libraries[274]

First person accounts:

- Bartrum, Katherine Mary. *A Widow's Reminiscences of the Siege of Lucknow.*[275], London: James Nisbet & Co., 1858. Online at A Celebration of Women Writers.[276]
- Inglis, Julia Selina, Lady, 1833–1904, *The Siege of Lucknow: a Diary*[277], London: James R. Osgood, McIlvaine & Co., 1892. Online at A Celebration of Women Writers.[276]
- Rees, L. E. Ruutz. *A personal narrative of the siege of Lucknow*[278], Oxford University Press, 1858. Digital copy on Google Books.
- *A Diary Kept by Mrs. R. C. Germon, at Lucknow* at Project Gutenberg

Other:

- Alfred Tennyson's "The Defence of Lucknow", is poem depicting the events leading up to the day of the first relief.

External links

Wikimedia Commons has media related to ***Siege of Lucknow***.

- Pakistan Defence Journal[279]

Coordinates: 26.8606°N 80.9158°E[280]

Central Indian campaign of 1858

The **Central India Campaign** was one of the last series of actions in the Indian rebellion of 1857. A small British and Indian Army (from the Bombay Presidency) overcame a disunited collection of states in a single rapid campaign, although determined rebels continued a guerrilla campaign until the spring of 1859.

Outbreak of the Rebellion

The area known to the British at the time as **Central India** is now occupied by parts of Madhya Pradesh and Rajasthan states. A large part of it was included in the region of Bundelkhand named after its former Bundela rulers. In 1857, it was administered as the Central India Agency and consisted of six large and almost 150 small states, nominally ruled by Maratha or Mogul princes, but actually controlled to a greater or lesser degree by Residents or Commissioners appointed by the British East India Company. Opposition to British control centred on the state of Jhansi, where the Rani Lakshmibai, widow of the last Maratha prince, opposed the British annexation of the state under the notorious doctrine of lapse. (Jhansi and Lalitpur districts are now in the state of Uttar Pradesh.)

The loyalty of the Indian soldiers (sepoys) of the East India Company's Bengal Army had been under increasing strain over the previous decade, and on 10 May 1857, the sepoys at Meerut, north of Delhi, broke into open rebellion. News of this outbreak spread rapidly, and most other units of the Bengal Army also rebelled.

Nine regiments of Bengal Native Infantry and three of cavalry were stationed in Central India. There was also a large **Gwalior Contingent**, raised largely from Oudh (or Awadh) and similar in organisation to the irregular units of the Bengal Army, but in the service of the Maharajah Jayajirao Scindia of Gwalior, who remained allied to the British. Almost all these units rose up against their officers during June and July. There were very few British units to oppose them, and Central India fell entirely out of British control.

At Jhansi, British officers, civilians and dependents took shelter in a nearby fort on 5 June. They emerged three days later after being assured of their safety and were immediately murdered by the rebellious sepoys and irregulars. Rani Lakshmibai had no complicity in this act but was nevertheless blamed by the British (the rebels were then the only armed force in the city and no British forces were there to oppose them).

Figure 93: *Lakshmibai, the Rani of Jhansi.*

Over the next few months, most of the former Company regiments marched to take part in the Siege of Delhi, where they were eventually defeated. The Gwalior Contingent remained largely inactive until October, when they were led to defeat at Cawnpore by Tantya Tope. These defeats deprived the rebels of a substantial body of trained and experienced troops, and made the subsequent British campaign easier. Meanwhile, most of the now independent princes began raising levies and warring with each other, or demanding ransoms from each other on threat of force. The Nawab of Banda, who induced several units of sepoys to join his service on the promise of loot, appears to have been particularly rapacious.[281]

One Mogul prince, Firuz Shah, attempted to lead an army into the Bombay Presidency to the south, but was defeated by a small force under the acting Commissioner for Central India, Sir Henry Durand. Durand then overawed the Holkar Tukojirao II (the ruler of Indore in southern Central India), into surrender.

Figure 94: *Tantia Topee's Soldiery*

The Campaign to the fall of Kalpi

The Central India Field Force, under Sir Hugh Rose took the field around Indore in late December 1857. The force consisted of two small brigades only. About half the troops were Indian units from the Bombay Presidency army, which had not been affected to the same extent by the tensions which led the Bengal Army to rebel. Rose was initially opposed only by the various armed retainers and levied forces of the Rajahs, whose equipment and efficiency were sometimes in doubt. Much of the rebel attention was focused to the north of the region, where Tatya Tope and other leaders were attempting to aid the rebels in Awadh, making Rose's campaign from the south comparatively easy.

Rose's first mission was to relieve the town of Saugor, where a small European garrison was besieged. He accomplished this on 5 February after some hard-fought battles against Afghan and Pakhtun mercenaries at Rathgar. Thousands of local villagers welcomed him as a liberator, freeing them from rebel occupation.[282] His force had then to wait at Saugor for several weeks while transport and supplies were collected.

Rose assembled his forces at Madanpur then advanced towards Jhansi by two routes, each column capturing and destroying numerous forts.[:494] When the British forces finally arrived at Jhansi they found that the city was well defended and the fort had heavy guns which could fire over the town and nearby

Figure 95: *Jhansi Fort*

countryside. Rose demanded the surrender of the city; if this was refused it would be destroyed.[283] After due deliberation the Rani issued a proclamation. "We fight for independence. In the words of Lord Krishna, we will if we are victorious, enjoy the fruits of victory, if defeated and killed on the field of battle, we shall surely earn eternal glory and salvation."[284] Rose ignored instructions from the Commander in Chief to detach forces to assist two "loyal" Rajahs, and laid siege to Jhansi on 24 March. The bombardment was met by heavy return fire and the damaged defences were repaired.

The defenders sent appeals for help to Tatya Tope.[285] An army of more than 20,000 headed by Tatya Tope was sent to relieve Jhansi but they failed to do so when they fought the British on 31 March. Even though he attacked at the most opportune moment, his scratch force was no match for Rose's troops, and he was defeated at the Battle of the Betwa the next day and forced to retreat. At the height of the hottest and driest part of the year, the rebels set fire to the forests to delay British pursuit, but the blaze disrupted their own army. They eventually retreated to Kalpi, abandoning all their guns.

During the battle with Tatya Tope's forces part of the British forces continued the siege and by 2 April it was decided to launch an assault. Jhansi was stormed on 3 April. The city wall had been breached and this was assaulted by one column, whilst other columns assaulted the defences at different points by attempting to scale the high walls, one on the left and two on the right of the breach. These troops came under heavy fire but were relieved by the breach assault column when it took control of the walls.:495 Two other columns had already entered the city and were approaching the palace together. Determined resistance was encountered in every street and in every room of the palace. Street fighting continued into the following day and no quarter was given, even to women and children. "No maudlin clemency was to mark the fall of the city" wrote Thomas Lowe.[286] The fighting stopped on 5 April when the defenders abandoned the fort.There were a number of atrocities committed by the attackers, and much looting and indiscipline. 5,000 defenders and civilians died. (British casualties were 343).

The Rani withdrew from the palace to the fort and after taking counsel decided that since resistance in the city was useless she must leave and join either Tatya Tope or Rao Sahib (Nana Sahib's nephew).[287] The Rani escaped in the night with her son, surrounded by guards, probably while Rose's cavalry were busy looting.

Rose was once again forced to pause while discipline and order was restored, but on 5 May he advanced towards Kalpi. Once again, the rebels attempted to fight in front of the city, and once again the British won a decisive although largely bloodless victory, at Kunch on 6 May. This led to demoralisation and mutual recrimination among the rebels, but their morale recovered when the Nawab of Banda reinforced them with his troops. On 16 May, they fought desperately to save the city, but were again defeated. Although there were few British battle casualties, many of Rose's soldiers were struck down by sunstroke.

The recapture of Gwalior

With the fall of Kalpi, Rose thought the campaign was over and applied to go on sick leave. The rebel leaders managed to rally some of their forces, and agreed on a plan to capture Gwalior from its ruler, Maharajah Scindia, who had continued to side with the British. On June 1, 1858 the Maharaja led his forces to Morar, a large military cantonment a few miles east of Gwalior, to fight a rebel army led by Tatya Tope, Rani Lakshmibai and Rao Sahib. This army had 7,000 infantry, 4,000 cavalry and 12 guns while he had only 1,500 cavalry, his bodyguard of 600 men and 8 guns. He waited for their attack which came at 7 o'clock in the morning; in this attack the rebel cavalry took the guns and most of the Gwalior forces except the bodyguard went over to the rebels (some deserted). The Maharaja and the remainder fled without stopping until they reached the British garrison at Agra.[288]

The rebels captured Gwalior, but there was no looting, other than from Scindia's treasury to pay the rebel troops. The rebels now wasted time celebrating and proclaiming the renewed rebellion. Rose had offered to remain

Figure 96: *Part of Gwalior Fort*

in the field until his replacement arrived, and on 12 June, he recaptured Morar, in spite of the great heat and humidity. Rani Lakshmi Bai was killed in a cavalry action near Kotah-ke-Serai on 17 June. Over the next two days, most rebels abandoned Gwalior while the British recaptured the city, although there was some desperate resistance before the fort fell.

Last actions

Most of the rebel leaders now surrendered or went into hiding, but Tatya Tope remained in the field. Aided by monsoon rains which delayed his pursuers, Tatya continued to dodge around Central India. Other leaders joined him, among them Rao Sahib, Man Singh, and Firuz Shah (who had been fighting in Rohilkhand). Eventually in April 1859, Tatya Tope was betrayed by Man Singh, and hanged.

Review

Indian historians criticise the conduct of the Indian princes, most of whom were self-interested or effete, and the lack of leadership among the sepoys. In the East India Company's Army, no Indian soldier could attain a rank greater than that equivalent to a subaltern or senior warrant officer. Most of the sepoys' officers were elderly men who had attained their rank through seniority while seeing little action and receiving no training as leaders. The rebellion therefore depended on charismatic leaders such as Tatya Tope and Rani Lakshmi Bai, who nevertheless were regarded with jealousy and animosity by many other princes.

In many cases, the defenders of cities and fortresses fought well at first but were demoralised when relieving forces were defeated, and then abandoned easily defended positions without fighting.

By contrast, Durand, Rose, and their principal subordinates had acted quickly and decisively. Many of their forces came from the Bombay Army, which was not disaffected to the same degree as the Bengal Army.

Awards

Victoria Cross

The Victoria Cross (VC) was awarded for gallantry to a number of participants in the campaign. (see List of Indian Mutiny Victoria Cross recipients)

Battle honour

The battle honour was awarded to the bulk of regiments of the British Indian Army (vide *Gazette of India* No 4 of 1864, to the Hyderabad Contingent (vide 1014 of 1866 and 178 of 1878) and to the Merwara and Deoli Regiments (vide 78 of 1887 and 1146 of 1912). The honour is repugnant.[289]

Units awarded this honour were:

- 4th Hyderabad Cavalry - 8th King George's Own Light Cavalry
- 3rd Bombay Cavalry - Poona Horse
- 1st Hyderabad Cavalry - Deccan Horse
- 1st Sindh Horse - Scinde Horse
- Madras Sappers and Miners
- Bombay Sappers and Miners
- 19th Madras Infantry - 3rd Battalion, the Madras Regiment
- 12th Bombay Infantry - 5th Battalion, The Grenadiers
- 13th Bombay Infantry - The Grenadiers Regimental Centre
- 10th Bombay Infantry - 3rd Battalion, Maratha Light Infantry now 2nd Battalion, the Parachute Regiment.
- 25th Bombay Infantry - 5th Battalion, Rajputana Rifles
- 2nd Bengal Infantry - 1st Battalion, Rajput Regiment, now 4th Battalion, the Brigade of Guards.
- 3rd Hyderabad Infantry - 2nd Battalion, Kumaon Regiment
- 5th Hyderabad Infantry - 4th Battalion, Kumaon Regiment

- 1st, 2nd Bombay Cavalry - 13th Duke of Connaught's Own Lancers (Pakistan)
- 24th Bombay Infantry - 1st Battalion, 10th Baluch Regiment (Pakistan)
- 50th Madras Infantry - Disbanded 1862
- 3rd Sindh Horse - Disbanded 1882
- 3rd Hyderabad Cavalry - Disbanded 1901
- 42nd Deoli Regiment - Disbanded 1921
- 44th Merwara Infantry - Disbanded 1921
- 1st Madras Infantry (1st Bn Madras Pioneers) - Disbanded 1933
- 1st, 2nd, 4th Batteries (Hyderabad Contingent) - Disbanded circa 1950

Indian Mutiny Medal

The Indian Mutiny Medal with Central India clasp was awarded for service in Central India January - June 1858, to all those who served under Major-General Sir Hugh Rose in actions against Jhansi, Kalpi, and Gwalior. Also awarded to those who served with Major-General Roberts in the Rajputana Field Force and Major-General Whitlock of the Madras Column, between January and June 1858.

References

- *Battles of the Indian Mutiny*, Michael Edwardes, Pan, 1963, ISBN 0-330-02524-4
- Edwardes, Michael (1975). *Red Year*. London: Sphere Books.
- *The Great Mutiny*, Christopher Hibbert, Penguin, 1978, ISBN 0-14-004752-2

Siege of Arrah

<indicator name="good-star"> ⊕ </indicator>

Siege of Arrah	
Part of the Indian Rebellion of 1857	
 *Defence of the Arrah House, 1857* (1858) by William Tayler.	
Date	27 July – 3 August 1857
Location	Arrah, Shahabad district, British India, modern day Bihar 25.5573°N 84.6658°E[290]Coordinates: 25.5573°N 84.6658°E[290]
Result	British victory
Belligerents	
East India Company United Kingdom	Mutinying Sepoys Kunwar Singh's Forces
Commanders and leaders	
Herwald Wake Hooken Singh Charles Dunbar † Vincent Eyre	Kunwar Singh
Strength	
Besieged party: 68 First relief: 400 Second relief: 225	Mutinying Sepoys: 2,500 – 3,000 Kunwar Singh's forces: 8,000 (Estimated)
Casualties and losses	
Besieged party: 1 wounded First relief: 170 killed 120 wounded Second relief: 2 killed	Unknown

File:India Bihar location map.svg
Location of Arrah in modern-day Bihar

The **Siege of Arrah** (27 July – 3 August 1857) took place during the Indian Mutiny (also known as the Indian Rebellion of 1857). It was the eight-day defence of a fortified outbuilding, occupied by a combination of 18 civilians and 50 members of the Bengal Military Police Battalion, against 2,500–3,000 mutinying Bengal Native Infantry sepoys from three regiments and an estimated 8,000 men from irregular forces commanded by Kunwar Singh, the local zamindar or chieftain.

An attempt to break the siege failed, with around 290 casualties out of around 415 men in the relief party. Shortly afterwards, a second relief effort consisting of 225 men and three artillery guns—carried out despite specific orders that it should not take place—dispersed the forces surrounding the building, suffering two casualties, and the besieged party escaped. Only one member of the besieged group was injured.

Background

On 10 May 1857, a mutiny by the 3rd Bengal Light Cavalry, a Bengal Army unit stationed in Meerut, triggered the Indian Mutiny, which quickly spread through the Bengal Presidency.[291] The town of Arrah, headquarters of Shahabad district, besides its local inhabitants, had a population at the time that included British and European employees of the East India Company and the East Indian Railway Company, and their respective families.[292,293] In addition, there was a local police force and a jail holding between 200 and 400 inmates, with 150 armed prison guards.[294,295] The population also included many sepoys from disbanded regiments[296] and retired sepoys living on their pensions.[297] Stationed in Dinapore, 25 miles (40.2 km) away, were two regiments of the British Army and three regiments of the East India Company's Bengal Native Infantry (part of the infantry component of the Bengal Army)—the 7th,

8th and 40th Regiments.[298] At the outbreak of the Indian Mutiny these were the only "native" troops in Shahabad district. They had been recruited entirely from Shahabad district and were loyal to the local zamindar (chieftain or landlord) Kunwar Singh[299] (also known as Koor,[300] Coer,[301] Koer,[299] Koowar,[302] or Kooer Sing[296]). Singh, who was around 80 years of age, had a number of grievances against the East India Company regarding deprivation of his lands and income,[303] and was described as "the high-souled chief of a warlike tribe, who had been reduced to a nonentity by the yoke of a foreign invader" by George Trevelyan in his 1864 book *The Competition Wallah*.[304]

On 8 June, a letter arrived from William Tayler, the commissioner of Patna district, warning that an outbreak of mutiny from the Bengal Native Infantry units in Dinapore was to be expected.[305] The European population in Arrah spent that night at the house of Arthur Littledale, a judge working in Arrah, and during the night it was decided that the European women and children were to be sent by boat to Dinapore, escorted by armed members of the European male population, where they would be taken into the care of the 10th Regiment of Foot—this decision was acted upon on the 9th.[306] The following morning a meeting was held at the house of Herwald Wake, the magistrate of Shahabad district, to discuss what to do next.[306] The East India Company civil servants stated that they did not intend to abandon the town and they would remain.[306] All but two of the remaining European male residents of Arrah who were not civil servants or Government employees decided to leave for the relative safety of Dinapore by boat or on horseback and did so the same day.[307] This reduced the European male population of Arrah to eight,[307] rising to sixteen over the next few weeks as men arrived in the town from the surrounding district.[308] The defence of the town was augmented on 11 June when a party arrived consisting of 50 sepoys and 6 sowars from the Bengal Military Police Battalion, known as Rattray's Sikhs (now the 3rd Battalion of the Sikh Regiment, Indian Army), under the command of Jemadar Hooken Singh.[309] The party had been sent from Dinapore, part of a larger detachment under their commander Captain Rattray whose presence in the area had been personally requested by Tayler, and placed under the direct command of Wake.[310]

Following a suggestion from Wake, Richard Vicars Boyle, District Engineer with the East Indian Railway Company, began to fortify his two-storey, 50 by 50 ft (15 by 15 m) outbuilding (originally intended as a billiard room) and completed his work by 17 June.[310] The arches of the verandah were filled in with bricks without mortar, leaving small holes in the walls for defenders to shoot through. Gaps between pillars on the second storey were filled with bricks and sandbags. Boyle stored food, water, wine and beer in the building in anticipation of unrest in the town.[311] Although it was suggested that the civil servants should immediately move their headquarters to Boyle's building, the

Mr. HERWALD WAKE.
(Taken just after the Mutiny).

Figure 97: *Herwald Wake (Taken just after the Mutiny) from A Turning Point in the Indian Mutiny (1910) by Isabel Giberne Sieveking*

suggestion was dismissed due to objections to its location, the close proximity of trees, outbuildings and other houses and the possibility that abandoning their current headquarters would lead to disorder in the town.[312] Throughout June and July, news arrived in Arrah about the widespread rebellion throughout the Bengal Presidency and there were rumours that outbreaks would take place within Shahabad district imminently, leading to the decision by the civil servants to mount nightly armed patrols.[313] On 17 July, an anonymous note was found on a table in Littledale's house saying that a mutiny of sepoys was "certain to take place" on 25 July; according to the note, Kunwar Singh was directly involved.[302] News arrived in the town on 22 July concerning the massacres that had taken place during the Siege of Cawnpore. Then on 25 July a letter arrived from Dinapore by express post, stating: "A revolt among the native troops is expected to occur this day. Stand prepared accordingly."[314]

Battle

The siege

Around 25 mi (40 km) east of Arrah, the 7th, 8th and 40th Regiments of Bengal Native Infantry were stationed in Dinapore, alongside the British Army's

10th and 37th Regiments of Foot. Throughout June, Tayler received anonymous letters warning him about the conduct of the sepoys, and he was informed that large sums of money were being distributed to the sepoys for unknown reasons.[315] Tayler also ordered the interception of all mail being sent to and from the three regiments,[316] leading to the discovery of plotters within Dinapore and nearby Patna who were then jailed.[317] Discussions had taken place between Tayler and his superiors about disarming the three regiments of Bengal Native Infantry stationed in Dinapore, and Governor-General Charles Canning delegated responsibility for the decision to Major General George Lloyd, military commander of the Dinapore division.[298] Instead of disarming the regiments, on the morning of 25 July Lloyd ordered the sepoys to hand in their percussion caps at 4:00 pm that day.[318] The 7th and 8th Regiments refused and fired on their officers. The 10th and 37th Regiments of Foot, also stationed in Dinapore, then opened fire on the mutineers. The 40th Regiment of Bengal Native Infantry, who had begun to comply with Lloyd's order, were also fired on in the confusion.[319] All three regiments of Bengal Native Infantry then left Dinapore heading toward Arrah. At the outbreak of the disturbance, Lloyd could not be located; by the time he was found aboard a river steamboat and orders were given to apprehend the mutineers, they were too far away to be caught. Lloyd, believing that his forces should remain in place to defend Dinapore, refused to order the pursuit of the mutineers.[320]

On the evening of 25 July, information arrived at Arrah that a disturbance was to be expected in the district. Wake had been told by a railway engineer stationed nearby that the boats used to cross the Son River would be destroyed; when Wake was informed on the morning of the 26th that the mutineers were crossing the river, he realised that the boats had in fact not been destroyed as promised. Wake, who had no information about the number of mutinying sepoys and other forces approaching Arrah, noted that the local police force had disappeared and he decided not to abandon the town. Eighteen civilians and fifty members of the Bengal Military Police Battalion[321] moved into Boyle's fortified building and bricked themselves up inside.[322] The building had stores of food, drink and ammunition (with gunpowder and lead to make more if required), entrenching tools and weapons the men had brought with them. The supplies were thought to be sufficient for a few days and, since they expected the mutineers to be followed by pursuing forces, the men anticipated a brief siege of no more than 48 hours.[323] Throughout the entire siege Wake kept a diary by writing on the walls of the building so there would be a record of events if the besieged party did not survive.[324] On the morning of 27 July the mutineers, joined by Kunwar Singh and his forces, arrived in Arrah. They released the prisoners from the jail and, joined by its guards, looted the treasury of 85,000 rupees. The mutineers and rebels (including the prison guards) then surrounded the house with drums and bugles playing, arranged themselves into

Figure 98: *Koor Sing, 'The Rebel of Arrah", and his attendants – From a photograph, from the Illustrated London News (1857)*

formation and charged. When the mutineers were within 100 yards the men inside opened fire on them, killing eighteen instantly and forcing the rest to stop their charge and take shelter behind the surrounding trees and buildings.[301]

Over the following seven days the besieged party faced constant musket fire, with fire from two artillery pieces after 28 July. When the party began to run out of water on 29 July, sepoys sneaked out of the building during the night, stole tools from their opponents and dug an 18 ft (5.5 m) well in about 12 hours.[325] When food began to run out, a small group was able to sneak out of the building on the afternoon of 30 July and return with some sheep that had been grazing within the compound.[326] Although an attempt was made to smoke the men out of the house by making a large fire of furniture and chilli peppers, a last-minute shift in wind direction blew the smoke away from the house.[327] Every evening, a voice loudly invited the Sikh sepoys in the house to slaughter the Europeans and join the mutineers, offering them 500 rupees each; it was met at first with sarcasm, and later by gunfire from the building.[328] The mutineers and rebel forces did not attempt another charge on the building, although its occupants expected an attack at any moment during the siege.

Figure 99: *Ross Mangles rescuing the wounded soldier from Thirty-Eight Years in India. From Juganath to the Himalaya Mountains (1882) by William Tayler*

First relief attempt

News reached Dinapore on 27 July that mutinying sepoys had attacked Arrah. General Lloyd was still unwilling to send troops to pursue the mutineers until he was persuaded to do so by pressure from magistrates, who were personal friends of the besieged party, and Tayler in his role as the Commissioner of Patna.[329] A party of 200 from the 37th Regiment of Foot, 50 from the Bengal Military Police Battalion and 15 loyal Sikhs from regiments that had mutinied, were sent, aboard the river steamer *Horungotta*,[330] to rescue the town's civil servants. News arrived in Dinapore the following day that the steamer was aground on a sandbank, and Lloyd ordered the party recalled. Under pressure from local government officials, he changed his mind and agreed to send, using the river steamer *Bombay*,[330] a large force of the 10th Regiment of Foot under Lieutenant Colonel William Fenwick to join up with the party on the first steamer and head to Arrah. *Bombay* already had a large complement of civilian passengers and attempts to have the passengers removed met with confusion and arguments with the captain of the steamer, causing a delay of around four hours.[331] As a result, only a reduced force of about 150 (including seven civilian volunteers) was able to embark. Fenwick, unwilling to carry out the mission with only 150 men, delegated its command to Captain Charles Dunbar[332] (who worked in the paymaster's bureau[333]) and *Bombay* departed

Figure 100: *William Fraser McDonell VC*

on 29 July at around 9:30 am. The two steamers met up, and the combined force of about 415 then headed towards Arrah.[334]

The expedition arrived at a place called *Beharee Ghat* on the western bank of the Son River and disembarked at about 4:00 pm.[335] Their path was then blocked by a large stream that could only be crossed using boats.[335] The party took three hours to cross the stream and head inland. After the expedition had marched 4 mi (6.4 km), Dunbar halted them 3 mi (4.8 km) from Arrah for one hour to see if his supplies would catch up to him. When the supplies did not arrive, he ordered the expedition to press on, despite warnings from his subordinate officers of the danger of hungry, tired men marching through unfamiliar territory at night.[333] Up to this point in the expedition, Dunbar had sent skirmishers as scouts ahead of his main body of troops; he now decided not to do so and the men advanced in a single body.[333] As the party neared Arrah, they spotted men on horseback, whom they took to be vedettes (mounted sentries), that rode away as they approached. When the expedition was about 1 mi (1.6 km) from Arrah, its route passed through a thick grove of mango trees. As the expedition was almost through the grove, they were fired on from three sides by a force they estimated as 2,000 to 3,000 in number.[336] Heavy casualties were suffered during the initial ambush, including Dunbar (who was killed instantly), and the force broke up in confusion. The besieged party in Arrah heard the sound of gunfire, growing louder as the expedition approached them, then becoming more distant as the expedition retreated, and they immediately inferred that something must have gone wrong.[335] A wounded member of the Bengal Military Police Battalion who was part of Dunbar's force was able to avoid the mutinying sepoys surrounding Boyle's building. Pulled up into the building with a rope, he told its occupants about the ambush.[337]

During the retreat from Arrah, Ross Mangles and William Fraser McDonell (civilian magistrates, and personal friends of Wake, who had volunteered to serve with Dunbar's expedition) earned the Victoria Cross—Mangles, despite being wounded, carried a wounded soldier from the 37th Regiment of Foot for several miles while under fire, and McDonnell exposed himself to heavy fire to cut a rope that was preventing a boat from making its escape, saving the lives of 35 soldiers. The steamer carrying the expedition returned to Dinapore on 30 July, and families and friends were waiting at the dock expecting to welcome home the victorious men. When the steamer docked outside the hospital instead of at its usual berth, the spectators realised something was wrong. In the words of Tayler: "The scene that ensued was heart-rending, the soldiers' wives rushed down, screaming, to the edge of the water, beating their breasts and tearing their hair, despondency and despair were depicted on every countenance."[338] Out of 415 men, the expedition had suffered 170 fatalities and 120 wounded.[335]

Second attempt

Major Vincent Eyre, a Bengal Artillery officer in command of the East India Company's Number 1 Company, 4th Bengal Foot Artillery—now 58 (Eyre's) Battery, 12th Regiment Royal Artillery, British Army—then stationed in Buxar, was under orders to head to Cawnpore with his battery. He had heard news of the situation in Arrah and, unaware of any relief expedition, decided on his own to collect troops to reinforce the expedition he believed would take place. Finding no troops available at Buxar, Eyre went to Ghazipur and was able to attach 25 men from the 78th (Highlanders) Regiment of Foot to his party. Upon returning to Buxar, Eyre found that 154 men from the 5th Regiment of Foot had arrived in his absence and he convinced their commander, Captain L'Estrange, to join him with the understanding that Eyre bore full responsibility. At this point, Eyre felt so confident of victory that he dismissed the men from the 78th Foot and went ahead without them.[339] Unable to locate horses to move his battery's guns, Eyre used bullocks (neutered bulls) instead and was able to procure two elephants to move the party's baggage.[340] After assembling a force of 225 men (including civilian volunteers) and three of his battery's guns, Eyre wrote to General Lloyd at Dinapore informing him of his intentions and requesting reinforcements. On 30 July, at about 4:00 pm, Eyre's expedition started for Arrah.[341]

Figure 101: *Sketch of Major Vincent Eyre from the Illustrated Naval and Military Magazine, 1 March 1888*

Lloyd's reply, informing Eyre of the failure of the first relief attempt and ordering him not to commence his mission, or to return to Buxar to await further orders if he had already started, arrived while the party was en route. Eyre disregarded Lloyd's order and continued towards Arrah.[342] On 2 August, still over 6 mi (9.7 km) from his objective, Eyre's force encountered an estimated 2,000 to 2,500 mutinying sepoys accompanied by Kunwar Singh's forces—including Kunwar Singh himself—headed to intercept him. Greatly outnumbered, Eyre's party became surrounded. He then ordered the infantry to charge with bayonets and the artillery to fire on the mutineers. This caused the mutinying sepoys to retreat, with an estimated 600 casualties.[343] Eyre's party, with only two killed, then continued towards Arrah. Blocked by a river, they built a bridge which they completed the following day. When they crossed the river on the morning of 3 August, a villager gave them a letter from Wake telling them that the besieged men had heard about their approach, stating "We are all well."[343]

Throughout the day of 2 August the besieged party heard distant cannon fire and saw people in the town hurriedly loading carts with their belongings.[344] The constant fire from muskets on the building lessened and finally ceased; it was approached by two men, who told the occupants that the besiegers were defeated and a relief force was expected to arrive in Arrah the following day.[345]

Figure 102: *House at Arrah fortified against the Dinapore Mutineers – From a sketch by Sir Vincent Eyre, 1857 from the Illustrated London News (1857)*

The occupants were sceptical, despite visual evidence, and sent out a small party at midnight to reconnoitre the area—they found no sign of the mutineers and brought in a large quantity of gunpowder and the mutineers' two artillery pieces. They then sent a party under cover of darkness to destroy a number of outhouses which the mutineers had been using as cover. This party discovered a mine dug directly under the foundations of the building by the mutineers, charged and ready to be primed, so this charge was destroyed by them. The following morning at about 7:00 am, two members of Major Eyre's expedition arrived at the house and the siege was officially broken.[346] Eyre, in his official report, wrote that Wake's defence of the building "seems to have been almost miraculous." About the outcome of the first relief attempt, he wrote: "I venture to affirm, confidently, that no such disaster would have been likely to occur, had that detachment advanced less precipitately, so as to have given full time for my force to approach direct from the opposite side, for the rebels would then have been hemmed in between the two opposing forces, and must have been utterly routed."

According to Wake's official report about the siege, "Nothing but cowardice, want of unanimity, and only the ignorance of our enemies, prevented our fortification being brought down about our ears." In his own report, Tayler wrote, "The conduct of the garrison is most creditable, and the gallantry and fidelity of the Sikhs beyond all praise."

Awards

For their actions during the siege, Wake was made a Companion of the Order of the Bath, and Boyle was made a Companion of the Order of the Star of India after the 1861 creation of the order. A few days after the relief of Arrah, the 50 besieged members of the Bengal Military Police Battalion received a gratuity of 12 months' pay as a reward for their loyalty and Jemadar Singh was promoted to Subedar upon Wake's recommendation. For its actions in Arrah the Bengal Military Police Battalion received the *Defence of Arrah (1857)* battle honour and was also given the *Bihar (1857)* battle honour for its role in safeguarding the area. These battle honours are unique to the Bengal Military Police Battalion as they were awarded to no other unit.[347] Major Eyre was recommended for the Victoria Cross by Sir James Outram, Commissioner of Oude and the overall military commander for the region, for his conduct in Arrah, but this was not awarded.[348]

Aftermath

Eyre, after receiving reinforcements, pursued Kunwar Singh's forces to Singh's palace in Jagdispur.[335] Many civilians who were besieged in Arrah, including Wake (still commanding the 50 men of the Bengal Military Police Battalion), volunteered to serve with him. Although Singh's forces were routed and the palace occupied by 12 August, Singh had fled. Eyre's force destroyed most of the town of Jagdispur including the palace (in the nearby jungle), Singh's brothers' houses and a Brahmin temple.[335] Eyre was publicly censured by Governor General Canning in *The London Gazette* for the temple's destruction. The Siege of Arrah marked the beginning of Singh's fight against the East India Company. Following Arrah he fought on, first leading his irregular forces to Lucknow, then keeping them together during an organised retreat back to Jagdispur. Singh died in April 1858. His irregular forces continued to fight, repelling an expedition sent to destroy them, until they finally laid down their arms in November 1858 as part of the general amnesty.[349] Following the general amnesty, unrest continued, and peace was not officially declared until 8 July 1859.[350]

The besieged building still stands on the grounds of Maharaja College, where it now houses a museum commemorating the life of Kunwar Singh, although according to Abhay Kumar of the *Deccan Herald*, as of May 2015 it "hardly has any item related to Kunwar Singh."

Legacy

After visiting the site in 1864, Trevelyan wrote:

> *Already the wall, on which Wake wrote the diary of the siege, has been whitewashed... a party-wall has been built over the mouth of the well in the cellars; and the garden-fence, which served the mutineers as a first parallel, has been moved twenty yards back. Half a century more, and every vestige of the struggle may have been swept away. But, as long as Englishmen love to hear of fidelity, and constancy, and courage bearing up the day against frightful odds, there is no fear lest they forget the name of "the little house at Arrah.'*[351]

References

Sources

<templatestyles src="Template:Refbegin/styles.css" />

- Best, Brian (2016). *The Victoria Crosses that Saved an Empire: The Story of the VCs of the Indian Mutiny*[352]. Barnsley: Frontline Books. ISBN 978-1-4738-5707-0.
- Boyle, Richard Vicars (1858). *Indian Mutiny, Brief Narrative of the Defence of the Arrah Garrison*[353]. London: W. Thacker & Co. OCLC 794643208[354].
- Dodd, George (1859). *The History of the Indian Revolt and of the Expeditions to Persia, China, and Japan, 1856–7–8: With Maps, Plans, and Wood Engravings*[355]. London: W. and R. Chambers. OCLC 248904480[356].
- Forrest, George (2006). *A History of the Indian Mutiny, 1857-58 (Volume III)*[357]. London (1904 original), New Delhi (2006 reprint): Gautam Jetley (reprint). ISBN 81-206-1999-4.
- Halls, John Jaoooooooooooooooooomes (1860). *Two Months in Arrah in 1857*[358]. London: Longman, Green, Longman and Roberts. OCLC 877907[359].
- O'Malley, Lewis Sydney Steward (1906). *Shahabad*[360]. Calcutta: The Bengal Secretariat Book Depot. OCLC 252001000[361].
- Prichard, Iltudus Thomas (1869). *The administration of India from 1859 to 1868: the first ten years of administration under the Crown*[362]. London: MacMillan & Company. OCLC 908361033[363].
- Sieveking, Isabel Giberne (1910). *A Turning Point in the Indian Mutiny*[364]. London: D. Nutt. OCLC 13203015[365].
- Singh, Sarbans (1993). *Battle Honours of the Indian Army 1757 – 1971*. New Delhi: Vision Books. ISBN 81-7094-115-6.

- Tayler, William (1858). *The Patna Crisis; Or, Three Months at Patna, During the Insurrection of 1857*[366]. London: J. Nisbet. OCLC 748092097[367].
- Trevelyan, George Otto (1864). *The Competition Wallah*[368]. London: MacMillan & Company. OCLC 308875870[369].

Appendix

References

[1]*The Gurkhas* by W. Brook Northey, John Morris. Page 58

[2]Dalrymple, *The Last Moghul*, pp.4–5

[3]Peers 2013, p. 64.

[4]//en.wikipedia.org/w/index.php?title=Template:Part_of_History_of_India&action=edit

[5]"The events of 1857–58 in India (are) known variously as a mutiny, a revolt, a rebellion and the first war of independence (the debates over which only confirm just how contested imperial history can become) ...(page 63)" UNIQ-ref-0-e8c5b5141a25ec89-QINU

[6]""The 1857 rebellion was by and large confined to northern Indian Gangetic Plain and central India." UNIQ-ref-1-e8c5b5141a25ec89-QINU

[7]"The revolt was confined to the northern Gangetic plain and central India."*The Gurkhas* by W. Brook Northey, John Morris. Page 58

[8]Although the majority of the violence occurred in the northern Indian Gangetic plain and central India, recent scholarship has suggested that the rebellion also reached parts of the east and north."Dalrymple, *The Last Moghul*, pp.4–5

[9]"What distinguished the events of 1857 was their scale and the fact that for a short time they posed a military threat to British dominance in the Ganges Plain."Peers 2013, p. 64.

[10], , and

[11]Metcalf & Metcalf 2006, pp. 100–103.

[12]Brown 1994, pp. 85–86.

[13]"Indian soldiers and the rural population over a large part of northern India showed their mistrust of their rulers and their alienation from them. .. For all their talk of improvement, the new rulers were as yet able to offer very little in the way of positive inducements for Indians to acquiesce in the rule."

[14]"Many Indians took up arms against the British, if for very diverse reasons. Explanations have therefore to concentrate on the motives of those who actually rebelled."

[15]"On the other hand, a very large number actually fought for the British, while the majority remained apparently acqueiscent.""The events of 1857–58 in India (are) known variously as a mutiny, a revolt, a rebellion and the first war of independence (the debates over which only confirm just how contested imperial history can become) ...(page 63)"

[16]The cost of the rebellion in terms of human suffering was immense. Two great cities, Delhi and Lucknow, were devastated by fighting and by the plundering of the victorious British. Where the countryside resisted, as in parts of Awadh, villages were burnt. Mutineers and their supporters were often killed out of hand. British civilians, including women and children, were murdered as well as the British officers of the sepoy regiments.""""The 1857 rebellion was by and large confined to northern Indian Gangetic Plain and central India."

[17]"The south, Bengal, and the Punjab remained unscathed, ...""The revolt was confined to the northern Gangetic plain and central India."

[18]"... it was the support from the Sikhs, carefully cultivated by the British since the end of the Anglo-Sikh wars, and the disinclination of the Bengali intelligentsia to throw in their lot with what they considered a backward Zamindar revolt, that proved decisive in the course of the struggle.Although the majority of the violence occurred in the northern Indian Gangetic plain and central India, recent scholarship has suggested that the rebellion also reached parts of the east and north."

[19]"(they) generated no coherent ideology or programme on which to build a new order.""What distinguished the events of 1857 was their scale and the fact that for a short time they posed a military threat to British dominance in the Ganges Plain."

[20]"The events of 1857–58 in India, ... marked a major watershed not only in the history of British India but also of British imperialism as a whole.", , and

[21]"Queen Victoria's Proclamation of 1858 laid the foundation for Indian secularism and established the semi-legal framework that would govern the politics of religion in colonial India for

the next century. .. It promised civil equality for Indians regardless of their religious affiliation, and state non-interference in Indians' religious affairs. Although the Proclamation lacked the legal authority of a constitution, generations of Indians cited the Queen's proclamation in order to claim, and to defend, their right to religious freedom." (page 23)Metcalf & Metcalf 2006, pp. 100–103.

[22]The proclamation to the "Princes, Chiefs, and People of India," issued by Queen Victoria on November 1, 1858. "We hold ourselves bound to the natives of our Indian territories by the same obligation of duty which bind us to all our other subjects." (p. 2)

[23]"When the governance of India was transferred from the East India Company to the Crown in 1858, she (Queen Victoria) and Prince Albert intervened in an unprecedented fashion to turn the proclamation of the transfer of power into a document of tolerance and clemency. .. they ... insisted on the clause that stated that the people of India would enjoy the same protection as all subjects of Britain. Over time, this royal intervention led to the Proclamation of 1858 becoming known in the Indian subcontinent as 'the Magna Carta of Indian liberties', a phrase which Indian nationalists such as Gandhi later took up as they sought to test equality under imperial law" (pages 38–39)Brown 1994, pp. 85–86.

[24]"In purely legal terms, (the proclamation) kept faith with the principles of liberal imperialism and appeared to hold out the promise that British rule would benefit Indians and Britons alike. But as is too often the case with noble statements of faith, reality fell far short of theory, and the failure on the part of the British to live up to the wording of the proclamation would later be used by Indian nationalists as proof of the hollowness of imperial principles. (page 76)""Indian soldiers and the rural population over a large part of northern India showed their mistrust of their rulers and their alienation from them. .. For all their talk of improvement, the new rulers were as yet able to offer very little in the way of positive inducements for Indians to acquiesce in the rule."

[25]"Ignoring ...the conciliatory proclamation of Queen Victoria in 1858, Britishers in India saw little reason to grant Indians a greater control over their own affairs. Under these circumstances, it was not long before the seed-idea of nationalism implanted by their reading of Western books began to take root in the minds of intelligent and energetic Indians.""Many Indians took up arms against the British, if for very diverse reasons. Explanations have therefore to concentrate on the motives of those who actually rebelled.""On the other hand, a very large number actually fought for the British, while the majority remained apparently acqueiscent."

[26]to

[27]*A Matter of Honour – an Account of the Indian Army, its Officers and Men*, Philip Mason, , page 261

[28]Essential histories, The Indian Rebellion 1857–1858, Gregory Fremont-Barnes, Osprey 2007, page 25

[29]From Sepoy to Subedar – Being the Life and Adventures of Subedar Sita Ram, a Native Officer of the Bengal Army, edited by James Lunt, , page 172

[30]Hyam, R (2002) Britain's Imperial Century, 1815–1914 Third Edition, Palgrave Macmillan, Basingstoke P135

[31]Headrick, Daniel R. "The Tools of Empire: Technology and European Imperialism in the Nineteenth Century". Oxford University Press, 1981, p.88

[32]The only troops to be armed with the Enfield rifle, and hence the greased cartridges, were the British HM 60th Rifles stationed at Meerut

[33]M. Edwardes, *Red Year: The Indian Rebellion of 1857* (London: Cardinal, 1975), p. 23

[34]G. W. Forrest, *Selections from the letters, despatches and other state papers preserved in the Military department of the government of India, 1857–58* (1893), pp. 8–12, available at archive.org https://archive.org/details/selectionsfroml00forrgoog

[35], ,

[36], ,

[37]Susanne Hoeber Rudolph, Lloyd I Rudolph. "Living with Difference in India", *The Political Quarterly*:71 (s1) (2000), 20–38.

[38]» Sepoy Mutiny of 1857 Postcolonial Studies @ Emory http://www.english.emory.edu/Bahri/Mutiny.html. English.emory.edu (23 March 1998). Retrieved on 12 July 2013.

[39]Seema Alavi *The Sepoys and the Company* (Delhi: Oxford University Press) 1998 p. 5

[40] Memorandum from Lieutenant-Colonel W. St. L. Mitchell (CO of the 19th BNI) to Major A. H. Ross about his troop's refusal to accept the Enfield cartridges, 27 February 1857, Archives of Project South Asia, South Dakota State University and Missouri Southern State University http://projectsouthasia.sdstate.edu/docs/history/primarydocs/War%20of%201857/Indian%20Mutiny--Ch1/letter%2031.htm

[41] "The Indian Mutiny of 1857", Col. G. B. Malleson, reprint 2005, Rupa & Co. Publishers, New Delhi

[42] Durendra Nath Sen, page 50 *Eighteen Fifty-Seven*, The Publications Division, Ministry of Information & Broadcasting, Government of India, May 1957

[43] Sir John Kaye & G.B. Malleson.: *The Indian Mutiny of 1857*, (Delhi: Rupa & Co.) reprint 2005 p49

[44] Dr. Surendra Nath Sen, pages 71–73 "Eighteen Fifty-Seven", Publications Division, Ministry of Information & Broadcasting, Government of India

[45] Dalrymple, *The Last Moghul*, pp.223–224

[46] Michael Edwardes, *Battles of the Indian Mutiny*, pp 52–53

[47] Zachary Nunn. The British Raj http://www.drake.edu/artsci/PolSci/ssjrnl/2001/nunn.html

[48] *Indian Army Uniforms under the British – Infantry*, W.Y. Carman, Morgan-Grampian Books 1969, p. 107

[49] A.H. Amin, Orbat.com http://orbat.com/site/cimh/india/bengalarmy1857.html

[50] Lessons from 1857 http://www.newstodaynet.com/guest/210607gu1.htm

[51] The Indian Army: 1765 – 1914 http://www.bharat-rakshak.com/LAND-FORCES/Army/Images-1765c.html

[52] The Indin Mutiny 1857–58, Gregory Fremont-Barnes, Osprey 2007, page 34

[53] God's Acre http://www.hindu.com/mp/2006/10/28/stories/2006102801590100.htm. The Hindu Metro Plus Delhi. 28 October 2006.

[54] 'The Rising: The Ballad of Mangal Pandey' http://www.jonathanforeman.com/movies/mangal.html . Daily Mail, 27 August 2005

[55] essential histories, the Indian Mutiny 1857–58, Gregory Fremont-Barnes, Osprey 2007, p.40

[56] *The story of Cawnpore: The Indian Mutiny 1857*, Capt. Mowbray Thomson, Brighton, Tom Donovan, 1859, pp. 148–159.

[57] Essential Histories, the Indian Mutiny 1857–58, Gregory Fremont-Barnes, Osprey 2007, page 49

[58] S&T magazine No. 121 (September 1998), page 56

[59] *A History of the Indian Mutiny* by G. W. Forrest, London, William Blackwood, 1904

[60] *Kaye's and Malleson's History of the Indian Mutiny*. Longman's, London, 1896. *Footnote, p. 257.*

[61] Edwardes, *Battles of the Indian Mutiny*, p.56

[62] Essential Histories, the Indian Mutiny 1857–58, Gregory Fremont-Barnes, Osprey 2007, page 53

[63] S&T magazine No. 121 (September 1998), page 58

[64] John Harris, The Indian mutiny, Wordsworth military library 2001, page 92,

[65] J.W. Sherer, *Daily Life during the Indian Mutiny*, 1858, p. 56

[66] Andrew Ward, *Our bones are scattered – The Cawnpore massacres and the Indian Mutiny of 1857*, John Murray, 1996

[67] Ramson, Martin & Ramson, Edward, *The Indian Empire, 1858*

[68] Michael Edwardes, *Battles of the Indian Mutiny*, Pan, 1963

[69] Units of the Army of the Madras Presidency wore blue rather than black shakoes or forage caps

[70] Essential Histories, the Indian Mutiny 1857–58, Gregory Fremont-Barnes, Osprey 2007, page 79

[71] Lachmi Bai Rani of Jhansi, the Jeanne d'Arc of India (1901), White, Michael (Michael Alfred Edwin), 1866, New York: J.F. Taylor & Company, 1901

[72] Charles Allen, *Soldier Sahibs*, p.276

[73] Charles Allen, *Soldier Sahibs*, pp. 290–293

[74] Hibbert, *The Great Mutiny*, p.163

[75] Charles Allen, *Soldier Sahibs*, p.283

[76]Dr Surendra Nath Sen, pages 343–344 *Eighteen Fifty-Seven*, Ministry of Information, Government of India 1957

[77]*John Sergeant's Tracks of Empire*, BBC4 programme.

[78]Turnbull, CM 'Convicts in the Straits Settlements 1826–1827' in Journal of the Malaysian Branch of the Royal Asiatic Society, 1970, 43, 1, P100

[79]Straits Times, 23 August 1857

[80]Arnold, D (1983) 'White colonization and labour in nineteenth-century India', Journal of Imperial and Commonwealth History, 11, P144

[81]The cost of the rebellion in terms of human suffering was immense. Two great cities, Delhi and Lucknow, were devastated by fighting and by the plundering of the victorious British. Where the countryside resisted, as in parts of Awadh, villages were burnt. Mutineers and their supporters were often killed out of hand. British civilians, including women and children, were murdered as well as the British officers of the sepoy regiments."The cost of the rebellion in terms of human suffering was immense. Two great cities, Delhi and Lucknow, were devastated by fighting and by the plundering of the victorious British. Where the countryside resisted, as in parts of Awadh, villages were burnt. Mutineers and their supporters were often killed out of hand. British civilians, including women and children, were murdered as well as the British officers of the sepoy regiments."

[82]*Sahib: The British Soldier in India 1750–1914* Richard Holmes HarperCollins 2005

[83]Punch, 24 October 1857

[84]Dalrymple, *The Last Moghul*, pp.374

[85]The Friend of India reprinted in South Australian Advertiser, 2 October 1860

[86]Rajit K. Mazumder, The Indian Army and the Making of the Punjab. (Delhi, Permanent Black, 2003), 11.

[87]W.Y. Carman, page 107 *Indian Army Uniforms – Infantry*, Morgan-Grampian London 1969

[88]Philip Mason, page 238 "A Matter of Honour",

[89]Philip Mason, page 319 "A Matter of Honour",

[90]Authorisation contained in General Order 363 of 1858 and General Order 733 of 1859

[91]First Indian War of Independence http://www.kamat.com/kalranga/itihas/1857.htm 8 January 1998

[92]A number of dispossessed dynasts, both Hindu and Muslim, exploited the well-founded caste-suspicions of the sepoys and made these simple folk their cat's paw in gamble for recovering their thrones. The last scions of the Delhi Mughals or the Oudh Nawabs and the Peshwa, can by no ingenuity be called fighters for Indian freedom *Hindusthan Standard, Puja Annual, 195 p. 22* referenced in the *Truth about the Indian mutiny* article by Dr Ganda Singh

[93]In the light of the available evidence, we are forced to the conclusion that the uprising of 1857 was not the result of careful planning, nor were there any master-minds behind it. As I read about the events of 1857, I am forced to the conclusion that the Indian national character had sunk very low. The leaders of the revolt could never agree. They were mutually jealous and continually intrigued against one another. .. In fact these personal jealousies and intrigues were largely responsible for the Indian defeat.Maulana Abul Kalam Azad, Surendranath Sen: Eighteen Fifty-seven (Appx. X & Appx. XV)

[94]German National Geographic article https://web.archive.org/web/20050503231048/http://www.nationalgeographic.de/php/entdecken/wettbewerb2/forum.php3?command=show&id=3118&root=3052

[95]The Empire, Sydney, Australia, 11 July 1857, or Taranaki Herald, New Zealand, 29 August 1857

[96]Michael Adas, "Twentieth Century Approaches to the Indian Mutiny of 1857–58," *Journal of Asian History,* 1971, Vol. 5 Issue 1, pp 1–19

[97]It includes essays by historians Eric Stokes, Christopher Bayly, Rudrangshu Mukherjee, Tapti Roy, Rajat K. Ray and others.

[98]For the latest research see Crispin Bates, ed., *Mutiny at the Margins: New Perspectives on the Indian Uprising of 1857: Volume I: Anticipations and Experiences in the Locality* (2013)

[99]Thomas R. Metcalf, "Rural society and British rule in nineteenth century India." *Journal of Asian Studies* 39#1 (1979): 111–119.

[100]M. Farooqui, trans (2010) *Besieged: voices from Delhi 1857* Penguin Books

[101] Kim A. Wagner, "The Marginal Mutiny: The New Historiography of the Indian Uprising of 1857," *History Compass* 9/10 (2011): 760–766, quote p 760

[102] See also

[103] Sabbaq Ahmed, "Ideology and Muslim militancy in India: Selected case studies of the 1857 Indian rebellion." (PhD Dissertation, Victoria University of Wellington (NZ), 2015). online http://researcharchive.vuw.ac.nz/xmlui/handle/10063/4660

[104] *The Indian Mutiny and Victorian Trauma* by Christopher Herbert, Princeton University Press, Princeton 2007

[105] *The History of the Indian Mutiny: Giving a detailed account of the sepoy insurrection in India* by Charles Ball, The London Printing and Publishing Company, London, 1860

[106] V.D. Savarkar argues that the rebellion was a war of Indian independence. *The Indian War of Independence: 1857* (Bombay: 1947 [1909]). Most historians have seen his arguments as discredited, with one venturing so far as to say, 'It was neither first, nor national, nor a war of independence.' Eric Stokes has argued that the rebellion was actually a variety of movements, not one movement. *The Peasant Armed* (Oxford: 1980). See also S.B. Chaudhuri, *Civil Rebellion in the Indian Mutinies 1857–1859* (Calcutta: 1957)

[107] The Indian Mutiny, Spilsbury Julian, Orion, 2007

[108] S&T magazine issue 121 (September 1988), page 20

[109] The communal hatred led to ugly communal riots in many parts of U.P. The green flag was hoisted and Muslims in Bareilly, Bijnor, Moradabad, and other places the Muslims shouted for the revival of Muslim kingdom." R. C. Majumdar: *Sepoy Mutiny and Revolt of 1857* (page 2303-31)

[110] Sitaram Yechury. The Empire Strikes Back http://hindustantimes.com/news/181_1896809, 00120001.htm . Hindustan Times. January 2006.

[111] http://www.oup.com/uk/catalogue/?ci=9780198731139

[112] http://www.thehistorypress.co.uk/index.php/victoria-s-scottish-lion-26465.html

[113] http://www.jamesleasor.com/the-red-fort/

[114] https://books.google.com/books?id=dyQuAgAAQBAJ

[115] //www.jstor.org/stable/23611115

[116] //doi.org/10.1017/S0026749X00016097

[117] //www.jstor.org/stable/312880

[118] //doi.org/10.1017/S0026749X00013913

[119] //www.jstor.org/stable/312615

[120] //doi.org/10.1006/jhge.2000.0236

[121] //doi.org/10.1093/past/142.1.169

[122] //www.jstor.org/stable/651200

[123] //doi.org/10.2307/3517586

[124] //www.jstor.org/stable/313141

[125] //doi.org/10.1080/0043824032000078072

[126] //www.jstor.org/stable/3560211

[127] //doi.org/10.1093/past/128.1.92

[128] //www.jstor.org/stable/651010

[129] //doi.org/10.1093/past/142.1.178

[130] //www.jstor.org/stable/651201

[131] //doi.org/10.1017/S0026749X00016115

[132] //www.jstor.org/stable/312882

[133] //doi.org/10.1017/s0018246x00010554

[134] //www.jstor.org/stable/2638016

[135] //www.worldcat.org/oclc/852404214

[136] http://www.csas.ed.ac.uk/mutiny/

[137] http://www.let.leidenuniv.nl/pdf/geschiedenis/EJES%20Erll%20final.pdf

[138] //www.jstor.org/stable/4419570

[139] //doi.org/10.2307/1345889

[140] //www.jstor.org/stable/1345889

[141] //doi.org/10.1111/j.1478-0542.2011.00799.x

[142] http://digital.library.upenn.edu/women/inglis/lucknow/lucknow.html

[143]http://digital.library.upenn.edu/women/writers.html
[144]https://www.britannica.com/technology/Lee-Enfield-rifle
[145]http://www.jamesleasor.com/follow-the-drum/.
[146]//tools.wmflabs.org/ftl/cgi-bin/ftl?st=wp&su=Indian+Rebellion+of+1857&library=OLBP
[147]//tools.wmflabs.org/ftl/cgi-bin/ftl?st=wp&su=Indian+Rebellion+of+1857
[148]//tools.wmflabs.org/ftl/cgi-bin/ftl?st=wp&su=Indian+Rebellion+of+1857&library=0CHOOSE0
[149]http://dsal.uchicago.edu/reference/schwartzberg/fullscreen.html?object=099
[150]http://defencejournal.com/dec99/1857.htm
[151]http://www.britishempire.co.uk/forces/armycampaigns/indiancampaigns/mutiny/mutiny.htm
[152]http://www.marxists.org/archive/marx/works/1857/india/index.htm
[153]Banke, Bardiya, Kanchanpur and Kailali, also known as "New Kingdom" were given to Jung Bahadur in 1860, 1 November.
[154]//en.wikipedia.org/w/index.php?title=Template:Part_of_History_of_India&action=edit
[155]//en.wikipedia.org/w/index.php?title=Template:Colonial_India&action=edit
[156]"Chapter 5: Early Modern India II: Company Raj", "Chapter 3: The East India Company Raj, 1772–1850", "Chapter 7: Company Raj and Indian Society 1757 to 1857, Reinvention and Reform of Tradition".
[157]Oxford English Dictionary, 2nd edition, 1989: Hindi, *rāj*, from Skr. *rāj*: to reign, rule; cognate with L. *rēx*, *rēg-is*, OIr. *rī*, *rīg* king (see RICH).
[158]James A. Williamson, *A Short History of British Expansion. The Old Colonial Empire*, Macmillan & Co Ltd, London, Third edition, 1955, p. 408.
[159]John Keay, *The Honourable Company, A History of the English East India Company*, Macmillan Publishing Company, New York, 1994, p. 319–324.
[160]Wickwire, p. 19
[161]http://www.indianmilitaryhistory.org/battles/baji%20rao%20I%20at%20Kharda.htm
[162], ,
[163]"in Council," *i.e.* in concert with the advice of the Council.
[164]Quoted in
[165]David Gilmour, *The Ruling Caste: Imperial Lives in the Victorian Raj* (2005)
[166]Colin Newbury, "Patronage and Professionalism: Manning a Transitional Empire, 1760–1870." *Journal of Imperial and Commonwealth History* (2013) 42#2 pp: 193-213.
[167]Majumdar, Mohini Lal. *The imperial post offices of British India, 1837-1914* (Phila Publications, 1990)
[168]Stockton and Darlington Railway
[169]Thorner, Daniel. "Great Britain and the development of India's railways." *Journal of Economic History* 1951; 11(4): 389-402. online http://journals.cambridge.org/abstract_S0022050700085120
[170]https://books.google.com/books?id=0oVra0ulQ3QC
[171]https://books.google.com/books?id=WJ7BNOmQvwcC
[172]https://books.google.com/books?id=Eq7tAAAAMAAJ
[173]https://books.google.com/books?id=hlf9u1asHTAC
[174]https://books.google.com/books?id=V73N8js5ZgAC
[175]https://books.google.com/books?hl=en&lr=&id=PQOtAgAAQBAJ
[176]https://books.google.com/books?id=wQJuAAAAMAAJ
[177]https://books.google.com/books?id=uzOmy2y0Zh4C&pg=PA271
[178]https://books.google.com/books?id=iuESgYNYPl0C
[179]https://books.google.com/books?id=6iNuAAAAMAAJ
[180]https://books.google.com/books?id=Es6x4u_g19UC
[181]https://books.google.com/books?id=GQ-2VH1LO_EC
[182]https://books.google.com/books?id=CDwwAQAAIAAJ
[183]https://books.google.com/books?id=0K3GZfqCabsC
[184]https://books.google.com/books?id=JT0wAQAAIAAJ
[185]https://books.google.com/books?id=lxkjJAAACAAJ
[186]https://books.google.com/books?id=MGJQKg4Tja0C
[187]https://books.google.com/books?id=fX2zMfWqIzMC

[188]https://www.amazon.com/Oxford-History-British-Empire-Nineteenth/dp/0199246785
[189]https://books.google.com/books?id=cE8Y_gAACAAJ
[190]//doi.org/10.2307/172481
[191]//www.jstor.org/stable/172481
[192]//doi.org/10.1111/j.1468-0289.2008.00438.x
[193]//doi.org/10.2307/2808021
[194]//www.jstor.org/stable/2808021
[195]//doi.org/10.1016/j.eeh.2007.11.002
[196]//doi.org/10.1017/S0026749X00013901
[197]//www.jstor.org/stable/312614
[198]//doi.org/10.2307/312523
[199]//www.jstor.org/stable/312523
[200]//www.jstor.org/stable/313141
[201]//doi.org/10.1086/649322
[202]//www.jstor.org/stable/301944
[203]//doi.org/10.1017/S0026749X00013986
[204]//www.jstor.org/stable/312868
[205]//doi.org/10.1257/089533002760278749
[206]//www.jstor.org/stable/3216953
[207]https://books.google.com/books?id=RlQBAAAAQAAJ&dq=%22employed+the+arm+of+political+injustice%22&cad=0
[208]//www.worldcat.org/oclc/63943320
[209]https://archive.org/details/historicaleccles00calciala
[210]https://archive.org/details/annalshonorable00brucgoog
[211]https://archive.org/details/annalshonorable01brucgoog
[212]https://archive.org/details/historyindiafro02marsgoog
[213]http://lcweb2.loc.gov/frd/cs/
[214]http://lcweb2.loc.gov/frd/cs/intoc.html
[215]http://lcweb2.loc.gov/frd/cs/pktoc.html
[216]https//www.academia.edu
[217]National Army Museum
[218]Dalrymple (2006), pp. 22–23
[219]Dalrymple (2006), p. 153
[220]Stokes (1973)
[221]Mason, Philip (1974), pages 203-204 A Matter of Honour", London: Holt, Rhinehart & Winston,
[222]Mason, Philip (1974), page 190 "A Matter of Honour", London: Holt, Rhinehart & Winston,
[223]Mason, Philip (1974), page 225 "A Matter of Honour", London: Holt, Rhinehart & Winston,
[224]Alavi (1998), p. 5
[225]Mason, Philip (1974), page 226 "A Matter of Honour", London: Holt, Rhinehart & Winston,
[226]Edwardes, p. 3
[227]Mason, Philip (1974), page 264 "A Matter of Honour", London: Holt, Rhinehart & Winston,
[228]Mason, Philip (1974), pages 226-228 "A Matter of Honour", London: Holt, Rhinehart & Winston,
[229]Mason, Philip (1974), page 236 "A Matter of Honour", London: Holt, Rhinehart & Winston,
[230]Mason, Philip (1974), pages 186 and 313 "A Matter of Honour", London: Holt, Rhinehart & Winston,
[231]Hibbert (1978), pp. 51-54
[232]Mason, Philip (1974), pages 291-292 "A Matter of Honour", London: Holt, Rhinehart & Winston,
[233]Mason, Philip (1974), pages 305-306 "A Matter of Honour", London: Holt, Rhinehart & Winston,
[234]Saul, David (2003), page 294 "The Indian Mutiny", Penguin Books,
[235]Mason, Philip (1974), page 263 "A Matter of Honour", London: Holt, Rhinehart & Winston,
[236]Wolpert (2009), p. 240
[237]Pionke (2004), pp. 86-87

[238] http://www.national-army-museum.ac.uk/exhibitions/indiaRising/
[239] https://books.google.com/books?id=OH6ml-qUK7sC&pg=PA87
[240] //doi.org/10.1093/past/58.1.136
[241] http://www.enfield-snider.com/Enfield%20P59.htm
[242] *Mangal Pandey: True Story of an Indian Revolutionary*, 2005, Rupa & Co. Mumbai
[243] Saul David, page 70, "The Indian Mutiny", Penguin Books 2003
[244] Saul David, page 69, "The Indian Mutiny", Penguin Books 2003
[245] pages 68-70 *The Great Mutiny*, Christopher Hibbert, 1978, Penguin Books
[246] Surendra Nath Sen, page 50 *Eighteen Fifty-Seven*, Publications Division, Ministry of Information & Broadcasting, Government of India, May 1957
[247] Surendra Nath Sen, page 48 *Eighteen Fifty-Seven*, The Publications Division, Ministry of Information & Broadcasting, Government of India, May 1957
[248] *Chambers 20th Century Dictionary*, W. & R. Chambers Limited, Edinburgh, 1983
[249] *Funk and Wagnall's New Standard Dictionary*, The Standard Dictionary Company, London and New York, 1929
[250] Mangal Pandey Park, Amusement Parks / Auditoriums / Clubs https://www.kmcgov.in/KMCPortal/jsp/KMCAmusementPark.jsp#a12, kmcgov.in
[251] http://www.tribuneindia.com/2005/20050814/spectrum/book10.htm
[252] http://www.indianexpress.com/res/web/pIe/print.php?content_id=72790
[253] Analysis of the 1857 War of Independence – Defence Journal http://www.defencejournal.com/dec99/1857.htm
[254] John Buckley (soldier), George Forrest (VC), William Raynor
[255] Defence Journal http://www.defencejournal.com/dec99/1857.htm
[256] Major A. H. Amin, orbat.com http://orbat.com/site/history/historical/india/bengalarmy1857.html
[257] The Bengal Fusiliers were "European" infantry, mainly Irish, raised by the Honourable East India Company. They were later absorbed into the British Army
[258] Commanding officer of the 52nd Foot, not to be confused with Sir Colin Campbell, soon to be appointed Commander-in-chief in India
[259] https://books.google.com/books?id=wYW5J-jQn8QC
[260] http://www.pinetreeweb.com/roberts-xiii.htm
[261] https://web.archive.org/web/20070926231205/http://www.kapadia.com/NativeNarrative/NarrativeofMunshiJeewanLal.htm
[262] G. W. Williams, "Memorandum", printed with Narrative of the Events in the NWP in 1857–58 (Calcutta, n.d.), section on Kanpur (hereafter Narrative Kanpur), p. 20: "A man of great influence in the city, and a government official, has related a circumstance that is strange, if true, viz. that whilst the massacre was being carried on at the ghat, a trooper of the 2nd Cavalry, reported to the Nana, then at Savada house, that his enemies, their wives and children were exterminated ... On hearing which, the Nana replied, that lfor the destruction of women and children, there was no necessity' and directed the sowar to return with an order to stay their slaughter". See also J. W. Kaye, History of the Sepoy War in India, 1857–58, 3 vols. (Westport, 1971 repr.), ii, p. 258. (This reprint of Kaye's work carries the title History of the Indian Mutiny of 1857–58.)
[263] Hibbert, Christopher. *The Great Mutiny: India, 1857*. Penguin, 1980, p. 212. 0140047522.
[264] Raugh, Harold E. *The Victorians at War, 1815–1914: An Encyclopedia of British Military History*. ABC-CLIO, 2004, p. 89. 1576079252.
[265] Kalpi Devi, "Nana Sahib's daughter Maina was burnt alive by Britishers", Vol. "Balindan", Hindupanch news report, 1858. (Hindi) http://www.philoid.com/epub/ncert/9/119/ihks105
[266] Kalpi Devi, "Nana Sahib's daughter Maina was burnt alive by Britishers", Vol. "Balindan", Hindupanch news report, 1858. (Hindi) http://www.philoid.com/epub/ncert/9/119/ihks105
[267] https://web.archive.org/web/20050510005945/http://www.geocities.com/Broadway/Alley/5443/indmut4.htm
[268] http://www.britishempire.co.uk/forces/armycampaigns/indiancampaigns/mutiny/cawnporeimages.htm
[269] //tools.wmflabs.org/geohack/geohack.php?pagename=Siege_of_Cawnpore¶ms=26.4607_N_80.3334_E_source:wikidata
[270] https://www.worldcat.org/oclc/200654

[271] http://www.thehistorypress.co.uk/index.php/victoria-s-scottish-lion-26465.html
[272] //tools.wmflabs.org/ftl/cgi-bin/ftl?st=wp&su=Siege+of+Lucknow&library=OLBP
[273] //tools.wmflabs.org/ftl/cgi-bin/ftl?st=wp&su=Siege+of+Lucknow
[274] //tools.wmflabs.org/ftl/cgi-bin/ftl?st=wp&su=Siege+of+Lucknow&library=0CHOOSE0
[275] http://digital.library.upenn.edu/women/bartrum/lucknow/lucknow.html
[276] http://digital.library.upenn.edu/women/writers.html
[277] http://digital.library.upenn.edu/women/inglis/lucknow/lucknow.html
[278] https://books.google.com/books?id=9msBAAAAQAAJ
[279] http://www.defencejournal.com/2000/mar/lucknow.htm
[280] //tools.wmflabs.org/geohack/geohack.php?pagename=Siege_of_Lucknow¶ms=26.8606_N_80.9158_E_source:wikidata
[281] Pakistan Defence Journal http://www.defencejournal.com/2000/feb/central-indian.htm
[282] *Essential Histories, the Indian Mutiny 1857-58 https://books.google.com/books?id=DVoNNeKsKmgC*, Gregory Fremont-Barnes, Osprey 2007, p. 79
[283] Edwardes (1975), pp.117-19
[284] Edwardes (1975), p.119, citing Vishnu Godse *Majha Pravas*, Poona, 1948, in Marathi, p.67
[285] Edwardes (1975), p.119
[286] Edwardes (1975), pp.120-21
[287] Edwardes (1975) p.121
[288] Edwardes, Michael (1975) *Red Year*. London: Sphere Books; p. 124
[289] Singh, Sarbans (1993) *Battle Honours of the Indian Army 1757 - 1971*. Vision Books (New Delhi)
[290] //tools.wmflabs.org/geohack/geohack.php?pagename=Siege_of_Arrah¶ms=25.5573_N_84.6658_E_type:event
[291] Dodd 1859, pp. 48–58.
[292] Sieveking 1910, pp. 18–19.
[293] Halls 1860, p. 9.
[294] Sieveking 1910, p. 18.
[295] Halls 1860, pp. 9–10.
[296] Sieveking 1910, p. 43.
[297] Trevelyan 1864, p. 92.
[298] Dodd 1859, p. 267.
[299] Sieveking 1910, p. 19.
[300] Sieveking 1910, p. 150.
[301] Trevelyan 1864, p. 89.
[302] Halls 1860, p. 33.
[303] Sieveking 1910, pp. 19–20.
[304] Trevelyan 1864, p. 90.
[305] Sieveking 1910, p. 21.
[306] Sieveking 1910, p. 22.
[307] Halls 1860, p. 14.
[308] Boyle 1858, p. 7.
[309] Halls 1860, p. 67.
[310] Sieveking 1910, p. 25.
[311] Boyle 1858, p. 8.
[312] Halls 1860, p. 26.
[313] Halls 1860, pp. 28–31.
[314] Halls 1860, p. 34.
[315] Tayler 1858, pp. 30–40.
[316] Trevelyan 1864, p. 72.
[317] Tayler 1858, pp. 39–40.
[318] Trevelyan 1864, p. 84.
[319] Forrest 2006, p. 417.
[320] Sieveking 1910, p. 50.
[321] O'Malley 1906, p. 128.
[322] Sieveking 1910, p. 28.

[323]Sieveking 1910, p. 46.
[324]Sieveking 1910, pp. 41–45.
[325]Forrest 2006, p. 438.
[326]Sieveking 1910, p. 44.
[327]Sieveking 1910, pp. 30–31.
[328]Trevelyan 1864, p. 93.
[329]Tayler 1858, p. 78.
[330]Dodd 1859, p. 270.
[331]Tayler 1858, pp. 79–81.
[332]Best 2016, Patna.
[333]Trevelyan 1864, p. 94.
[334]Sieveking 1910, pp. 51–53.
[335]Dodd 1859, p. 271.
[336]Sieveking 1910, p. 58.
[337]Halls 1860, pp. 46–48.
[338]Tayler 1858, p. 83.
[339]Forrest 2006, p. 448.
[340]Sieveking 1910, p. 83.
[341]Sieveking 1910, p. 81.
[342]Sieveking 1910, p. 74.
[343]Sieveking 1910, p. 90.
[344]Trevelyan 1864, p. 109.
[345]Halls 1860, pp. 52–53.
[346]Halls 1860, p. 54.
[347]Singh 1993, p. 10.
[348]Sieveking 1910, p. 80.
[349]Trevelyan 1864, pp. 91–92.
[350]Prichard 1869, p. 43.
[351]Trevelyan 1864, p. 111.
[352]https://books.google.com/?id=JmZGDAAAQBAJ&pg=PT45&lpg=PT45&dq=Charles+Dunbar+siege+of+Arrah#v=onepage&q=Charles%20Dunbar%20siege%20of%20Arrah&f=false
[353]https://books.google.com/?id=f10oAAAAYAAJ&printsec=frontcover&pg=GBS.PA3
[354]//www.worldcat.org/oclc/794643208
[355]https://archive.org/stream/historyofindianr00doddrich#page/n7/mode/2up
[356]//www.worldcat.org/oclc/248904480
[357]https://books.google.com/?id=VDmS9noPkbkC&pg=PA414&lpg=PA414&dq=dinapore+mutiny#v=onepage&q=dinapore%20mutiny&f=false
[358]https://archive.org/details/twomonthsinarrah00hallrich
[359]//www.worldcat.org/oclc/877907
[360]https://archive.org/details/shahabadbylssoma00omal
[361]//www.worldcat.org/oclc/252001000
[362]https://archive.org/details/administrationof01pricuoft
[363]//www.worldcat.org/oclc/908361033
[364]https://archive.org/details/turningpointinin00sieviala
[365]//www.worldcat.org/oclc/13203015
[366]https://archive.org/details/patnacrisisorthr00taylrich
[367]//www.worldcat.org/oclc/748092097
[368]https://archive.org/details/competitionwall01trevgoog
[369]//www.worldcat.org/oclc/308875870

Article Sources and Contributors

The sources listed for each article provide more detailed licensing information including the copyright status, the copyright owner, and the license conditions.

Indian Rebellion of 1857 *Source:* https://en.wikipedia.org/w/index.php?oldid=853536324 *License:* Creative Commons Attribution-Share Alike 3.0 *Contributors:* 564dude, AAJ KHAN, Abecedare, Adamgerber80, Adv Avijit Ghoshal, Alexf, Appu man123, Arjayay, Billywebs, Buistr, CASSIOPEIA, CLCStudent, CambridgeBayWeather, Ch sonuu, Chewings72, Chris the speller, Clarityfiend, ClueBot NG, Cplakidas, Dahiyapulkit, Daniel Case, Daphne Lantier, Darylgolden, DatSyrupGuy, Deadwikipedian, Dipak pambhar, Donner60, DuncanHill, Ehudtal, El C, Eragonshadowslasher, Exemplo347, FRibeiro66, Fowler&fowler, Future12340, FuzhouneseMinpride, Gautam Sah, Gazal world, GeneralizationsAreBad, GenuineArt, Georgestar99, Gewingewin, Gilliam, Gladamas, Gotnolifewhatsoever, GreenMeansGo, GrindtXX, Guffydrawers, HLGallon, Haha12345433216678, Happygolucky2005, Heatlineheard, HelgeRieder, Highpeaks35, Hijiri88, HyperGaruda, Imdabes7, Indian Writer2, Infinenoi, Irondome, Jalaluddin Muhammad, Jim1138, Jiten D, Joihazarika, Jon C., Jonesey95, Jop2～enwiki, JosephusOfJerusalem, Kautilya3, Kavitha Shankaran, Kulsin567, KylieTastic, Laszlo Panaflex, Laughing sandbags, Lawrence501, Leventio, Liberal Humanist, LindsayH, Lovely amit, MBlaze Lightning, Magioladitis, Mallu Techiez, Materialscientist, MatthewVanitas, Mccapra, Md183, Necrothesp, New786678, Newblog 32, Nizil Shah, Notthebestusername, ParadiseDesertOasis8888, Peterbruce01, Pharaoh of the Wizards, Polylerus, Rattans, ReagentsParks, RegentsPark, Rjwilmsi, Robertkamau, Sakshi Dalla, Salociin, ScrapIronIV, Sennacannavaro, Serols, Shellwood, Simplexity22, Sirius86, Sjö, Skysmith, Slatersteven, Slugsheir, Socialawareness1, Stumink, Sufalbepari2, Trappist the monk, Umairsy, Utcursch, Wbm1058, Worldbruce, Zingarese, 152 anonymous edits 1

Company rule in India *Source:* https://en.wikipedia.org/w/index.php?oldid=852147199 *License:* Creative Commons Attribution-Share Alike 3.0 *Contributors:* A2soup, Acad Ronin, Ad Orientem, Altetendekrabbe, Amit20081980, Anarcho-statist, AnwarInsaan, Arimaboss, Atticusfinch123, Aumnamahashiva, BD2412, Barthateslisa, Bazonka, Beland, Bender235, Bgwhite, Bhonsale, Bonadea, Bonopartee))mediterin, Boven, Burbak, CAPTAIN RAJU, Candalua, Catpals, Chewings72, ClueBot NG, Colonies Chris, CommonsDelinker, Comp.arch, Credema, DadaNeem, DalQ95, Dananuj, Devgowri, Dewritech, DiscantX, Dispenser, DocWatson42, Donaldduck100, Donner60, DuncanHill, EdwardElric2016, FaisalAbbasid, Faizhaider, Fatbuu, Flyer22 Reborn, Fowler&fowler, Frankalbertson, Furius, G S Palmer, GDibyendu, Gob Lofa, Green daemon, Gryffindor, Gulumeemee, Guy Macon, HLGallon, Hmains, HyperGaruda, Indopug, Italia2006, Jasca Ducato, Jayadevp13, Jethwarp, Jim1138, John of Reading, John.kakoty, Josve05a, K6ka, KH-1, Kapitop, Karada, Knight of BAAWA, L235, Lakun.patra, Lalmohan Babu, Linguist6666, Lkjgfstyugfd, Lobsterthermidor, Locomotive999, Lubiesque, Martinr2006, Materialscientist, Mauls, MilborneOne, Missvain, Msundqvist, Muhammad Umair Mirza, Narky Blert, Needlenose, Newblog 32, NikNaks, O.Koslowski, Ohconfucius, Omnipaedista, Pawyilee, PhnomPencil, Pktlaurence, Plantdrew, Pooyaf, Pratyya Ghosh, Pukkativa, Punyaboy, Quizer SHK, R'n'B, Rattans, Ravi agasarahalli, RedTomato, RegentsPark, Ricky81682, Rjensen, Rjwilmsi, Rodw, SJK, SQGibbon, Salih, Scyfie, Sitush, Skinsmoke, Solomon7968, Srich32977, Srnec, StAnselm, StringRay, Sundostund, Sushilkumarmishra, Sushilmishra, Syz2, Tamravidhir, The Anomebot2, The C of E, The Dawn of Husk, Tinkurider, Titodutta, Tobby72, Trusilver, Twsx, UY Scuti, UsmanKhanDiri, Utcursch, Vgy7ujm, Vigyani, Vilij, WatermillockCommon, Widr, Wikid77, William Harris, Woohookitty, Worldbruce, XavierGreen, Xurei, Yutsi, Zaketo, फ़िलप्रो, ვაჟა მ, 148 anonymous edits 67

Causes of the Indian Rebellion of 1857 *Source:* https://en.wikipedia.org/w/index.php?oldid=852548762 *License:* Creative Commons Attribution-Share Alike 3.0 *Contributors:* 65sharad, ASIM MEMON, Anilbhx, AshLin, Audacity, AusLondonder, AvalerionV, Babitaarora, Buistr, Chinmaya1011, Chip123456, ClueBot NG, Cnwilliams, Colonel Flashman, Crystallizedcarbon, DavidLeighEllis, Discospinster, Drajay1976, Dthomsen8, Echosmoke, Fayenatic london, Flaming Scimitar, Francis Davey, Gilliam, Glane23, Haldraper, Hrishikesh Lokhande, I dream of horses, IWPCHI, Italia2006, Iwilsonp, Jakernet, Jbergste, Jim1138, John of Reading, Jon Acheson, Jon Huggett, KConWiki, Khestwol, Krj373, KylieTastic, Liance, Liberal Humanist, Lightmouse, Magioladitis, Mark Arsten, Materialscientist, Maxis ftw, Metroplex801, Mogism, Monty845, Moonraker, Neveselbert, Niceguyedc, Nizil Shah, Noyster, O.Syed, Ohconfucius, Oshwah, Otolemur crassicaudatus, Piast93, Piguy101, Qzd, R'n'B, Rich Farmbrough, Rjwilmsi, Robcraufurd, Rsloch, Sahiluliik, Sct72, ShakespeareFan00, Shaunagm, Shirik, SilverplateDelta, Sitush, Slatersteven, Sldkdjcslkzxdjszlkxj, Smalljim, SomeRandomUserGuy, Sona haldar, Sphilbrick, Stefanomione, Teles, Temporaluser, Timawesomeness, Tom.Reding, Trappist the monk, Utcursch, Vibh96, Widr, Zocke1r, 159 anonymous edits 117

Mangal Pandey *Source:* https://en.wikipedia.org/w/index.php?oldid=847064036 *License:* Creative Commons Attribution-Share Alike 3.0 *Contributors:* 220 of Borg, AKS.9955, Abhijit Tiwary, Abhinav5696, Adamgerber80, Aditya.tiwari83, Akandkur, Angeldeviltanya, AsceticRose, Ashish Kumar Pandey Delhi university, Avskbhatta, Baddu676, Bgwhite, Bishonen, Bolti bandh, Bpandey89, Buistr, CAPTAIN RAJU, Capankajsmilyo, Chrishitch, Citizen Canine, ClueBot NG, Crystallizedcarbon, Dan Koehl, Dinnypaul, Discospinster, DrSachinYadav, Emerald-wiki, Enock4seth, Eurodyne, Exemplo347, Flyer22 Reborn, Frosty, Gavinkmccarthy, Gopaljirai, Harinarayanan02, HimanginiS, Ibaman, Indiangovt.83, Jethwarp, Jim1138, Jon C., Jupitus Smart, Jusdafax, KGirlTrucker81, Kkm010, MBlaze Lightning, Materialscientist, Mcmatter, MelbourneStar, Muhidden012x2, MusikAnimal, Nadeem 1999, Neatsfoot, Niceguyedc, Noyster, Olidog, Onel5969, Pan nikh, Pandit4580, Parth.297, PrairieKid, Pranavpalliyil, Rajeevranjan1414, Randhirreddy, RegentsPark, Rich Farmbrough, Roland zh, Sakina54322, Serols, Shubham niitvns, Shweta.may8, Sitush, Srinidhikukkila, Strike Eagle, Subhash 008, Tachs, TaqPol, Utcursch, Vchau96, Verbum Veritas, Widr, Winged Blades of Godric, Yamaguchi先生, 212 anonymous edits 126

Siege of Delhi *Source:* https://en.wikipedia.org/w/index.php?oldid=841704767 *License:* Creative Commons Attribution-Share Alike 3.0 *Contributors:* Abecedare, Amerijuanican, Andrwsc, Anjela taneja, Ardfern, Aryan hindustan, Az81964444, Badbuu1000, Baddu676, Beaumont, Ben Ben, Benea, Binggo666, Britmax, Carlson288, Chaosactor, Charles Matthews, Cpt.a.haddock, DBigXray, DemolitionMan, Diggers2004, Dpv, DuncanHill, Duncharris, Ekabhishek, Evecurid, Exemplo347, Faizhaider, Favonian, Fergus the widget, Fowler&fowler, Ginkomithu, GraemeLeggett, Gryffindor, Gwinva, HLGallon, Jaraalbe, John of Reading, Kapitop, Karhana, Kingbird1, LeCalum, LilHelpa, Magicpiano, Mogism, Moxy, Neddyseagoon, NikNaks, Nosaj777, Ohconfucius, Olivander, Omnipaedista, Pahari Sahib, Peltirasia, Profitoftruth85, Quadell, Quibik, Rama's Arrow, Rao Ravindra, Risingstar12, Rjwilmsi, RobotG, Rollingcontributor, Rsloch, SCGC, SOS136, Salociin, Sandip90, Sardanaphalus, Shyamsunder, Sidsahu, Sirlanz, Sitush, Sminthopsis84, SoLando, Srichrome, Sstrauch1955, StAnselm, Tabletop, TeriEmbrey, The Anomebot2, Therash09, Thomas Peardew, Tim!, Tom.Reding, Twas Now, UnbiasedVictory, Wally Wiglet, Wilson44691, Ânes-pur-sàng, Валерий Пасько, 43 anonymous edits 135

Siege of Cawnpore *Source:* https://en.wikipedia.org/w/index.php?oldid=853192459 *License:* Creative Commons Attribution-Share Alike 3.0 *Contributors:* A protohominid, Alfietucker, American Idiot1, Andrew Gray, Ardfern, Arjayay, BD2412, BS Thurner Hof, Baddu676, Bakeysaur99, Bgwhite, Bilsonius, Bookgrrl, Bravo Foxtrot, Buckshot06, Bullzeye, Chandan Guha, Chris the speller, Citation bot 1, Clarityfiend, ClueBot NG, Crowmagnon, Dabbler, Dave6, DemolitionMan, Djbuck1, DocWatson42, Dr doris, DuncanHill, Eselquinoa, Faizhaider, Fatcud, Felix Folio Secundus, Fowler&fowler, Frankly Man, Gmanacsa, GraemeLeggett, Graham87, HLGallon, Harshal1981, Heatlineheard, Honeyabigale, Hongooi, Iridescent, Italia2006, JRPG, JaGa, Jheald, Jocme, KF, Kaayay, KylieTastic, LilHelpa, Lmcelhiney, Materialscientist, Momo san, Moogwrench, MrTwitchy, Mukogodo, Neutrality, Nizil Shah, Nocowardsoulismine, O.Koslowski, Ohconfucius, Ohnoitsjamie, Olivander, Oskanpur, Paradise won, Peripitus, QueenCake, Rcbutcher, Risingstar12, Rocksays23, SDC, SOS136, Salociin, Sardanaphalus, Shellwood, Shyamal, Shyamsunder, Smeat75, Southdevonian, Squid603, StAnselm, Tamagosh, Tbirdofparadise, The Anomebot2, Themightyquill, ThinkingTwice, Tim!, Tom.Reding, Tristan benedict, Urprakhar, Utcursch, Valenciano, Welsh, Worldbruce, Xufanc, Yoc2007, ZfJames, Валерий Пасько, 218 anonymous edits 153

Siege of Lucknow *Source:* https://en.wikipedia.org/w/index.php?oldid=848965209 *License:* Creative Commons Attribution-Share Alike 3.0 *Contributors:* AMCKen, ARAZATI, Aipbookslko, Aitias, Alexbook, Anupam, Apalonius, Arch dude, Ardfern, BS Thurner Hof, Baddu676, Bakeysaur99, Bobblewik, Bobby Awasthi, Brenont, Brookie, Buckshot06, California Girl 21, Carlson288, Chandan Guha, Chris the speller, Chuntuk, Cjrother, Clarityfiend, ClueBot NG, CommonsDelinker, DMacks, Daemonic Kangaroo, Dahliarose, DaltonCastle, DanielCD, DemolitionMan, Dewritech, DivermanAU, Djkeddie, DocWatson42, Dvavasour, ElinorD, Enigmaman, Everyking, Faizhaider, Gaintes, GraemeLeggett, Grenod, Gujuguy, HLGallon, Hairy Dude, Hantsheroes, Hemlock Martinis, Historian, Hlhfoster, Howcheng, Hugo999, IceKarma, IndianGeneralist, Irmgard, Italia2006, Jack1956, Jackyd101, Jainrajat11, Jameswilson, Jaraalbe, JayKiskel, Jnc, John of Reading, Johnalex1, Johnxxx9, Jonathunder, Katieh5584, Keith D, Kingbird1, Knife-in-the-drawer, LiniShu, Lobsterthermidor, Lotje, MAG1, MPS1992, Mandarax, Mary Mark Ockerbloom, Materialscientist, MayerG, McZusatz, Mike hayes, Moxy, Mvdejong, NHSavage, Nauticashades, Navigator1027, Neddyseagoon, Niceguyedc, Nicklott, Nikhilmn2002, Nizil Shah, Ntsimp, Ohconfucius, Old Nol, PBS, PaleoNeonate, Petri Krohn, Pharring, Pinkville, Pramanick, Presidentman, PythosIsAwesome, RFBailey, RP459, Rama's Arrow, Rcbutcher, Remy B, Renata3, RetiredUser2, Rich Farmbrough, Risingstar12, Robertgreer, RobotG, Ruzulo, Salociin, Sandytowel, Sardanaphalus, Ser Amantio di Nicolao, Sharononline, Shell Kinney, Shyamsunder, SlaveToTheWage, Socrates2008, Student7, Susiemorgan, Talon Artaine, Tassedethe, TathD, TeriEmbrey, The Anome, The Anomebot2, The Madras, ThinkingTwice, Tinkswiki, Tjmayerinsf, Tom.Reding, Tomandlu, Tristan benedict, Umairsy, UnbiasedVictory, Utcursch, Vanisaac, Victuallers, Waerloeg, Wally Wiglet, Wee Jimmy, Wikiboy2364, Wikipodiumz, Ânes-pur-sàng, Валерий Пасько, 102 anonymous edits 172

Central Indian campaign of 1858 *Source:* https://en.wikipedia.org/w/index.php?oldid=824587576 *License:* Creative Commons Attribution-Share Alike 3.0 *Contributors:* Ardfern, AshLin, Belovedfreak, Buckshot06, Chandan Guha, Faizhaider, Felix Folio Secundus, Gadget850, HLGallon, Jaraalbe, Jim Sweeney, MKar, Mail2amitabha, Modify, Moonraker, Ndkl, Nizil Shah, R'n'B, Rjwilmsi, RobotG, Sardanaphalus, Sassf, Sfan00 IMG, Shyamsunder, Slatersteven, Srnec, Tavilis, Titodutta, Trident13, Utcursch, Vivek Sarje, Wiki-uk, Ânes-pur-sàng, Валерий Пасько, 7 anonymous edits 192

Siege of Arrah *Source:* https://en.wikipedia.org/w/index.php?oldid=853208214 *License:* Creative Commons Attribution-Share Alike 3.0 *Contributors:* Abductive, Acad Ronin, Anotherclown, Applodion, AustralianRupert, BD2412, Casliber, Charles Matthews, Damien2016, Dank, Exemplo347, GeneralizationsAreBad, HJ Mitchell, Howcheng, Hugo999, I dream of horses, Iazyges, KCVelaga, KConWiki, Kulsin567, Llammakey, Miniapolis, Mr Stephen, PratyushSinha101, Redtigerxyz, Salociin, The Rambling Man, Tim!, Vensatry, Zackmann08, 2 anonymous edits 199

Image Sources, Licenses and Contributors

The sources listed for each image provide more detailed licensing information including the copyright status, the copyright owner, and the license conditions.

Image *Source:* https://en.wikipedia.org/w/index.php?title=File:Indian_Rebellion_of_1857.jpg *License:* Public Domain *Contributors:* Athaenara, File Upload Bot (Magnus Manske), Grandiose, Krinkle, Nizil Shah, OgreBot 2, Rd232, Roland zh, Yann, 1 anonymous edits 1

Image *Source:* https://en.wikipedia.org/w/index.php?title=File:Flag_of_the_British_East_India_Company_(1801).svg *License:* Public Domain *Contributors:* User:Yaddah 1

Image *Source:* https://en.wikipedia.org/w/index.php?title=File:Gwalior_flag.svg *License:* Public Domain *Contributors:* Robert Alfers 1

Image *Source:* https://en.wikipedia.org/w/index.php?title=File:Flag_of_the_Maratha_Empire.svg *License:* Public Domain *Contributors:* DarkEvil 1

Image *Source:* https://en.wikipedia.org/w/index.php?title=File:Flag_of_Awadh.svg *License:* Creative Commons Attribution-Sharealike 3.0 *Contributors:* User:Utcursch 1

Image *Source:* https://en.wikipedia.org/w/index.php?title=File:Flag_of_the_United_Kingdom.svg *License:* Public Domain *Contributors:* Anomie, Good Olfactory, Jo-Jo Eumerus, MSGJ, Mifter 1

Image *Source:* https://en.wikipedia.org/w/index.php?title=File:Flag_of_Nepal_(19th_century-1962).svg *License:* Creative Commons Attribution-Sharealike 3.0 *Contributors:* Orange Tuesday 1

Image *Source:* https://en.wikipedia.org/w/index.php?title=File:Flag_of_Tibet.svg *License:* Public Domain *Contributors:* A ri gi bod, Abu-Dun, Alkari, Anime Addict AA, Arilang1234, BartekChom, ChongDae, Cmadler, Daphne Lantier, Denelson83, Fry1989, Gryffindor, Homo lupus, Hottentot∼commonswiki, Inhorw, MAXXX-309, MB298, Marco Plassio, Mattes, Nightstallion, Reisio, Sarang, SiBr4, Sweeper tamonten, Theo10011, Thisisbossi, Triton, Vinne2, W., Wereldburger758, Wylve, 12 anonymous edits 1

Image *Source:* https://en.wikipedia.org/w/index.php?title=File:Drapeau_Ajaigarh.png *License:* GNU Free Documentation License *Contributors:* User Nataraja on fr.wikipedia 2

Image *Source:* https://en.wikipedia.org/w/index.php?title=File:Alwar_flag.svg *License:* Public Domain *Contributors:* Robert Alfers 2

Image *Source:* https://en.wikipedia.org/w/index.php?title=File:Flag_of_Bharatpur.svg *License:* Public domain *Contributors:* Orange Tuesday (talk) 2

Image *Source:* https://en.wikipedia.org/w/index.php?title=File:Drapeau_Bhopal.svg *License:* Public Domain *Contributors:* User:Ricordisamoa 2

Image *Source:* https://en.wikipedia.org/w/index.php?title=File:Flag_of_Bikaner.svg *License:* Public Domain *Contributors:* Robert Alfers 2

Image *Source:* https://en.wikipedia.org/w/index.php?title=File:Bundi.svg *Contributors:* - 2

Image *Source:* https://en.wikipedia.org/w/index.php?title=File:Asafia_flag_of_Hyderabad_State.png *License:* Public Domain *Contributors:* Yenemus 2

Image *Source:* https://en.wikipedia.org/w/index.php?title=File:Flag_of_Jaipur.svg *License:* Public Domain *Contributors:* Robert Alfers 2

Image *Source:* https://en.wikipedia.org/w/index.php?title=File:Jaoraflag.png *License:* Creative Commons Attribution-Sharealike 3.0 *Contributors:* OgreBot 2, Xufanc 2

Image *Source:* https://en.wikipedia.org/w/index.php?title=File:Flag_of_Jodhpur.svg *License:* Public Domain *Contributors:* PD 2

Image *Source:* https://en.wikipedia.org/w/index.php?title=File:Kapurthala_flag.svg *License:* Public Domain *Contributors:* Robert Alfers 2

Image *Source:* https://en.wikipedia.org/w/index.php?title=File:Flag_Jammu_Kashmir.png *License:* Public Domain *Contributors:* Mikrobølgeovn 2

Image *Source:* https://en.wikipedia.org/w/index.php?title=File:Keonjharflag.jpg *License:* Creative Commons Attribution-Sharealike 3.0 *Contributors:* Mikhail Ryazanov, Slimguy, Xufanc 2

Image *Source:* https://en.wikipedia.org/w/index.php?title=File:Nabha_flag.svg *License:* Public Domain *Contributors:* Robert Alfers 2

Image *Source:* https://en.wikipedia.org/w/index.php?title=File:Patiala_flag.svg *License:* Public Domain *Contributors:* Robert Alfers 2

Image *Source:* https://en.wikipedia.org/w/index.php?title=File:Rampur_flag.svg *License:* Public Domain *Contributors:* Robert Alfers 2

Image *Source:* https://en.wikipedia.org/w/index.php?title=File:Rewaflag.png *License:* Creative Commons Attribution-Sharealike 3.0 *Contributors:* OgreBot 2, Xufanc 2

Image *Source:* https://en.wikipedia.org/w/index.php?title=File:Sirohi.svg *Contributors:* - 2

Image *Source:* https://en.wikipedia.org/w/index.php?title=File:Mewar.svg *License:* Public Domain *Contributors:* Robert Alfers 2

Image *Source:* https://en.wikipedia.org/w/index.php?title=File:Flag_of_Kingdom_of_Mysore.svg *License:* Creative Commons Zero *Contributors:* User:Samhanin 2

Image *Source:* https://en.wikipedia.org/w/index.php?title=File:Flag_of_Kingdom_of_Travancore.svg *Contributors:* Washiucho 2

Image *Source:* https://en.wikipedia.org/w/index.php?title=File:Skull_and_crossbones.svg *Contributors:* Andux, Andy0101, AnselmiJuan, Bayo, BotMultichill, BotMultichillT, Coyau, D0ktorz, Derbeth, Eugenio Hansen, OFS, Franzenshof, Ies, J.delanoy, JMCC1, Jahoe, Juliancolton, Karelj, MarianSigler, Natr, Sarang, Shuhazmir, Sidpatil, Silsor, Stas1995, Stepshep, Str4nd, Sven Manguard, SweetCanadianMullet, The Evil IP address, Tiptoety, Túrelio, W!B:, Wknight94, 22 anonymous edits 2

Image *Source:* https://en.wikipedia.org/w/index.php?title=File:Jhansi_state_flag.png *License:* Creative Commons Attribution-Sharealike 3.0 *Contributors:* User:Xufanc 2

Image *Source:* https://en.wikipedia.org/w/index.php?title=File:North_Gateway_-_Rear_Side_-_Stupa_1_-_Sanchi_Hill_2013-02-21_4480-4481.JPG *License:* Creative Commons Attribution 3.0 *Contributors:* Biswarup Ganguly 3

Figure 1 *Source:* https://en.wikipedia.org/w/index.php?title=File:India1765and1805b.jpg *License:* Public Domain *Contributors:* Edinburgh Geographical Institute. 5

Figure 2 *Source:* https://en.wikipedia.org/w/index.php?title=File:India1837to1857.jpg *License:* Public Domain *Contributors:* Edinburgh Geographical Institute. 5

Figure 3 *Source:* https://en.wikipedia.org/w/index.php?title=File:Two_Seapoy_Officers;_A_Private_Seapoy.jpg *License:* Public Domain *Contributors:* Clusternote, Jacklee, Ranveig, Roland zh 7

Figure 4 *Source:* https://en.wikipedia.org/w/index.php?title=File:Charles_Canning,_1st_Earl_Canning_-_Project_Gutenberg_eText_16528.jpg *License:* Public Domain *Contributors:* BotMultichill, Tagishsimon 10

Figure 5 *Source:* https://en.wikipedia.org/w/index.php?title=File:Dalhousie.jpg *License:* Public Domain *Contributors:* Sir William Lee-Warner 10

Figure 6 *Source:* https://en.wikipedia.org/w/index.php?title=File:Rani_of_jhansi.jpg *License:* Public Domain *Contributors:* Amenhtp, Aschroet, BotMultichill, Felix Folio Secundus, Martin H., Roland zh, Sankalpdravid 11

Figure 7 *Source:* https://en.wikipedia.org/w/index.php?title=File:Bahadur_Shah_II_of_India.jpg *License:* Public Domain *Contributors:* Gryffindor, Kürschner, Marcus Cyron, OgreBot 2, TRAJAN 117 12

Figure 8 *Source:* https://en.wikipedia.org/w/index.php?title=File:Indian_Mutiny_Map_Showing_Position_of_Troops_on_1st_May_1857.jpg *Contributors:* Internet Archive Book Images 14

Figure 9 *Source:* https://en.wikipedia.org/w/index.php?title=File:The_Sepoy_revolt_at_Meerut.jpg *Contributors:* DarwIn, Exemplo347, Hohum, Roland zh, Sridhar1000 16

Figure 10 *Source:* https://en.wikipedia.org/w/index.php?title=File:1857_mutineers_mosque_meerut2.jpg *License:* Public Domain *Contributors:* Major Robert Christopher Tytler (1818–1872) 16

Figure 11 *Source:* https://en.wikipedia.org/w/index.php?title=File:Massacre_of_officers_by_insurgent_cavalry_at_Delhi,.jpg *License:* Public Domain *Contributors:* DarwIn, Exemplo347, Roland zh, Sridhar1000, 1 anonymous edits 18

Figure 12 *Source:* https://en.wikipedia.org/w/index.php?title=File:1858_Delhi_flag_tower.jpg *License:* Public Domain *Contributors:* Amenhtp, Aschroet, BotMultichill, Ekabhishek, Martin H., Roland zh, 1 anonymous edits 18

Figure 13 *Source:* https://en.wikipedia.org/w/index.php?title=File:Indian_revolt_of_1857_states_map.svg *License:* Creative Commons Attribution-Sharealike 3.0 *Contributors:* Abhishekjoshi, Juliancolton, Nikotins, Planemad, Roland zh, WOSlinker, Wknight94, Zykasaa, 3 anonymous edits 20

Figure 14 *Source:* https://en.wikipedia.org/w/index.php?title=File:Troops_of_the_Native_Allies.jpg *License:* Public Domain *Contributors:* Alonso de Mendoza, Charles Matthews, Innotata, Napoleon 100 20

Figure 15 *Source:* https://en.wikipedia.org/w/index.php?title=File:Looting_sikhs.jpg *License:* Public Domain *Contributors:* Roland zh, Sridhar1000, 1 anonymous edits 21

Figure 16 *Source:* https://en.wikipedia.org/w/index.php?title=File:Fugitive_British_officers_and_their_families_attacked_by_mutineers..jpg *License:* Public Domain *Contributors:* Hilohello, Piggy58 23

Figure 17 *Source:* https://en.wikipedia.org/w/index.php?title=File:NyneeTal1857.jpg *Contributors:* User:Fowler&fowler 24

Figure 18 *Source:* https://en.wikipedia.org/w/index.php?title=File:"Attack_of_the_Mutineers_on_the_Redan_Battery_at_Lucknow,_July_30th,_1857,.jpg *License:* Public Domain *Contributors:* Denniss, Hsarrazin, Jarould, Nyttend, Rcbutcher, Roland zh, Sridhar1000, Vinkje83, Wally Wiglet, WikiOriginal-9 25

License

Index

www.ingramcontent.com/pod-product-compliance
Lightning Source LLC
Chambersburg PA
CBHW021139090426
42740CB00008B/850
* 9 7 8 9 3 5 2 9 7 9 2 0 2 *